CHARLES
Victim or Villain?

Also by Penny Junor

Diana, Princess of Wales
Margaret Thatcher: Wife, Mother and Politician
Burton: The Man Behind the Myth
Charles
Charles and Diana: Portrait of a Marriage
John Major: From Brixton to Downing Street

CHARLES
Victim or Villain?

PENNY JUNOR

HarperCollins*Publishers*

To Jane

HarperCollins*Publishers*
77–85 Fulham Palace Road,
Hammersmith, London W6 8JB

Published by HarperCollins*Publishers* 1998
1 3 5 7 9 8 6 4 2

Copyright © Penny Junor 1998

The author asserts the moral right to
be identified as the author of this work

A catalogue record for this book is
available from the British Library

ISBN 0 00 255900 5

Set in Sabon

Printed and bound in Great Britain by Clays Ltd, St Ives plc

Contents

The author and publishers are grateful to the following for
permission to use copyright photographic material:

Section One:
1 photograph © Mike Forster/Solo Syndication; **2** © Solo Syndication;
3, 4, 5, 8, 10, 13, 14 © Rex Features; **6** © PA News Photo Library;
7 © Popperfoto; **9, 16** photographs by Tim Graham; **11** © Alpha;
12 © Wakehams; **15** photograph by Les Chudzicki

Section Two:
1 photograph by Tim Graham; **2, 4, 10** © UK Press; **3, 6, 7, 9, 12, 14**
© Rex Features; **4** © Solo Syndication; **8** photograph © Mike
Forster/Solo Syndication; **11** photograph © Adrian Sherratt/South
West News Service; **13** photograph © Darren Fletcher/South West
News Service; **15** photograph © John Giles/PA News Photo Library;
16 photograph © Chuck Stoody/Associated Press; **17** photograph
© Paul Ashton/South West News Service

Acknowledgements

This book could not have been written without the huge generosity of so many people who gave up their time to talk to me. I will not list them, since some spoke in confidence, but simply say thank you to each and every one of them. I would also like to thank the people, who again must remain nameless, who read the manuscript and corrected errors. Thanks are also due to so many people at St James's Palace, particularly in the Prince of Wales's press office, who were so helpful in finding me the information I needed.

My agent, Jane Turnbull, has been quite fantastic throughout, a huge support and fount of encouragement, as has Eddie Bell, Executive Chairman and Publisher at HarperCollins. They both believed in an idea at a very early stage, and kept faith even when the outcome was by no means certain. Everyone at HarperCollins has been a very great pleasure to work with, and I owe a particular debt of gratitude to Val Hudson and Andrea Henry, who worked magic on my manuscript in what must be record time. Other people that warrant particular mention are Adrian Bourne, Adrian Laing, Kim Dawe, Heather Rogers, Katie Fulford, Rachel Smyth, Mel Haselden and James Annal.

Photographer, Les Wilson, has also been a star. The quality of illustrations are entirely down to his encyclopedic knowledge of royal photographs and where to find them – and, like everyone, he has worked with astonishing speed and with great good humour.

I am grateful to one or two friends who have been amazing in their support and help. And last, but by no means least, I thank my family without whom...

~

Books Consulted

There are two books in particular from which I have drawn: *Diana – Her True Story/In Her Own Words* by Andrew Morton (Michael O'Mara Books, 1997), and *The Prince of Wales* by Jonathan Dimbleby (Little, Brown, 1994). Both provided unique source material, and I am grateful to the authors and publishers.

Other books include: *The Monarchy and the Constitution* by Vernon Bogdanor (Clarendon Press, 1995); *Highgrove, Portrait of an Estate* by HRH The Prince of Wales and Charles Clover (Chapmans Publishers, 1993); *A Greater Love, Charles and Camilla* by Christopher Wilson (Headline Book Publishing, 1995); *The Royal Encyclopedia* edited by Roland Allison and Sarah Riddell (Macmillan Press, 1991); *Diana in Private: The Princess Nobody Knows* by Lady Colin Campbell (Smith Gryphon, 1992).

List of Illustrations

14 The Prince of Wales and Mrs Camilla Parker Bowles.

15 The Princess of Wales and Major James Hewitt.

16 The Prince and Princess of Wales and their two sons at Highgrove.

Section Two

1 The Prince of Wales with his dog, Harvey.

2 The Prince and Princess of Wales on their Korean tour.

3 The Princess of Wales and Prince Harry at Thorpe Park.

4 The Princess of Wales carrying the ashes of her father, Earl Spencer.

5 The Princess of Wales's last official engagement.

6 The Prince of Wales and Mrs Camilla Parker Bowles leave Balmoral.

7 The Princess of Wales greets Carolyn Bartholomew.

8 The Prince of Wales with his arm in a sling.

9 The Princess of Wales on 'Panorama'.

10 Diana appears for her public on the evening of Prince Charles's Dimbleby programme.

11 Mrs Camilla Parker Bowles with the Beaufort Hunt.

12 The first public sighting of Mrs Camilla Parker Bowles following her divorce.

13 Mrs Camilla Parker Bowles arrives at Highgrove for her fiftieth birthday party.

14 Diana, Princess of Wales, on holiday in the South of France with Mohamed al Fayed and his daughter Jasmin al Fayed, Prince William and Prince Harry.

15 The Prince of Wales playing basketball at his first official engagement following the death of Diana, Princess of Wales.

16 The Prince of Wales wearing a hat from the Canadian Olympic team.

17 Mrs Camilla Parker Bowles and her daughter Laura.

Introduction

Opinion polls suggest that the reputation of the Prince of Wales is beginning to recover after the emotional turmoil of Diana's death in August 1997. It had not been good before she died, largely because of his relationship with Camilla Parker Bowles, but in the days that followed the fatal crash it plumbed new depths, as the nation's anger at the loss of the Princess it loved so dearly turned on the monarchy and, more particularly, the heir to the throne. When Diana's brother, Charles Spencer, gave his address at her funeral, and said that he would rescue her sons from the clutches of the Royal Family, the nation cheered – literally – as his voice was relayed to those inside and outside Westminster Abbey.

The Prince's new-found popularity is no doubt gratifying, and has much to do with the way he has been seen to care for his children in the wake of their mother's death. A significant percentage of the population would even sanction his marriage to Camilla Parker Bowles. However, a popular misconception undermines this growing acceptance: the belief that the Prince always loved Camilla and made no attempt during his years of marriage to Diana to shut his mistress out of his life.

Few would deny that it takes two to make a marriage, and two to break it. Yet millions of people the world over have been led to believe that the Prince of Wales destroyed his marriage, alone and unaided, because of his obsession with Mrs Parker Bowles. In 1992,

Andrew Morton told Diana's story – one side of the story – in a book that brought about the end of the 'fairytale' marriage. *Diana – Her True Story*, which was reissued after Diana's death and renamed *In Her Own Words*, gave a picture of Charles and Diana's life together and the part his mistress had to play in it, which is not quite what those who knew both Charles and Diana best remember.

So far, no one has attempted to tell the complete story. While Diana was alive the Prince would never allow it because he didn't want to hurt either her or their children. In all their years together and apart, and despite intense provocation, he never spoke ill of her in any way. Now that she is dead Charles is even more determined that he will not defend himself and that history alone shall be his judge. If that means waiting until he is long dead, so be it. He has no qualms about meeting his maker. The evidence to support what really happened – letters, diaries, tapes, medical records, which explain the true nature of the relationship – is under lock and key at the Royal Family Archive at Windsor. One day in the future, when they are released, the whole truth will be told.

In the meantime, a number of his family and friends feel he has suffered enough and believe there should be some attempt to correct at least some of the misconceptions.

Diana said some terrible things about Charles, which she later regretted quite bitterly. Not, however, before millions of people were led to believe that she was taken 'like a lamb to the slaughter' into a loveless union, in order to produce an heir for a man who had no intention of honouring his marriage vows. On the strength of Diana's words, there are many who believe that he carried on an affair with his mistress throughout his marriage, even sleeping with her the night before his wedding and resuming their affair immediately after the honeymoon. They believe Charles was a cold and insensitive husband and a cold and insensitive father, who only now, after Diana's death, is beginning to show a little affection for his children. Some people even blame Charles for Diana's death. And, because Diana said so on prime time television, in an interview for 'Panorama' in 1995, many believe he is not fit to be king.

It is hard to imagine Prince Charles's emotions as he walked behind Diana's cortège that September morning, their sons by his side, bravely fighting back their tears. Never had there been such public outpourings of love and grief for someone so few had ever met. The world had loved her, admired her, worshipped her. He had rejected her, divorced her. Why?

Charles: Victim or Villain? tries to explain what really happened in that marriage; to give a more objective view than Diana's, and reveal more clearly than ever before the part Camilla Parker Bowles played in it. Not for the sake of the Prince of Wales – who, like Diana, is not entirely blameless – but for the sake of the millions of people who have lived through this royal soap opera and have never had an alternative account of what happened on which to form a judgement for themselves. At the moment there is only Diana's account, which is flawed and inevitably partial, as even her friends will admit in private.

It is an attempt to describe why Charles married Diana, what life was like for them both, and what went so badly wrong that she felt compelled to tell the world and take very public revenge on her husband. What possessed Charles to confess his infidelity on camera – as he did to Jonathan Dimbleby in a two-and-a-half-hour documentary about his life in June 1994 – and how did he feel when he faced the public after the embarrassment of the Camillagate tapes that exposed his late-night ramblings on the telephone to his mistress?

The two young princes, William and Harry, have lived through it all – the embarrassment, the affairs, the divorce and, finally, the traumatic death of their mother. How are they faring as a family today? What do they think of Mrs Parker Bowles? What is the future likely to hold for them all?

This is a portrait of the Prince of Wales at fifty. A very private man, with a public role, in an intrusive media world. A single parent and future king, a man emotionally handcuffed by his upbringing and damaged by the failure of his marriage. He is a man who inspires great love and loyalty, but a man of contradictions. He can be the greatest company or the most sombre; the kindest, most considerate of human beings or the most selfish. He has warmth and charisma, and a wicked sense of fun but, when he doesn't get what he wants, a fearsome temper that in fifty years he has never learnt to control. He is a man who cares about the disadvantaged, and the sick and dying, no less than the planet we pass on to future generations and the English we teach our children. A man who is cocooned from the real world, who has butlers and valets, helicopters and fast cars, yet who has seen more deprivation and who understands despair better than most politicians. A man whose life has been given over to duty to the institution he was born into, and who longs to modernise it, but who is thwarted by the very people his wife called 'the enemy' – the courtiers who rule royal life – and who must wait for the death of the mother he loves before he can begin his task. He is a man who cares above all else – even above his own happiness – for the future well being of his sons. While they are children he can protect them, but he knows that as they come of age he will be powerless to stop the intrusion, the criticism and pressure that very nearly destroyed him.

ONE

Death of a Princess

'They tell me there's been an accident. What's going on?'
Charles in the early hours of 31 August 1997

The first call alerting the Royal Family to Diana's accident came through to Sir Robin Janvrin, the Queen's deputy private secretary, at one o'clock on the morning of Sunday 31 August. He was asleep in his house on the Balmoral estate in Aberdeenshire. It was from the British ambassador in Paris, who had only sketchy news. There had been a car crash. Dodi Fayed, it seemed, had been killed, although there was no confirmation yet. The Princess of Wales, who had been travelling with him, was injured but no one knew how badly. Their car had smashed into the support pillars of a tunnel under the Seine. It had been travelling at high speed while trying to escape a group of paparazzi in hot pursuit on motorbikes.

Janvrin immediately telephoned the Queen and the Prince of Wales in their rooms at the castle. He then telephoned the Prince's assistant private secretary, Nick Archer, who was staying in another house on the estate; also the Queen's equerry and protection officers. They all agreed to meet in the offices at the castle, where they set up an operations room and manned the phones throughout the night.

Meanwhile, in London, the Prince's team were being woken and told the news, ironically, by the tabloid press. The first call to Mark Bolland, the Prince's deputy private secretary, came at 1 a.m. from the *News of the World*. Having gone to bed at his flat in the City after a very good dinner party, he let the answering machine take the call, and when he heard something about an accident in Paris dismissed it as the usual Saturday night fantasy. It was not until he heard the voice of Stuart Higgins, then editor of the *Sun*, a paper not published on a Sunday, speaking into the machine ten minutes later, that he realised something very odd was going on and picked up the phone. Higgins had much the same news as the Embassy. The reports were conflicting but it sounded as though Dodi had been killed and Diana injured.

The Prince's press secretary, Sandy Henney, had also just gone to bed at her home in Surrey, having seen the last guest out after a fortieth birthday party for her sister-in-law. She too was woken by a journalist with a very similar story. The media, getting news directly from the emergency services, were in many ways better informed than the Embassy that night and provided a real service to the Prince's staff.

Mark Bolland immediately rang Stephen Lamport, the Prince's private secretary, at his home in west London, then Sandy Henney, and within minutes the phone lines across the capital and between London and Scotland were buzzing.

The Prince telephoned Bolland in London. 'Robin tells me there's been an accident. What's going on?'

He wanted details. Shocked and unable to believe what he was hearing, he asked the same questions over and over again: What had caused the accident? What had Diana been doing in that situation? Who was driving? Where had it happened? Why had it happened? Questions to which, for the time being, there were no answers. They spoke for almost an hour.

There was no more concrete news. Reports one minute said Diana was seriously hurt, and the next suggested she had walked away with superficial injuries.

The Queen was also awake in her suite of rooms next door to her son's on the first floor of the castle. Her private secretary, Sir Robert Fellowes, was on holiday in Norfolk, but like the Prince's staff her own people were in constant touch with one another. The Prince's private secretary on duty in Scotland was Nick Archer, but it was

Stephen Lamport and Mark Bolland in London who were calling the shots.

Bolland telephoned Robin Janvrin to tell him that the Prince would be flying to Paris later that day to visit Diana in hospital, and needed a plane. 'He's going,' he said. 'This is not a matter for discussion. He is going to see his ex-wife.'

His request did not go down well initially. Was it the right thing to do? wondered Janvrin. An aeroplane of the Queen's Flight couldn't be ordered without the Queen's specific agreement, and that was unlikely to be forthcoming.

'Okay, fine,' said Bolland. 'We'll take a scheduled flight from Aberdeen.' The Queen would be irritated, no doubt, that yet again Diana was disrupting everyone's lives. She had lost patience with Diana long ago, and as the week wore on she was confirmed in her belief that everything to do with her former daughter-in-law was always extraordinarily complicated.

Unbelievably, although the Queen and Prince Charles were just feet away from one another in their separate rooms, divided by paper-thin walls, it was their staff who were discussing the rights and wrongs of asking the Queen's permission for Charles to use her aeroplane. Never was the true nature of this mother–son relationship more starkly demonstrated. Closely knit though the family appears, there is very little real communication between them. The Prince loves his parents dearly but they don't talk. The Queen and the Duke of Edinburgh had not known quite how serious the problems with their son's marriage had been until 1987, when two friends wrote to the Queen, having decided independently and simultaneously that she ought to know what was going on. Their letters landed on her desk on the same day. They had witnessed some odd incidents, like Diana falling down the stairs at Sandringham, and Diana had told them on one occasion that her life with the Prince was impossible because of Mrs Parker Bowles, but they had not discussed the problems with their son.

That Sunday, Charles, William and Harry had all been planning to fly to London. The boys' summer holiday was almost over and they were due to meet up with their mother, who was flying back from Paris. Diana always had the children for the last few days before they went back to school at the start of a new term, so that she could get everything ready and make sure they had the right kit. The Prince would spend a few days at Highgrove, his home in Gloucestershire, before heading for Provence, in the South of France, his habitual haunt in early September.

The Prince was in no doubt that he wanted to go and see Diana in Paris that morning, but uncertain whether he should take the children. He was worried that her injuries would be too upsetting for them. Clearly no decision could be made until they knew how bad her injuries were. And as the hours crept painfully past, he talked about the Princess, whom he still loved and prayed for every night, despite the failure of their marriage, despite the hurt that had existed between them.

'I always thought it would end like this,' he said, 'with me having to nurse Diana through some terrible injury or illness. I always thought she'd come back to me and I would spend the rest of my time looking after her.'

The walls in Balmoral are so thin that there is no keeping of secrets. One regular visitor says that if you want to have a private conversation you have to put the plug in the wash basin and talk quietly, or it will be all round the castle. Inevitably, with this kind of drama going on, most of the family were by now awake and watching the television or listening to the radio, which was already given over to news of the accident. The Duke of York was staying in the castle at the time, also Princess Anne's son Peter Phillips, then aged nineteen, two friends of the Queen and Princess Margaret, the Queen's sister. William and Harry were asleep and it became a priority to get their radios out of their bedrooms and the television out of the nursery, to prevent them waking up and switching one of them on.

At about 3.30 a.m., Mark Bolland rang Robin Janvrin again to find out how he was doing with the plane, and whether he had woken up the people at RAF Northolt, in Greater London, where it was based. In the middle of the conversation, at 3.45, they were interrupted by a telephone call that came through from the Embassy in Paris for Janvrin, and he put Bolland on to Nick Archer while he took the call.

'We can't muck about with his plane,' Bolland was saying. 'Make sure Robin is quite clear what is going to happen …'

'Oh, Mark, I think we're going to have a change of plan.'

In the background Archer could hear Robin Janvrin breaking the news to the Prince of Wales on the telephone. 'Sir, I'm very sorry to have to tell you, I've just had the Ambassador on the phone. The Princess died a short time ago.'

The announcement that went out at 4.30 a.m. said she had died at four o'clock. It had actually been earlier.

The Prince immediately rang Mark. 'Robin has just told me she's dead, Mark, is this true? What happened? What on earth was she doing there? How could this have happened? They're all going to blame me, aren't they? What do I do? What does this mean?'

Mark's first reaction was to ring Camilla Parker Bowles to tell her that Diana had died, and warn her that she could expect a call at any moment from the Prince, in a state of serious distress. He had rung a number of close friends that night, and Camilla and the Prince had already spoken several times. She was shocked to the core by the news that Diana was dead, and utterly devastated for the boys; also terrified for the Prince, of what would happen to him, what people's reaction would be.

Diana's death came as a terrible shock to everyone. All the news had indicated that she had survived the crash, and with some reports having suggested she had walked away from the car, people were totally unprepared. The truth was that she had sustained terrible chest and head injuries. She had lost consciousness very soon after the impact, and never regained it. She had been treated in the wreckage of the Mercedes at the scene for about an hour and was then taken to the Pitié-Salpêtrière hospital four miles away, where surgeons had fought for a further two hours to save her life, but in vain. The reaction was total horror and disbelief.

The Prince's first thought was for the children. Should he wake them and tell them or let them sleep and tell them in the morning? He was absolutely dreading it, and didn't know what to do for the best. The Queen felt strongly that they should be left to sleep and he took her advice and didn't wake them up until 7.15. William had had a difficult night's sleep and had woken many times. He had known, he said, that something awful was going to happen.

The Prince, like Camilla, realised only too well what the public reaction might be, and what the media would say. 'They're all going to blame me,' he said. 'The world's going to go completely mad, isn't it? We're going to see a reaction that we've never seen before. And it could destroy everything. It could destroy the monarchy.'

'Yes, sir, I think it could,' said Lamport with brutal honesty. 'It's going to be very difficult for your mother, sir. She's going to have to do things she may not want to do, or feel comfortable doing, but if she doesn't do them, then that's the end of it.'

The Queen's first difficulty was upon her before dawn had broken. The Prince decided he should be the one to go to Paris to collect Diana's body, but the Queen was against the idea and was strongly supported by her private secretary. The Princess was no longer a member of the Royal Family, argued Sir Robert Fellowes; it would be wrong to make too much fuss.

Robin Janvrin came up with the remark that clinched it. 'What would you rather, Ma'am,' he said; 'that she came back in a Harrods' van?' There was no further argument.

Diana's love affair with Dodi Fayed had been a source of deep concern to everyone at court, not least the Prince of Wales. Not because he resented her happiness – it was his deepest wish that Diana would find happiness – but because he feared it would end in disaster. He feared that Diana was in danger of being used by the al Fayed publicity machine. Dodi's father, Mohamed al Fayed, the high-profile Egyptian owner of Harrods, was a controversial figure. Long denied British citizenship, he had tried relentlessly to ingratiate himself with the establishment. He had done some inspired matchmaking that summer between his playboy son and the Princess of Wales in the South of France, and had milked it for all it was worth. He had scarcely been out of the news for a month: he had been photographed with William and Harry, the Queen's grandsons, who had been his guests on board his yacht, and was hoping for the greatest coup of all, to secure the mother of a future king of England as a daughter-in-law.

Dodi was a serious member of the international jet set, a kind and gentle man, but with more money than intellect, and a string of conquests to his name amongst the world's most beautiful women. While he was busy wooing Diana, another woman thought she was engaged to marry him. He dabbled in the film business, but was essentially financed by his rich father, who denied him nothing. Dodi and Diana did appear to be in love, and may well have gone on to marry had things turned out differently. She would have been the biggest catch in the world for him. He would have provided the wealth she needed, even after her divorce settlement, to finance her enormously expensive lifestyle, and it would have been the ultimate two-fingered gesture to the Royal Family she so despised.

The boys had not enjoyed their holiday on board al Fayed's yacht. They had not taken to Dodi or his father and had hated the publicity – as a result William had had a terrible row with his mother – and the whole trip had been extremely uncomfortable. And to add insult to injury, at the end of their stay, their two royal protection officers were taken aside by a Fayed aide, and handed a brown envelope each, stuffed with notes. 'Mr al Fayed would like to thank you for all you have done,' he said. In a panic, they immediately telephoned Colin Trimming, the Prince's detective and head of the royal protection squad, and told him what had happened. 'You've got to give it back,' he said.

'We've tried,' they said, 'but we were told that Mr al Fayed would be very upset if we didn't accept it.' The money went back.

The mention of Harrods to the Queen was enough to trigger Operation Overlord – the plan, which had been in existence for many years but never previously needed, to return the body of a member of the Royal Family to London. There is a BAe146 plane ear-marked for the purpose, which can be airborne at short notice from RAF Northolt. It had always been thought the Queen Mother might be its first passenger, which given she was then ninety-seven years old was not unreasonable. No one in their wildest dreams could have guessed it would be used for Diana, still so young and beautiful, super-fit and brimming with health and vitality.

The plane left Northolt at 10 a.m. that Sunday morning, bound for Aberdeen, with Stephen Lamport, Mark Bolland and Sandy Henney on board. First stop was RAF Wittering in Rutland, where it collected Diana's sisters, Lady Sarah McCorquodale, who lived nearby, and Lady Jane Fellowes. It was Robert Fellowes who had broken the news to Diana's family, and the Prince had telephoned Sarah to suggest they might like to go with him to collect the body, whereupon Jane had driven up from Norfolk to join her sister. From Wittering they flew to Aberdeen, where they collected the Prince of Wales, and then on to Paris. The Prince had decided this was not a trip for the children and so they stayed at Balmoral with Tiggy Legge-Bourke, who, as the Queen said, 'by the grace of God' had just arrived in Scotland ready to take the Princes down to London to meet their mother. She and their cousin Peter Phillips were utterly brilliant with William and Harry that day and for the remainder of the week.

Diana's sisters spent most of the flight to Paris in tears. The Prince was controlled but clearly very shaken. Stephen Lamport took everyone through what would happen at the other end. There was a possibility, he warned Sarah and Jane, that Mohamed al Fayed might be at the hospital and if he was the Prince would have to speak to him; how did they feel about that? Both sisters were adamant they wanted nothing to do with Mr al Fayed; they didn't even want to see him.

In the event he wasn't there. By the time the Prince's party arrived al Fayed had already taken his son's body home for prayers in Regent's Park Mosque, followed by a Muslim burial that night at a cemetery in Woking, Surrey. On arrival at the hospital the Prince was met by President Chirac, who had come in person to express his nation's great sadness at the death of the Princess.

With protocol observed, the Prince and the two sisters were taken to see Diana's body. A doctor accompanied them into the small room on the first floor of the hospital, as well as a priest, whom they had specifically asked for. It was a distressing sight for which none of them was adequately prepared. Diana's body was laid out in a coffin which had been flown to Paris earlier that morning on a Hercules from RAF Brize Norton in Oxfordshire. Levertons, the north London family firm of undertakers, were an integral part of Operation Overlord. The Princess had been embalmed and was wearing a dress that her butler, Paul Burrell, had flown out with earlier, but the body that lay so still and cold and empty looked nothing like the Diana they had known. Her head had been badly damaged in the crash and her face was distorted. The Prince told Diana's sisters how glad he was that he had not taken William and Harry to Paris with him. It would have been much too distressing for them.

They stayed with Diana's body for seven minutes. Sarah and Jane were sobbing helplessly when they left and were taken to a room for some privacy while they recovered. The Prince was not crying when he came back into the corridor, but it was obvious that he had been, and was visibly very distressed. His eyes were quite red, his face racked with pain. A small crowd was waiting in the corridor, most of them hospital staff, and also a number of men in dark suits. The Prince came out of the door, stopped, closed his eyes and bit his lip. Then after a moment's pause, while he fought to regain his composure, he set off down the corridor, a private man no longer, to shake hands with the doctors and nurses and thank them for all they had done. As someone watching remarked, 'He went from human being to Windsor' – as nearly fifty years of training ensured he would. Duty above all else. When he heard that the parents of the Welsh bodyguard, Trevor Rees-Jones, employed by the al Fayeds, who had been the sole survivor in the accident, were at the hospital, he immediately said he must talk to them.

Moments later the coffin, by now closed and draped with the maroon and yellow of the Royal Standard, was carried out of the room. It was suddenly obvious that the men in dark suits were the undertakers, and without a word needing to be said, everyone in the corridor spontaneously formed two lines and silently bowed their heads as the coffin passed between them and down the stairs into a waiting Renault Espace.

There were thousands of people in the streets outside. The whole of Paris seemed to know who was in the Espace and what was going on. To a man, woman and child they were silent. As the motorcade made its way slowly through the city and out on to the périphérique towards the airport, the people on the pavements bowed their heads in silence, people in street cafés stood up as the cars passed, each one flanked by two large motorbikes on either side, and no one made a sound. The Prince was deeply moved, and in the silence that enveloped the aircraft on the flight home, with everyone wrapped up in their own thoughts and emotions, he said, 'Wasn't it wonderful that everybody stood up.'

But if the tribute paid to Diana by the Parisians had been moving, the arrangements that had been made unbeknownst to him for the next stage of her journey enraged him. While Sarah and Jane disappeared into another part of the cabin to have a cigarette, the Prince asked what arrangements had been made after they touched down at Northolt. The Prime Minister, Tony Blair, would be there, he knew, also the Lord Chamberlain, Lord Airlie, who is the most senior member of the Queen's household. He wanted to know how many RAF people would be there to carry the coffin, whether the flowers he had said he wanted had been sorted out, whether there would be a proper hearse to carry the coffin, and where they were planning to take Diana's body. The answer to that final question was the mortuary in Fulham, commonly used by the Royal Coroner.

'Who decided that? Nobody asked me. Diana is going to the Chapel Royal at St James's Palace. Sort it. I don't care who has made this decision. She is going to the Chapel Royal.'

Sandy Henney spent much of the remainder of the flight on the plane's telephone ensuring that the Prince's instructions were carried out to the last detail.

The decision had almost certainly been made by Robert Fellowes, doing what he imagined the Queen would have wanted, without actually asking her, but his second guessing was not far off the mark. There is no doubt that in the course of the days leading up to Diana's funeral, the hostility that both the Queen and the Duke of Edinburgh had felt towards their erstwhile daughter-in-law came dangerously close to the surface on several occasions. She had caused nothing but trouble and embarrassment over the years, and here she was, in death, still managing to cause mayhem.

The Prince's relationship with Diana had been turbulent and troubled and they were no longer man and wife, but Diana was still the mother of his children and, in a way, he still loved her. He wanted her treated with the dignity she deserved. After Sandy's hasty and heated phone calls from the plane, the plan about the mortuary was changed and it was agreed that the Princess of Wales would be taken to the Chapel Royal at St James's Palace, just yards from the office they shared so disastrously until their divorce. She was also to have outriders. And while he was at it, her sisters Sarah and Jane were to be given a plane to take them wherever they wanted to go, and if they wanted to go with the body into London first, then so be it. So at the Prince's bidding, the plane which had brought the Prime Minister from his constituency to Northolt to meet the returning party was kept on hold, but in the end was not required. The sisters accompanied the body into London and chose to make their own ways home.

The plane carrying the coffin touched down at Northolt and taxied out of sight of the reception party, where it came to a halt. One of the crew climbed out and opened up the cargo hatch, and the group onboard listened in silence to the bolts holding the coffin in place being loosened beneath them. The plane then taxied on and came to a halt in front of the airport building where Tony Blair, David Airlie and 150 or so photographers and pressmen were waiting quietly on the tarmac. In silence the coffin was unloaded and carried to the waiting hearse. The only sound to be heard was the Royal Standard flapping in the breeze.

Wrapped in thought, his emotions in turmoil, the Prince of Wales climbed back aboard the aircraft, accompanied by Stephen Lamport, to fly back to Balmoral and be with his grieving sons, while the hearse made its way slowly down the A40 into west London.

It was only then that the real enormity of what had happened began to dawn on the Palace staff. The motorway, the bridges and embankments – and when they ran out, the roads and pavements – were full of cars and people who had come to watch and weep as Diana's coffin passed by. Tributes had started pouring in from all over the world, and flowers were being laid at the gate of every building with which Diana was associated.

This, they realised, was going to be unlike anything anyone had ever seen before.

TWO

A Nation Mourns

'A girl given the name of the ancient goddess of hunting was,
in the end, the most hunted person of the modern age.'
Charles Spencer

In the days following Diana's death, the future of the monarchy
hung perilously in the balance. As the mountain of flowers outside
her Kensington Palace home grew ever higher, spreading further and
further into the park, the people of Britain, stunned, shocked and
numb with grief, looked for someone to blame for their awesome
sense of loss.

The national reaction to Diana's death bordered on hysteria. Few
of the people who mourned had ever met the Princess, yet her
compassion and vulnerability had touched a chord deep in the
public psyche. Everyone grieved for the stranger whom they felt they
knew, with a depth of feeling never before shown for a public figure.
Months later, counsellors were still treating people who had been
unable to come to terms with their grief. In a rather studied tribute,
the Prime Minister, Tony Blair, called her 'the people's Princess', and
it was the perfect epithet: the people felt she cared and spoke for
them, and in a curious way she probably took greater comfort from
her relationship with strangers than with almost anyone else.

'I feel like everyone else in this country,' said Tony Blair. 'I am
utterly devastated. We are a nation in a state of shock, in mourning,
in grief. It is so deeply painful for us. She was a wonderful and a
warm human being. Though her own life was often sadly touched
by tragedy, she touched the lives of so many others in Britain and
through the world, with joy and with comfort. She was the people's

Princess and that is how she will remain in our hearts and memories for ever.'

Whatever the psychological and sociological explanations for the nation's reaction to her death might be, there was not only grief, but also anger on the streets of London – anger directed in very large part at the Royal Family. As Charles had instinctively feared would happen, some went so far as to suggest that he was responsible for her death. Had he loved her instead of his mistress, they said, this would never have happened. They would still have been married and she would never have been in a car racing through the streets of Paris with Dodi Fayed. Yet at the same time others were leaving tributes to both of them outside Kensington and all the other palaces, 'To Diana and Dodi, together for ever', and paying eulogies to the man who had brought Diana true love and happiness.

There was also anger at the tabloid press, which encouraged the paparazzi by paying such huge sums of money for photographs and stories. In the weeks before her death, the red-top papers, and some of the broadsheets too, had been full of long-lens photographs of Diana and Dodi canoodling on his father's yacht in the South of France. Diana's brother, Earl Spencer, had not held back when he heard the news at his home in South Africa. 'I always believed the press would kill her in the end,' he said. 'But not even I could imagine that they would take such a direct hand in her death as seems to be the case.' At that time it was thought the paparazzi were entirely responsible for the accident; and he said that the editors and proprietors of every newspaper which had paid money for intrusive pictures of his sister had 'blood on their hands'. The public, of course, had not been slow to buy these newspapers, all of which argued a vicious circle of supply and demand. But this was not the time to draw too much attention to hypocrisy.

Strangely, no blame was ever levelled at Dodi, or even his father, who had provided the car they were travelling in, and who also employed the driver, Henri Paul. He had not been the regular driver and, it soon transpired, he had been several times over the drink-driving limit that night. The proper driver had been sent off in a decoy car. It was an elaborate attempt to try to foil the paparazzi, who were all waiting outside the Ritz Hotel, where they had had dinner that night, ready to follow them home. Yet Dodi failed to make the driver slow down, and he was doing well over 100 mph when he ploughed into the underpass. Almost overnight, the paparazzi ceased to be seen as the sole cause of the accident. Afraid that the tables might turn and that, as Henri Paul's employer, he might find himself liable, Mohamed al Fayed shared his own private theory about the crash with the press. It was, he suggested, a conspiracy cooked up by the Queen and the security services to assassinate Diana so that she would not marry Dodi; such a marriage would have given William, second in line to the throne of England, a Muslim and Egyptian step-father. It was a ludicrous notion invented by a man who had spent the months since his son's death telling lies about Diana's last words, which medical evidence suggested could never have been uttered. Yet in the spring of 1998 he was given airtime on Channel 4 television to explain why he believed the Queen had murdered Diana and Dodi. His words were picked up not only in Britain but in Egypt, and as a result the Queen's life is now at risk. Her security arrangements have necessarily been stepped up considerably, so much so that a friend whom she was visiting recently said over dinner, 'Ma'am, I thought things were supposed to be better with the IRA these days.'

'No,' the Queen replied. 'They think there's a good chance I'm going to be killed by a Muslim.'

The Queen would no doubt have been horrified by a marriage between Diana and Dodi, and William and Harry no less appalled. And they would not have been alone. Millions of people were shocked by the overtly sexual nature of the relationship, which Diana seemed to be flaunting so brazenly to the press. No one was labouring under the illusion that she was still the shy, blushing innocent Princess. Her various well-documented affairs had put an end to that. Apart from the much publicised revelations about James Hewitt, she had been publicly blamed by the wife of rugby player Will Carling for destroying their marriage. In his autobiograpy, published in October 1998, Carling was coy about the relationship, saying, 'I was attracted to her but I never made a pass at her. To be honest, if I had had a sexual relationship with her I wouldn't say I had. I don't think that would be right.' At the time, however, he boasted quite openly to his friends about the sexual nature of his relationship with Diana.

The press was becoming increasingly critical of Diana's conduct. She had subjected her boys to Dodi and, worse still, to his father, and she was paying the price.

'The sight of a paunchy playboy groping a scantily-dressed Diana must appal and humiliate Prince William ...' wrote Lynda Lee-Potter in the *Daily Mail* on 27 August. 'As the mother of two young sons she ought to have more decorum and sense.'

'Princess Diana's press relations are now clearly established,' wrote Bernard Ingham for the 31 August edition of the *Express*. 'Any publicity is good publicity ... I'm told she and Dodi are made for each other, both having more brass than brains.'

On the same day, Chris Hutchins wrote in the *Sunday Mirror*, 'Just when Diana began to believe that her current romance with likeable playboy Dodi Fayed had wiped out her past liaisons, a new tape recording is doing the rounds of Belgravia dinner parties. And this one is hot, hot, hot! I must remember to take it up with Diana next time we find ourselves on adjacent running machines at our west London gym.'

But then, suddenly, the music stopped and, as in the party game, all those who were still moving were caught out. Overnight, Diana found instant beatification; pity those columnists who had committed their thoughts to print on the Saturday afternoon, little knowing that their target would be a saint by the time their words hit the streets on Sunday.

'She was the butterfly who shone with the light of glamour which illuminated all our lives,' wrote Ross Benson in the *Express*; 'A beacon of light has been extinguished,' said Lady Thatcher, the former Prime Minister; 'A comet streaked across the sky of public life and entranced the world,' wrote Simon Jenkins in *The Times*; and

Paul Johnson in the *Daily Mail* called her 'A gem of purest ray serene.'

Her love affair with Dodi was given new status: she had found 'true love at last', and the couple may very well have been on the brink of announcing their engagement. It was a week of instant judgements and media saturation, and while one pundit after another filled the airwaves or the column inches on the loss to the nation, the nation itself displayed its distress on the streets of every town and city. People of all ages and from all walks of life wept openly and clasped one another for comfort. They queued, in some places for hours, to sign books of condolence, and in many instances people sat down and wrote in the books for half an hour. In London, they pilgrimaged from one royal palace to another to lay flowers with messages to Diana and Dodi.

Meanwhile the Royal Family sat, stoic and silent, in Scotland, and the nation's anger grew. It was assumed they didn't care about the nation's grief. If they had cared – the received wisdom went – they would have come to London to be with the people. There had been no statement about Diana's death, so it was assumed they didn't care about that either. Instead, it was business as usual. That the family had even gone to church on the morning of Diana's death – just hours after hearing the news – and taken the boys with them, and that there was not so much as a quivering lower lip to be seen, provoked more outrage. What further proof could there be that everything the Princess had said about this cold, heartless family she had married into was absolutely true?

Yet in the privacy of their own home there had been plenty of tears. The Prince of Wales is an emotional man, and does cry, but he was brought up to keep emotion of all sorts to himself: a characteristic which, in a less touchy-feely, emotionally transparent society, was never questioned. Indeed, to keep one's grief to oneself was a sign of strength. Yet in 1997 it was taken as a sign of insensitivity. It is not a cold heartless family, as close friends know, but it is rare for anyone outside that charmed inner circle to see a display of either emotion or affection.

In a more religious age, taking a grief-stricken family to church would have been seen as the natural thing to do. In the material nineties it was seen as insensitive and unfeeling. In fact, they had gone to church that Sunday before Charles set out for Paris because Prince William had specifically said that he would like to 'talk to Mummy'. It was a week in which the children were given choices about everything, when their needs came before public relations. Church has always been a central part of the family routine and in the emotional turmoil of that Sunday, the familiarity, routine and permanence of a church service was comforting to them all.

God is very much a part of the Prince's life and his thinking and philosophy. He doesn't wear it on his sleeve, but he is a sincere believer that having a spiritual dimension to life, having faith of some sort or another – whether it is in God, Mohammed, Buddha or anyone else – is important to the human soul. He also believes that religious and cultural diversity is a real strength, and fears for Scotland and Wales breaking away from the rest of the UK for much the same reason.

His own choice of religion is Prayer Book Church of England, and he is a regular churchgoer no matter where he is. When he is at Highgrove on a Sunday, he will attend one of five village churches run by Chris Mulholland, vicar of the neighbouring village of Leighterton, who holds services in rotation. He has boycotted Tetbury Church ever since the vicar, John Hawthorne, denounced the Prince in the pages of most national newspapers for his adultery with Mrs Parker Bowles. It did not endear him to the Prince, particularly as Charles had given his support to a number of Tetbury Church fundraising initiatives.

Among the Prince's great loves are old churches – an enthusiasm he discovered he shared with Matthew Butler, his assistant private secretary, who introduced him to one or two he had never seen before. Fitting an old church or two into the schedule at the end of a day was a great treat for the Prince and when, at the end of his secondment, Matthew returned to his career in business and was awarded an MVO, he chose to receive it in Cardiff Castle, which was unusual for someone used to working in London and who lived in Tetbury. 'Matthew, what are you doing here?' asked the Prince as he ceremoniously handed over the medal. He explained that having organised the Prince's twenty-fifth anniversary tour of Wales it seemed more appropriate than Buckingham Palace. 'Oh, I suppose so,' said the Prince, then, suddenly lighting up, 'Matthew, I saw this wonderful church the other day …'

Of the churches they visited together, there was one in Staunton Harold in Leicestershire which the Prince found particularly poignant. It had been built by Sir Robert Shirley, Baronet, a Royalist, and ancestor of the present Earl of Ferrers, during the Commonwealth in 1649, after the turbulent reign of Charles I. Like the King, he was beheaded for his pains. There was an inscription over the door, which the Prince seemed to take to heart:

'All things sacred were throughout the nation either demolished or profaned.'

With his religious conviction running deep, the Prince firmly believes in life after death. He talks about death being 'the next great journey in our existence', and is dismayed that as westerners we have become separated from the cycles of Nature, and what they have to teach us. Speaking at a Macmillan Fund anniversary a few years ago, he said, 'The seasons of the year provided for our ancestors a lesson which could not be ignored; that life is surely followed by death, but also that death can be seen as a doorway to renewed life. In Christianity the message is seen in the mystery of resurrection, and in the picture of Christ as a seed dying in the ground in order to produce the new life that supplies bread, and sustenance.'

The subject of death has fascinated the Prince for a long time. He has suffered great personal loss on a number of occasions – most notably the death of his cousin Prince William of Gloucester in an air crash in 1972, and the brutal murder of Lord Mountbatten, Nicholas Knatchbull and others by the IRA in 1979. Despite the difference in age, his great-uncle Mountbatten was closer to him than anybody else, and the news that he had been suddenly and mercilessly blown to bits by a terrorist bomb while out fishing with his family in Ireland had been completely devastating. Charles was also with his friend Major Hugh Lindsay when he was killed in a horrifying skiing accident in Switzerland in 1988. He has watched friends die, and the children of friends, and visited hospices and hospitals and talked to strangers about their experiences of death, as Diana herself did so sympathetically.

For Charles, death is a mystery and a painful parting, but not something to fear, and Diana had much the same view. She too believed in life after death and frequently consulted mediums and clairvoyants. She was quite certain that her paternal grandmother, Cynthia, Lady Spencer, who had died in 1972 when Diana was a child, kept guard over her in the spirit world.

Balmoral is the Royal Family's spiritual home, the place where they instinctively feel relaxed and at ease, where they adopt an informality that is not seen in any of the Queen's other residences. They had stayed there because it was the most sensible place for the boys to be, and that week William and Harry were the top priority. They love Balmoral like the rest of the Royal Family. They love the freedom, the walking, the fishing, the stalking, riding, go-karting; and in that week when their entire world had been turned upside down, they needed the comfort and familiarity of home. Buckingham Palace is little more than the Royal Family's institutional headquarters, and to have brought the boys to London would have been to imprison them within four walls. At Balmoral they could be certain of some privacy in which to begin to take in the enormity of what had happened, and to prepare for their mother's funeral and the most traumatic ordeal of their young lives.

Yet in London, the anger was mounting. People wanted a public display of grief. 'They're up in bloody Scotland,' was the common cry. 'They should be here. Those children should be down here.'

The whole Royal Family was well aware of the negative atmosphere building up in the south. They could see for themselves what was going on in the media and there was also a constant stream of news, views and advice coming in from politicians, friends, historians and VIPs from all over the world. But the Prince recognised it was not for him to take the lead. There was nothing he could usefully say which could have helped anyone. He had brought Diana's body home from Paris; but if he also made a statement about how very saddened he was by her death, the public would have called him a hypocrite.

The *Daily Mail* headline on Tuesday morning – 'Charles weeps bitter tears of guilt' – only exacerbated the problem. It was an obscene headline over a picture of Charles taken some months before which the newspaper swiftly recognised had been a misjudgement. The Royal Family was appalled, and from that morning onwards stopped putting the newspapers out on display for everyone to read at Balmoral, as they previously had. It seemed that the Prince's only option was to keep a low profile and look after his sons, but by the middle of the week, when his mother's advisers still saw no need to put on a public display of emotion, he became more forceful.

Meanwhile arrangements were underway for the funeral, and once again, there was fierce disagreement between the Prince's office at St James's Palace and the Queen's at Buckingham Palace. Robert Fellowes was in an unenviable position. He was torn between duty to his wife, whom he adored, and his employer. Jane was very deeply distressed by the death of her sister and, like the rest of the Spencer family, had very definite ideas about how Diana's funeral should be handled. While wanting to respect her wishes, Fellowes also had to think of what was the best course of action for the monarchy. The Spencer family wanted a very small, private funeral, and the Queen, inclined to agree to a minimum of fuss, strongly supported this wish to keep it small and for family only. The Prince, however, felt very strongly that Diana should have nothing less than a full royal funeral at Westminster Abbey, and had told Sarah and Jane on the plane coming back from Paris that he thought it would be impossible to do anything else. Although reluctant at first, once they saw the public reaction they began to realise that this was no family affair; they couldn't keep it to themselves. There were bitter exchanges between the two camps. Even once a state funeral had been agreed upon, Earl

Spencer and Sir Robert Fellowes thought that it should only be Spencers who walked behind the cortège. The Prince disagreed, and the question was not to be resolved until the last minute.

There were yet more rows over who should sit on the Funeral Committee, set up on the day of Diana's death, chaired by Lord Airlie, the Lord Chamberlain, which met throughout the week in the Chinese Room at Buckingham Palace. The Prince of Wales wanted Downing Street represented on the committee, as did Tony Blair. The Queen didn't, and it was left to Robin Janvrin to persuade Robert Fellowes that they needed help from Number 10.

As the week progressed, the absence of a flag flying at half mast at Buckingham Palace became another issue, upon which much of the public's anger and emotion was focused. Outside the Palace, the piles of flowers grew ever more mountainous; flags were flying at half mast all over the country, and yet none of the Queen's men could reach a decision about Palace protocol. The Royal Standard never flies at half mast over Buckingham Palace because the sovereign is never dead. The minute one dies, he or she is immediately succeeded by another: 'The King is dead, long live the King.'

This was one occasion, however, where it was clear that the people of Britain didn't give a damn about protocol. They wanted to see some feeling, some indication that the Royal Family was affected by the death of the Princess, and there appeared to be no such feeling. None of them had spoken publicly, none of them had been seen, and the most elementary of gestures, the lowering of a flag, had not been observed. To the press and to the nation this embodied everything that was irrelevant and out of touch about the monarchy in the nineties, and stood in stark contrast to the warmth and compassion of the Princess, which the public had so admired. It caused a furious row internally and, in the heat of the moment, it was suggested that Sir Robert Fellowes might 'impale himself on his own flag staff'.

Finally Stephen Lamport spoke to Prince Charles. 'You've got to talk to your mother. You've got to make her understand. You're the only person who can do it.'

The Queen and the Duke of Edinburgh were entirely taken aback by the reaction to Diana's death, and were not pleased at being told how to behave in order to appease public opinion. The Queen was so often castigated for being a remote mother who always put the country before her children. Now, on the one occasion on which she was putting her grieving grandchildren first, she was being castigated for not being in London when her country needed her. After discussing the matter with David Airlie, the Queen was persuaded that a public sign of grief was required and agreed on the Thursday that a Union Flag would fly at half mast from Buckingham Palace.

That same day the family ventured out of the gates of Balmoral for the first time since the morning of Diana's death, as a means of gently preparing William and Harry for the funeral that was to be held two days later. The Prince of Wales had asked Sandy Henney, his press secretary, to come and have a chat with them. She had been in London for most of the week and witnessed what was going on there. She had felt the mood, and was one of the many people who had been feeding information up to Scotland all week, saying, 'You can't read about this, you can't even see it on television. There is real hatred building up here, and the public is incensed by your silence.'

She took the children aside. 'Mummy's death has had the most amazing impact on people,' she said. 'They really miss her, and when you go down to London you will see something you will never ever see again and it may come as a bit of a shock. We want you to know about it so you will be ready for it.'

Flowers had been piling up outside the gates of Balmoral, although in nothing like the quantity at Buckingham Palace, St James's or Kensington Palace in London. So the following day, when the children expressed the desire to go to church again, the Prince of Wales took the opportunity to give them a taster of what was awaiting them in the capital, and let them walk amongst the bouquets, reading the messages.

About sixty members of the press were waiting outside the gates of Balmoral that day, yet they uttered not a single word as the

Queen, the Duke of Edinburgh, Peter Phillips, the Prince of Wales, William and Harry climbed out of their cars to look at the flowers and tributes. The only sound to be heard, apart from the clicking of the camera shutters, were the voices of the royal party. Five days after their mother's death, the country had its first view of the boys, and it was a touching scene. All three Princes, father and sons, were visibly moved by what they saw and taken aback by the messages attached to most bouquets.

'Look at this one, Papa,' said Harry, grabbing hold of his father's hand and pulling him down. 'Read this one.'

Captured on film, the gesture sent shock waves around the world. The Prince of Wales did seem to have a heart after all. He actually held his son's hand, something no one could ever have imagined before. He also seemed to have aged.

Of all the criticism Diana threw at the Prince during their bitter war of words and television, that he was unfeeling and cold was the one that hurt him most. It was demonstrably untrue, as anyone who has seen Charles with his children knows very well. Diana knew it too, and later regretted her words.

The sight of the Prince of Wales and his sons did much to soften the public mood, and when the Queen made a surprising live television broadcast that Friday evening before the funeral, the mood softened further. The fact that it was only the second time during her reign that she had broadcast to the nation other than at Christmas – the first being during the Gulf War – made it an additionally impressive gesture.

'Since last Sunday's dreadful news we have seen, throughout Britain and around the world, an overwhelming expression of sadness at Diana's death.

'We have all been trying in our different ways to cope. It is not easy to express a sense of loss, since the initial shock is often succeeded by a mixture of other feelings: disbelief, incomprehension, anger – and concern for all who remain.

'We have all felt those emotions in these last few days. So

what I say to you now, as your Queen and as a grandmother, I say from my heart.

'First, I want to pay tribute to Diana myself. She was an exceptional and gifted human being. In good times and bad, she never lost her capacity to smile and laugh, nor to inspire others with her warmth and kindness.

'I admired and respected her – for her energy and commitment to others, and especially for her devotion to her two boys.

'This week at Balmoral, we have all been trying to help William and Harry come to terms with the devastating loss that they and the rest of us have suffered.

'No one who knew Diana will ever forget her. Millions of others who never met her, but felt they knew her, will remember her.

'I for one believe that there are lessons to be drawn from her life and from the extraordinary and moving reaction to her death.'

The Queen's words were delivered in the nick of time.

The decision about who should walk behind the cortège was not made until the very last moment. The Prince of Wales wanted to walk as a mark of respect to the Princess, who despite everything had been his wife for fifteen years, and he wanted his sons to walk too. He felt intuitively that this was something they should do for their mother and that it would aid the grieving process. Earl Spencer, backed by Sir Robert Fellowes, had been against it. He had wanted to walk behind his sister's cortège on his own. There was a bitter exchange on the telephone between the Prince and the Earl in which Earl Spencer hung up on the Prince of Wales. Over dinner on the Friday night, when the whole Royal Family was together at Buckingham Palace, the Duke of Edinburgh put an end to the argument by saying that he would walk too. The next morning Earl Spencer was told what was going to happen, and the three men and two boys all walked together.

It was a long walk from St James's Palace, where they joined the cortège, to Westminster Abbey, with every bite of the lip and tremble of the chin exposed to the world's media and the millions of people lining the route. Some threw flowers, some cried, some wailed. It was an ordeal that called for huge courage from the boys, and they did their mother – and their nation – proud. They walked slowly and steadily, struggling at times to hold back tears, but their composure never wavered, until they were inside the Abbey, when at times the music, the poetry and the oratory were too much for them. But by then the cameras were off them, forbidden to focus on the family. The boys displayed maturity beyond their years, which touched everyone. It was an ordeal for the Prince too, worrying as he was about whether the boys would be all right, but at the same time knowing that so many of the people weeping for Diana blamed him for her death. Fears that he might have been booed by the crowd were unfounded.

There were millions of people in London that Saturday and many millions more watching all over the world. Many of those in the capital had walked the streets for much of the night, or held candle-lit vigils in the park – even Diana's mother had been walking quietly amongst the mourners. Some had brought sleeping bags and had been soaked through by torrential rain the afternoon before. They did not care. United in their grief, strangers talked to strangers, as they had seventeen years before, when the Royal Wedding united them in joy.

Earlier in the week, around the royal parks and palaces the atmosphere had not been so good humoured, and felt almost intimidating at times, but by the morning of the funeral, the sun shone gloriously and although emotions were still very raw, there were tears but there was laughter too.

The funeral itself was immensely moving, and a masterpiece of organisation – the British doing what they do best: the precision timing, the military professionalism, the ceremonial pageantry, but mixed with a refreshingly human touch so perfect for Diana. Tony Blair gave a rather ham reading of 1 Corinthians 13, and Elton John sang a specially re-written version of 'Candle in the Wind' which left not a dry eye. An American film cameraman outside Kensington Palace, watching on a television monitor, said that in the silence before Elton John began to play, a sudden gust of wind, in an otherwise perfectly still morning, whipped through the millions of flowers laid at the gates, rustling the cellophane wrappings. It then disappeared just as suddenly as it had come, at the very moment Elton hit the opening chords. At the same time a small grey cloud hung over Buckingham Palace, leaving this hardened cameraman distinctly unnerved.

The denouement of the service, which no tabloid editor had been allowed to attend, was Earl Spencer's tribute to his sister. Grievously insulting to the Royal Family sitting just feet away from him, it was applauded by those within the Abbey and cheered loudly by the thousands listening on the sound relay outside.

'Diana was the very essence of compassion, of duty, of style, of beauty. All over the world she was a symbol of selfless human-ity. All over the world she was the standard bearer for the rights of the truly downtrodden, a very British girl who transcended nationality. Someone with a natural nobility who was classless and who proved in the last year that she needed no royal title to continue to generate her particular brand of magic.

'There is a rush to canonise your memory; there is no need to do so. You stand tall enough as a human being of unique qualities not to need to be seen as a saint. Indeed to sanctify your memory would be to miss out on the very core of your being, your wonderfully mischievous sense of humour with a laugh that bent you double.

'Diana explained to me once that it was her innermost feel-ings of suffering that made it possible for her to connect with her constituency of the rejected.

'And here we come to another truth about her. For all the status, the glamour, the applause, Diana remained throughout a very insecure person at heart, almost childlike in her desire to do good for others so she could release herself from deep feelings of unworthiness, of which her eating disorders were merely a symptom.

'She talked endlessly about getting away from England, mainly because of the treatment that she received at the hands of the newspapers. I don't think she ever understood why her genuinely good intentions were sneered at by the media, why there appeared to be a permanent quest on their behalf to bring her down. It is baffling.

'My own and only explanation is that genuine goodness is threatening to those at the opposite end of the moral spectrum. It is a point to remember that, of all the ironies about Diana, perhaps the greatest was this – a girl given the name of the ancient goddess of hunting was, in the end, the most hunted person of the modern age.

'She would want us today to pledge ourselves to protecting her beloved boys William and Harry from a similar fate, and I do this here, Diana, on your behalf. We will not allow them to suffer the anguish that used regularly to drive you to tearful despair.

'And beyond that, on behalf of your mother and sisters, I pledge that we, your blood family, will do all we can to continue the imaginative way in which you were steering these two exceptional young men so that their souls are not simply immersed by duty and tradition but can sing openly as you planned.'

It was a deeply moving tribute, bravely delivered as the Earl struggled against his own tears. But the last sentence was a shocking kick in the teeth to the Prince of Wales; it was thoroughly insensitive of the Earl to have criticised William and Harry's father and grandparents – indeed, one half of their relatives – in front of them on the day they buried their mother.

What really offended the Prince, however, was being forced to sit and be lectured about parental responsibility by a man who had a disastrous marriage of his own: four young children, a wife who had been ill-treated for years, and a history of adultery – all of which became very public during a bitter divorce some months later. What is more, Spencer had the gall to bring his latest mistress, Josie Borain, to the funeral. She sat beside him in the Abbey and accompanied him – on the royal train with the Prince of Wales – to the Spencer family home in Northamptonshire, Althorp, for Diana's interment immediately afterwards. Diana was buried on an island in the middle of a lake in the grounds, not in the family crypt as she had requested. It was thought that the small village churchyard would be unable to cope with the number of people that might come to visit her grave.

Charles Spencer and Diana had not been particularly close in recent years. The relationship had been up and down, as it was with most of her family. She was particularly upset that after her divorce her brother told her she could not have a particular cottage she wanted to move into on the Althorp estate. Charles, who had inherited Althorp after their father's death in 1991, said she couldn't have the cottage she wanted because it was near the gates of the estate and he was worried about the media interest she would attract. He had offered her others to choose from but Diana had set her heart on this particular cottage and felt badly let down.

Ironically, in burying Diana on the island, the Earl has turned the estate into a Mecca. He has created a museum in memory of his sister in the old stable block at Althorp, where all the hundreds of books of condolence, her dresses and various other bits of memorabilia are housed, and where videos of her, both as a child and a Princess, play constantly throughout the day. Visitors are taken around a small section of the house and then herded out to the lake, and to the shrine to the Princess that has been built on the water's edge. Some of her words are inscribed on it, and some of his from his funeral tribute.

There is a rumour, however, that Diana is not there. A very select group was invited to attend the burial, and many people believe that her body is actually in the family crypt at the churchyard in the village of Great Brington, alongside the remains of her father, the eighth Earl, and the grandmother she so adored, Cynthia Spencer, who had been her guide, she always felt, in the spirit world.

THREE

The Young Prince

'I've fallen in love with all sorts of girls ...'
Charles

Nothing could have been further from the truth than the *Daily Mail*'s claim that Charles had wept 'bitter tears of guilt' as he walked the lonely moors in the immediate hours after Diana's death. He wept bitterly for the loss of the girl he had once loved, whose life had been so sad, he wept bitterly for his children, whose grief he knew would be unimaginable. He was terrified about having to break the news to them. But there was no guilt, either about Diana's death or about his affair with Camilla Parker Bowles. He knew that he was not responsible in any way for what had happened in that Parisian tunnel. Although he had failed, he knew that he had done everything in his power to make his marriage to Diana work; and he knew that no headline writer could ever begin to understand the reasons why.

If the Prince of Wales felt at all guilty, it was because of all the emotions he felt about Diana's death, the principal one was relief. Relief that the pain and the suffering was now over, that his children would no longer be torn in opposite directions, confused and upset by their mother's bizarre behaviour, and that he would no longer be spied upon – she had always tried to find out what he was doing, who he was seeing, where he was going – but be free to get on with his life. He wept bitterly because of the sheer tragedy of it all. Their life together had begun with such promise and such joy, but had ended in such acrimony and anger. But mostly he wept for William and Harry, whose lives would never be the same again, who would never have the comforting arms of their mother around them and who would carry that loss for the rest of their lives. No one, he knew, would ever be able to take away their pain.

He understood. He knew the numbing, hopeless, gnawing emptiness of grief. He had known it when Lord Mountbatten was murdered. Learning to make sense of living without this mainstay in his life had seemed impossible. How much worse for William and Harry, still so young and vulnerable, to lose their mother.

So he cried for them, and he cried for his failure to help Diana. He had tried desperately, but she had been beyond any help he had been able to provide. And he cried for the failure of his marriage – as he had done many times before. He cried for all the people they had let down, and for all the lost hopes that they both had cherished in the early days, to create a secure, happy and loving home for each other and their children.

He had wanted this, just as much as she had. They had both passionately believed in the importance of family. He wanted Diana to be the person with whom he might share his life and interests, who could be friend, companion and lover. Sadly, neither he nor Diana knew what a happy home was. Neither of them had grown up with a normal loving relationship to observe, on which they might base theirs; and both were crippled by low self-esteem and lack of confidence, and a desperate need to be loved.

By 1980 the pressure on the Prince of Wales to find a wife had been intense. Guessing who it might be had been an international obsession during the seventies, which reached the height of absurdity one summer's day when the *Daily Express* announced his imminent engagement to Princess Marie-Astrid of Luxembourg, whom he had never even met. Dubbed Action Man, Charles cut a very dashing figure, particularly on the polo field, and he had had a string of attractive girlfriends, some suitably aristocratic, others glamorous and highly unsuitable starlets. The press followed every romance with fascination, especially the French and German magazines, and it was they who began the long-lens paparazzi style of photography that came to make everyone's life such a misery.

The Prince had never been short of pretty female company, but he was always handicapped because of his position. No one ever behaved normally in his company, and there was always a danger that he was attractive to women for no better reason than because they wanted to be seen with the Prince of Wales. When this was the case he was never the best person to spot it. He had always been shy and awkward and, with little opportunity to gain experience, he was ignorant about women and how to treat them. He had been to ordinary schools and university, and he had done a spell in the Navy, but most of his life had been spent in a rarefied atmosphere. With a handful of exceptions, men and women alike bowed and curtsied when they met him and called him 'sir'. Even Diana called him 'sir' until they were engaged. It is as much a mark of respect for the title as it is for the individual, but it is enough to keep a very strong barrier between him and the real world.

Charles would take girlfriends to watch him play polo at Smiths Lawn, or he would take them to the opera or the ballet and bring them home to his apartment at Buckingham Palace for supper afterwards. But there was little room for spontaneity, and certainly none for privacy. He couldn't even be alone with them in his car. Ever since a gunman ambushed Princess Anne as she was being driven down the Mall in 1974, security for all the family has been tight – and on any journey there will be a detective in the car and a backup car behind. The Prince's staff would make the arrangements and girls were usually brought to wherever he happened to be, which understandably made encounters awkward and forced. And if the formality didn't kill a burgeoning relationship, then the other hazard of dating the Prince of Wales – being splashed all over the gossip columns – usually did.

Lord Mountbatten had encouraged Charles to take girlfriends to his Hampshire estate – he was a great believer that the Prince should 'sow his wild oats' before settling down – and Broadlands afforded greater privacy (as well as the chance for Mountbatten to vet the latest conquest), but it was still an unhappy situation, and one from which most suitable girls ran a mile. Far more relaxing, Charles discovered, was the company of married women. There was no pressure on him, no expectation from them, and best of all the press left him alone. This was how he became so friendly with Camilla Parker Bowles, although she was only one of several he was close to.

He had first got to know Camilla Shand, as she then was, in 1972, when he was in the Navy. She was single at the time, but she had been going out with Andrew Parker Bowles for six years. He was a cavalry officer, nine years older than her, and hugely attractive, but hopelessly faithless. He had swept her off her feet when she was just eighteen – as he swept many girls before and since, including Princess Anne – and she hoped he would marry her, but he took her for granted, and treated her badly, knowing that she would always be there to take him back.

It was while he was stationed in Germany and their relationship was going through an off patch that Camilla and the Prince of Wales had a brief affair in the autumn of 1972. The Prince fell in love with Camilla. She was the most wonderful girl he had ever met. She was pretty and bubbly and laughed easily, and at the same sort of puerile dirty jokes he enjoyed. She loved the Goons and silly voices and put on accents that made him laugh, and she had no pretensions or guile of any sort. She loved horses and hunting, loved watching polo, loved the countryside, and was relaxed and exciting to be with.

He saw a lot of her at the end of that year and fell ever more deeply in love. He even began to think that he might have found someone he could share his life with. To his great joy she seemed to feel the same way about him, but he was only just twenty-four and too reticent to say anything to her – and certainly too reticent to discuss the possibility of any future together. Three weeks before Christmas their time together came to an enforced end. Duty called, and he went off to join the frigate HMS *Minerva*, as Acting Sub Lieutenant, which was due to set sail for the Caribbean in the New Year, and would keep him away for eight months. Before he left, Camilla came down to have lunch on the ship, once with Lord Mountbatten, with whom she had stayed with Charles at Broadlands, and on another weekend on her own.

By the time Charles came back Camilla had married Andrew Parker Bowles. They had become engaged in March, two months after he set sail, and were married at the Guards Chapel in London in July. This was what she had been waiting seven years for. He was one of the most attractive and desirable men in England and she adored him. When Charles heard of the engagement he was deeply upset. As he wrote to a friend, it seemed particularly cruel that after 'such a blissful, peaceful and mutually happy relationship' fate had decreed that it should last no more than six months. 'I suppose the feeling of emptiness will pass eventually.'

Despite the bitter disappointment, he and Camilla remained friends, and during the next seven years, when he was dating other girls with enthusiasm, she was someone he could talk to. When the Parker Bowles's first child, Tom, was born in 1975, Camilla asked Charles to be his godfather. For many years there was nothing sexual in their relationship, but because they had had such a happy and intimate affair during those six months, there remained a closeness and trust and friendship that was special. He confided in Camilla and spent a lot of time on the telephone to her. They also met at polo, parties and royal gatherings – Andrew Parker Bowles's mother had been a friend of the Queen and he was distantly related to the Queen Mother. Camilla and her family had also been on the periphery of royalty. Her father, Bruce Shand, was a wealthy wine merchant and businessman, and her mother, Rosalind, a member of the hugely rich Cubitt family – her father was Baron Ashcombe. Camilla's great-grandmother, Alice Keppel, had been mistress to King Edward VII, who was the Prince's great-great-grandfather, and Camilla enjoyed the idea of history repeating itself. She and Andrew were frequently invited to stay at Sandringham, Windsor and Balmoral, and Charles went to spend weekends with Camilla and Andrew and the children in Wiltshire. Their daughter Laura was born in 1979.

The friendship only became physical again after Laura's birth, long after Camilla realised that the philanderer she had pursued for seven years before their marriage had continued in much the same way after marriage. What was so hurtful was that as often as not the women Andrew bedded were friends of hers. As time passed, she spent a lot of time on her own in the country, looking after the children and horses, while Andrew lived in London, where he escorted other women quite openly. Under those circumstances, who was to mind if she had a fling with the Prince of Wales? It was not serious, it couldn't go anywhere, it was just a bit of fun, and although there were occasional references to Camilla in the satirical magazine *Private Eye*, and the odd gossip column, it was the Prince's single starlets that attracted the headlines.

The Duke of Edinburgh disapproved of the playboy image that the Prince was acquiring, and when he passed his thirtieth birthday, and still showed no signs of settling down, told him what he thought. Charles knew it was his duty to provide an heir for the future security and stability of the monarchy, but he wanted to find the right wife and had repeatedly spoken about choosing someone who would know what she was letting herself in for.

'I've fallen in love with all sorts of girls and I fully intend to go on doing so, but I've made sure I haven't married the first person I've fallen in love with. I think one's got to be aware of the fact that falling madly in love with someone is not necessarily the starting point to getting married,' he once said. '[Marriage] is basically a very strong friendship ... I think you are lucky if you find the person attractive in the physical and the mental sense ... To me marriage seems to be the biggest and most responsible step to be taken in one's life.

'Whatever your place in life, when you marry you are forming a partnership which you hope will last for fifty years. So I'd want to marry someone whose interests I could share. A woman not only marries a man; she marries into a way of life – a job. She's got to have some knowledge of it, some sense of it, otherwise she wouldn't have a clue about whether she's going to like it. If I'm deciding on whom I want to live with for fifty years – well, that's the last decision on which I want my head to be ruled by my heart.'

Despite the girlfriends, the Prince was fundamentally lonely and longed to find someone to share his life with. He wanted to settle down, be domestic, have a garden and dogs and children, and all the things that his friends had. He had spent his life in search of love and reassurance and was dogged by a sense of worthlessness, which his parents had done nothing to help him overcome. They are not demonstrative people, and praise for one another's achievements is not something that comes naturally in the Royal Family.

Those who have known the family since Charles was a child say that the Queen adores her eldest son, as she adores all her children – there is no doubting the affection – but sadly it is not in her nature to be overtly affectionate. Some remember her sitting him on her knee at afternoon tea when he was small, and playing games with him, but that physical closeness disappeared as he grew older. The Queen inherited the throne when he was three years old on the death of her father, George VI, and her duties as monarch inevitably competed with motherhood, taking her away more than she would have chosen. She made it a rule to be with her children at bath and bedtime, whenever possible, and to be at home during the school holidays, but day to day care was left to much-loved nannies, which was normal in upper-class families of that period. The one time she was away for a sustained period was for the Coronation tour in 1953–54, when she and the Duke of Edinburgh were gone for six months, including Christmas. It was then that Charles saw so much of the Queen Mother and, although the Prince adores his mother, the relationship never developed the real warmth or intimacy that he shares with his grandmother.

Even on the night Diana died, when his mother was on the other side of a thin partition wall, he sat and talked and worried not with her, but with his friends and his advisers. When he thought Diana was injured and was undecided about whether to get on a plane and go to Paris, he didn't ask his mother's advice, he asked his private secretary; and in the arranging of the plane, his advisers spoke to her advisers. This is no ordinary mother–son relationship: Charles has been in awe of her all his life and, even at fifty, is still delighted beyond reason when she compliments him on something she has noticed he has done well.

His father is equally loving and proud of his eldest son, but no less sparing in showing it. He was rough with Charles as a child and witnesses say he frequently reduced the boy to tears. Charles was a sensitive, shy and uncertain little boy, in contrast to his sister Anne, who was tough and sure of herself and could do no wrong. The Duke probably thought this kind of treatment would make a man of Charles, but it only served to undermine his confidence still further. Charles was frightened of his father, and desperate for his approval, but try as he might to please him, he seldom could.

There are not many men of fifty, with independent means, who are still trying so hard to please their parents – certainly not men with the kind of physical courage that the Prince of Wales indisputably has. But the family that Charles was born into is not like any other family in Britain and he was conditioned to accept, without question, a way of life that normal people would find quite intolerable. Duty to Queen and country comes before any other consideration. Charles is never entirely alone: a detective is within earshot twenty-four hours a day. He never goes anywhere without someone knowing. He has no privacy, therefore, and is dependent upon the discretion of the men who shadow him.

There is no heart to the family: it is a business, an institution, and participation is not an option, it is duty. There is very little communication between members of the family. When there is, it is often by memo, or via private secretaries. And, except for holidays and ceremonial fixtures, there is very little contact between them. Their lives are run to a formula, from which there is no deviation or spontaneity, and the formality with which the Queen runs her household is from another age.

Apart from the companionship, which he craved, Charles had no need for a wife. His life was ordered: his meals were cooked; his clothes bought, laundered and laid out for him; his every whim catered for; his friends numerous, understanding and sufficiently fawning; his office compliant; his love life exciting; and his sporting activities and holidays strategically organised from one year to the next to fit in around official fixtures, functions and the call of duty.

He had houses in the country and convenient apartments at Buckingham Palace; he had horses, dogs and cars, and a fleet of royal helicopters, planes and trains, not to mention the royal yacht at his disposal, plus holiday homes in all the places he most liked to be. He only had to click his fingers and what he wanted arrived or was fixed. The only benefit a wife could bring, which he could get nowhere else, was an heir.

By an accident of birth the Prince of Wales was cursed with a life in which his waking hours are mapped out six months in advance, and there are fixtures in his diary which will be there on the same day every year for the rest of his life. He is surrounded by people who tell him what they think he wants to hear; he is paraded like a performing poodle on high days and holidays, and his every twitch and grunt recorded and analysed by the tabloid press. His right to exist is debated regularly, as though he had some say in the matter, and his character and physique considered fair game for whoever fancies taking a passing punch. This is how it has been since he was three years old, when his mother became Queen.

He is an uneasy mix of old and new, half expecting the deference, service and lifestyle of another era, and half wanting to be a modern man of the people in an egalitarian age. But he is hampered by being kept at one remove from the life modern man leads. Diana had one huge advantage over the Prince: she did understand how the other half lived, because she had grown up in the real world. The Prince, try as he might, has never been given a chance. He has wanted to meet people in their own environment, but he is always cushioned. Try as he might to empathise, he will never know what it is like to queue for hours in a hospital casualty department or have petty bureaucrats be rude to him. He will never be elbowed out of the way in the rush for the first bus to appear in twenty minutes, know the frustrations of a train being cancelled, or have to hang around an overcrowded airport lounge. And if it starts to rain, someone will appear with an umbrella to keep him dry.

When he was forty minutes late for an Order of the Bath ceremony at Westminster Abbey with the Queen not long ago, he was incandescent with rage. The helicopter had been unable to land at Highgrove because of fog, so he was told to drive to RAF Lyneham nearby, only to discover that the fog was just as bad and the helicopter couldn't land there either. There was no alternative but to drive all the way to London, which made him late. Some unfortunate person had got it wrong, and he hit the roof. When his staff once failed to organise his supper menu on the royal train because they had been working exceptionally hard on a very tricky weekend of engagements that had gone like clockwork, he was furious. The chef said he could do him one of three dishes: some salmon, a salad or steak and kidney pie. He petulantly said he didn't like any of them. When a member of staff once failed to call him 'sir' or 'Your Royal Highness' – terrified by the experience of meeting the Prince for the first time – he said, 'Do you think you could ask that chap to call me something when he meets me?' Friends will say, 'He only lets people know who he is when they forget,' but it evidently depends upon what sort of mood he is in, and during the difficult times in his marriage, his moods were highly unpredictable.

Employees see this side of the Prince more than friends, which perhaps makes it all the more reprehensible.

Yet at other times he is relaxed and will laugh when things go wrong. A trip to the United World College in Trieste some years ago fell during the transition period between two private secretaries. The one who had done the recce – when the precise details are worked out of where HRH will go, who he will speak to, and how long it will all take – was not the one there on the day. Thus with great élan, but no certainty about where they were going, the Prince and accompanying entourage were led off down an alley way, only to discover it was a dead end which led to the dustbins. Covered in confusion the party did a swift U-turn and with photographers swarming around them beat a hasty retreat. The incoming private secretary, Major-General Sir Christopher Airy, a highly efficient man, was mortified, but the Prince simply laughed.

He was also amused by an encounter with Chris Eubank, the champion boxer, who had been running a fitness workshop at a

Prince's Trust residential course in Brighton. He was standing at the end of a line-up to meet the Prince and was obviously very nervous, so the private secretary went across to try and calm him down. 'Don't worry,' he said, 'the Prince is very easy to talk to, just enjoy it.'

After they had met, he went up to Eubank to see how it had gone. 'Yes, of course it was okay,' said Eubank. 'I wasn't frightened. If you've been in the ring with Nigel Benn you're not frightened of the Prince of Wales. So it was absolutely fine.'

The private secretary beat a retreat. A little later Eubank called him back. 'Anyway, I hope I did the right thing. I called him Mr Windsor. I'm Chris Eubank, so I'm Mr Eubank. He's Charles Windsor, so he must be Mr Windsor. Right?'

'Yes,' said the private secretary, fearing for his profile. 'That's absolutely fine.'

Charles does have a sense of humour and a great sense of the absurd, but anyone who knows him well knows how important it is to judge his mood before ever presuming familiarity. His children are the exception; they can say and do what they like to him and if he starts to get testy or pompous about it, they simply tease him out of it. They are sensitive enough, though, to know who not to tease him in front of.

One other person who can stop the Prince taking himself too seriously, and get away with it, is Mrs Parker Bowles; but she too picks her moments and would never embarrass the Prince in front of anyone other than his closest friends. They all acknowledge she has a miraculous effect on him, and whenever invitations to dinner at Highgrove are issued, they desperately hope Camilla will be there. If she is, the evening will be relaxed and good fun, with a great deal of gossip, jokes and giggling. Without her, the Prince is likely be serious and if he's feeling down – which without her he often is – he can be fairly leaden company.

Thousands of young people whom he has helped during the course of the last twenty-one years rightly regard him as someone very special: without him they might never have had a chance in life. He has helped when no bank manager would have considered their application – even if they had known how to apply for a loan. He believed in their potential and has put time, thought, effort and money into helping through the Prince's Trust and its various offshoots. The Prince's Trust was just the beginning. He has spread himself over a wide range of interests and concerns, and he has done a huge amount of good in his fifty years, much of it unrecognised by the majority of the population. He has exploited his privilege and his position to very good ends, and there is no doubt that he is an extremely sensitive man, who cares desperately and sincerely. Yet he remains intrinsically very selfish and very spoilt.

The problem is that Charles has no social equal, and few people have ever been brave enough over the years to say what needed to be said. There have been a few exceptions, and whenever rebuked for behaving in an inconsiderate manner to someone, the Prince has always been deeply ashamed. On one occasion, speaking at a Queen's Silver Jubilee Trust dinner, the Prince made some rather barbed remarks about a couple of people in the room who were dragging their feet about taking up one of his ideas. At the end of the evening, Michael Colborne told the Prince he thought he had been unnecessarily harsh on the two individuals. Colborne had known the Prince during his time in the Navy and joined his staff in 1974. He felt so strongly that over the following weekend he sat down and put his feelings on paper, and sent the letter to the Prince, who was by then staying on a Duchy farm. A week later Charles was back at Highgrove, and called Colborne into his office.

'You know that letter you wrote me?' he said. 'Do you know what I did with it? I read it and I screwed it up into a ball and I kicked it round the bedroom.'

'Oh you did, did you, sir?' said Colborne with a slight smile. 'Why was that?'

'Because unfortunately you were right. I wasn't very nice to those two men that night.'

FOUR

The Discovery of Diana

'She was a sort of wonderful English schoolgirl
who was game for anything.'
Friend of Prince Charles

When Charles first met Diana she was a nondescript schoolgirl of sixteen – his girlfriend's little sister. He was in the midst of a lengthy and enjoyable relationship with Sarah, and they met at Althorp, where he had been invited to a shoot. Diana was nothing more than a slightly plump, noisy teenager, but he made a profound impression on this particular teenager and Diana secretly set her heart on him then and there and determined that she would become Princess of Wales.

Sarah's romance with Charles came to an end when she spoke candidly to the press about it, saying, 'I wouldn't marry anyone I didn't love, whether it was the dustman or the King of England. If he asked me I would turn him down.' But they remained friends, and the Prince invited Sarah and Diana to his thirtieth birthday party at Buckingham Palace a year later, and a few months after that, in January 1979, they were both invited as guests of the Queen to a shooting weekend at Sandringham. That very weekend, their father, Earl Spencer, had come out of hospital following a brain haemorrhage that very nearly killed him.

Later that year Diana was staying with her sister, Jane Fellowes, in her house at Balmoral to help with Jane's new baby, while the Royal Family was in residence at the castle. But the first time Charles saw her as anything more than a jolly and bouncy young girl whom he enjoyed taking out from time to time as one of a group to make up numbers was in July 1980, when they were both invited to a weekend party with mutual friends in Sussex. He had just had a dramatic and humiliating bust up with his latest passion, Anna Wallace, and he and Diana were sitting side by side on a hay bale while their hosts prepared a barbecue, when the conversation turned to Mountbatten, who had died the previous August. What Diana said touched the Prince deeply – as she knew it would.

'You looked so sad when you walked up the aisle at Lord Mountbatten's funeral,' she said. 'It was the most tragic thing I've ever seen. My heart bled for you when I watched. I thought, "It's wrong, you're lonely – you should be with somebody to look after you."'

It is ironic that her sensitivity about Lord Mountbatten should have triggered Charles's interest in Diana as a future bride, for Mountbatten would not have approved of the match. In losing his beloved great-uncle, his 'Honorary Grandfather', the Prince had lost his mentor; also, for a considerable time, he had lost his way in life. Mountbatten would have applauded Diana's sweet nature, her youth, her beauty, her nobility and her virginity; but he would have seen that the pair had too little in common to sustain them through fifty years of marriage. He might also have spotted her acute vulnerability and the damage sustained by her painful start in life, and known that the Prince, with his own vulnerability and insecurity, was not the right man to cope with her needs.

Mountbatten's murder had an unimaginable impact on the Prince's life; it knocked him entirely off-balance. As he wrote in his journal on the evening he heard the news, 'Life has to go on, I suppose, but this afternoon I must confess I wanted it to stop. I felt supremely useless and powerless …

'I have lost someone infinitely special in my life; someone who showed enormous affection, who told me unpleasant things I didn't particularly want to hear, who gave praise where it was due as well as criticism; someone to whom I knew I could confide anything and from whom I would receive the wisest of counsel and advice.'

Mountbatten had criticised the Prince of Wales, most notably for his selfishness, but he also made him feel he was loved and valued, which neither of his parents had ever been able to do. Where his father had cut the ground from under his feet, Mountbatten had built him up, listened to his doubts and his fears, rebuked him when he felt he had behaved badly, encouraged him, cajoled him, provided a sounding board for his wackier ideas, a shoulder to cry on, and given him some much needed confidence. There was no one else in his life at that time who could do this.

From the time when Charles was so touched by their exchange on the hay bale, to the announcement of their engagement, the romance was brief – less than seven months – and their moments alone were rare, but throughout the course of the relationship, Diana was in charge. She knew what she wanted and she went all out to get it. She had cherished her dream of marrying the Prince since their first meeting three years before, and with great cunning ensured her dream came true. She had always said since she was a small child that when she grew up she was going to be someone special. Her siblings called her 'Duch' – because she was determined to be a duchess at the very least. When the opportunity arose, she threw herself at the Prince, quite blatantly and brazenly. Yet it was only the more astute of Charles's friends who realised what was going on. He didn't appear to notice. Like most men he was easily flattered, particularly by a pretty young woman who professed great interest in everything he said and did, and manifested great sympathy and understanding for the trials and tribulations of his life. He found her quite intoxicating, and she was willing and amenable to do whatever might please him. She slotted neatly into whatever plans he already had, she talked about her love of the country and of shooting and her interest in taking up horse riding, and she liked his friends. And crucially, she made him laugh. She was fun.

But it was all a sham. Diana didn't like any of these things. She hated the countryside, had no interest in shooting or horses, or dogs, and she didn't even really like his friends. She found them old, boring and sycophantic. What she enjoyed was the city. She liked shopping in expensive Knightsbridge department stores, and lunching in smart London restaurants. She liked cinema and pop music.

Diana was a victim, who needed love and attention and constant reassurance – needs she carried to an exaggerated degree from her childhood. Her mother, Frances Shand Kydd, had run away from a violent and unhappy marriage when Diana was six years old and the experience of that loss – her feeling of rejection that followed when her mother disappeared – left deep scars in Diana's psyche.

Frances Shand Kydd has been unfairly maligned for deserting her children, not least by Mohamed al Fayed when they attended an investigative meeting in Paris in June 1998 about the crash that killed both their children. He lashed out at her, saying, 'She didn't give a damn about her daughter ... If you leave a child when she's six years old how can you call yourself a good mother?'

Whatever her qualities as a mother, Frances had every expectation when she left home for good just before Christmas in 1967 that it would be a temporary separation. She intended to sue her husband for divorce on the grounds of cruelty, and it was unthinkable for a mother in these circumstances not to be given custody of young children. Her husband, Johnnie Althorp, who later became the eighth Earl Spencer on his father's death, was a well-respected, genial, if rather dim, member of the aristocracy. He had been an equerry to George VI, then to Queen Elizabeth II.

Abuse ran in the Spencer family marriages and their thirteen years together had not been happy. To compound her misery, Frances had lost a child, a baby boy called John, born after Jane and Sarah, in January 1960, who only lived for ten hours. Diana was born eighteen months later, and then in May 1964 Frances gave birth to another boy, Charles, the son and heir her husband so badly wanted.

Shortly afterwards she met and fell in love with Peter Shand Kydd, a wealthy married businessman. Their affair broke up both marriages, and Frances seized the opportunity to escape. In the autumn of 1967 she and Johnnie had a trial separation, and at

Christmas it became permanent and she left the family home. But her plans to sue for cruelty went badly awry. Shand Kydd's wife, Janet, sued him for divorce on the grounds of his adultery with Frances. With that proven, Frances had no defence when Johnnie also sued for divorce because of their adultery. The cruelty suit was thrown out, and in the custody proceedings that followed, he brought some of the most influential people in the land to speak up for him – including her own mother, Ruth, Lady Fermoy, a considerable snob, who was said to have been appalled that her daughter had run off with a man 'in trade' – albeit a millionaire.

As a result, custody of Jane, Sarah, Diana and Charles was given to their father, who employed a string of itinerant nannies to take care of them. Frances was only allowed to have them on specified weekends and parts of the school holidays.

Diana said, 'It was a very unhappy childhood ... Always seeing my mother crying ... I remember Mummy crying an awful lot and every Saturday when we went up for weekends, every Saturday night, standard procedure, she would start crying. On Saturday we would both see her crying. "What's the matter, Mummy?" "Oh, I don't want you to leave tomorrow."'

One of Diana's other early memories was hearing her younger brother Charles sobbing in his bed at the other end of the house from her room, crying for their mother. She understood none of what had gone on between her parents. All she could see, like any small child in a similar situation, was that her mother didn't want her any more. She told Andrew Morton that she began to think she was a nuisance, and then worked out that because she was born after her dead brother, she must have been a huge disappointment to her parents. 'Both were crazy to have a son and heir and there comes a third daughter. "What a bore, we're going to have to try again." I've recognised that now. I've been aware of it and now I recognise it and that's fine. I accept it.'

Rightly or wrongly, Diana felt rejected, worthless and unwanted. Those were the feelings she nursed throughout her childhood and teenage years and, three weeks after her twentieth birthday, took with her into marriage. She was still desperately seeking love and reassurance.

Her mother's departure was not the end of the trauma in Diana's young life. In June 1975, shortly before her fourteenth birthday, her paternal grandfather died and her father inherited the title and the ancestral home, Althorp. It meant an upheaval from Norfolk, where she had friends and roots, to Northamptonshire, where she knew no one. Worse still, her father, whom the children had had more or less to themselves for the last eight years, had taken up with a formidable woman, Raine, Countess of Dartmouth, daughter of the romantic novelist, Barbara Cartland, mother of four and former member of Westminster City Council, the London County Council and the Greater London Council. To the children's horror, the couple were married just over a year later, and the woman one of her friends described as 'not a person but an experience' took over Althorp and all who lived in it.

Diana's education was poor. After prep school at Riddlesworth Hall in Norfolk, she followed her sisters to West Heath, another boarding school in Kent, where she passed no O-Levels, despite two attempts, and left in December 1977 at the age of sixteen. She went from there to finishing school in Switzerland but didn't enjoy it; she came home after six weeks and refused to go back. She did some brief nannying jobs, learnt to drive, did a short cookery course, and briefly worked as a student teacher at Betti Vacani's children's dancing school in Knightsbridge. But that too she gave up. One day she simply didn't arrive for work, and when she was telephoned and asked what the problem was, she said she had hurt her leg. The truth was that whenever the going got tough, Diana quit. After that she did cleaning jobs for her sister and any friends who wanted their flats vacuuming or their laundry done. She had been obsessively clean and tidy ever since she was a small child. At school she had done far more washing than anyone else. It was the one thing she was prepared to stick at.

On 1 July 1979, her eighteenth birthday, Diana came into money which had been left in trust for the Spencer children by her American great-grandmother, Frances Work, and was encouraged by her mother, as her sisters had been before her, to buy a flat with some of the money. The flat she bought was 60 Coleherne Court, said to have cost £50,000, which she shared initially with two friends. By the time she began seeing the Prince of Wales, she had three flatmates, Carolyn Pride, Virginia Pitman and Anne Bolton; and was working three afternoons a week as an assistant at the Young England Kindergarten in Pimlico, run by the sister of a schoolfriend of Jane.

Diana's problem was that she had had no discipline in her life. Like so many children of divorced parents, she had been indulged. She was an extremely rich, extremely spoilt young woman, who was used to getting her own way. In marrying the Prince of Wales she was taking on one of the most disciplined ways of life in Britain.

The Prince of Wales was quite besotted by Diana at the time he asked her to marry him, and when she came to Balmoral in the late summer of 1980 everyone fell in love with her. She was a fresh, delightful, funny girl, with a podgy face and pudding basin haircut, who told jokes, had no clothes so borrowed everyone else's, asked daft questions, knew nothing about anything, and made everyone helpless with laughter. Charles couldn't believe his luck, that this lovely girl, whom all his friends seemed to find so attractive and engaging, said she loved *him*.

Charles's excitement at finding Diana, who seemed to be perfect in every way, was quite touching. In public, the mask behind which he hides is impenetrable. In private, he has never been able to hide his emotions, and since he was a small child, if asked, he has always blurted out everything he is thinking and feeling. He has no guile, and over the years most of these thoughts and emotions have been committed to paper in letters and notes to friends and relations. As his feelings for Diana began to run away with him, his older and wiser friends told him that he should slow down and keep his cool, lest he blow it.

In August 1980, several of Charles's friends were with him on board the royal yacht *Britannia* for Cowes Week on the Isle of

Wight, the oldest yachting regatta in the world and one of the great events of the social season. He invited Diana, and confided to one of his friends that he had met the girl he intended to marry. Oliver Everett, an assistant private secretary, who had accompanied her to the yacht, returned to his colleagues in the office saying, 'I think this is serious.' In September the Prince invited her to Balmoral, again with his friends. By then he was confessing that he was not yet in love with her, but felt that because she was so lovable and warm-hearted, he very soon could be. The friends could see no objection. At nineteen she was younger than most of them by many years, but she was friendly and easy company and most of them warmed to her. She was fun and bubbly, and told Charles how completely at home she was in the country. As one of his friends said, 'We went walking together, we got hot, we got tired, she fell into a bog, she got covered in mud, laughed her head off, got puce in the face, hair glued to her forehead because it was pouring with rain ... She was a sort of wonderful English schoolgirl who was game for anything, naturally young but sweet and clearly determined and enthusiastic about him, very much wanted him.'

The Prince taught Diana to fish on the River Dee, and it was while she was out alone with him one afternoon that she was spotted by James Whitaker, at that time royal correspondent of the *Daily Star*, who had been pursuing Charles for many years to secure the scoop of the decade – the girl who would be Queen – and his tenacity can only be marvelled at. It was a matter of hours before Diana's name, address and pedigree were all over Fleet Street and her flat in Coleherne Court in Chelsea was under siege by seldom fewer than thirty photographers. They followed her every move, telephoned her at all hours of the day and night, pointed long lenses at her bedroom window from the building opposite, and made her life totally intolerable until the engagement was announced five months later and she was able to move into the sanctuary of Buckingham Palace.

Charles was badly smitten, but his decision to ask Diana to marry him in February was not born out of spontaneity or conviction.

It was a pitiful combination of poor communication, media manipulation and pressure that he no longer had the strength to resist. Diana was clearly suitable and in every way might have been tailor made. She came from a family that had been connected to the Royal Family for years, she understood the protocol, she was comfortable around them all. She was sexy, pretty and fun to be with. She was interested in all the things he was interested in, and young enough to fit in with his lifestyle without too much difficulty. The newspapers loved Diana, and the country wanted him to marry her.

It was still early days, but because the media had reached fever pitch – not entirely discouraged by Diana, who developed quite a warm relationship with people like James Whitaker during that time – Charles was forced into making a decision that he was not yet ready to make. Everyone wanted him to find a wife. The pressure from inside and outside the family was intense, and there were not many candidates by the 1980s who fitted the job description. Diana seemed as close to perfect as he had known. She appeared to love him very much, so, hoping for the best, the Prince allowed himself to be led by others.

There was one other decisive factor. It was one of the most inexplicable episodes, which has remained a mystery ever since and probably always will. In November, a story appeared in the *Sunday Mirror* entitled 'Love in the Sidings', which claimed that a blonde woman of Diana's description had driven from London in the middle of the night, and been secreted on to the royal train for a few hours with the Prince while it was parked at a siding in Wiltshire. She had been telephoned and asked for a comment and said the story was quite untrue. Bob Edwards, the editor, was so convinced it was true that he published anyway, and was shocked by the unprecedented reaction from the Queen's press secretary, Michael Shea. He demanded a retraction, calling the story 'total fabrication'. Some years later, Edwards had a Christmas card from his friend Woodrow Wyatt which simply said, 'It must have been Camilla.' Camilla and the Prince both say the incident never happened –

Camilla has never been on board the royal train – and neither they, nor any of the Prince's staff who were around at the time have ever been able to get to the bottom of where the story could possibly have come from. The royal train is heavily guarded by British Transport police – it is their big moment – and when it stops overnight, there are patrols walking up and down both sides of the train, men on bridges, cars everywhere, plus a large crew on board. It is inconceivable that anyone could have been smuggled on to the train undetected, and if someone had seen a blonde woman smuggled into the Prince's compartment, whether Camilla or not, the story would have been out long ago.

However, it was pivotal to Charles and Diana's relationship, and it would not have been beyond the cunning of Diana to have tipped off the *Sunday Mirror* herself – nor some years later, consumed with jealousy for Camilla, suggested the blonde was Camilla.

The clear implication from the story was that Diana had slept with the Prince, which cast doubt on her virtue. The fact that the Queen should have been so quick to protect her virtue gave Diana a special status. She had not stepped in to protect any of the other women the Prince had been with. It further fuelled speculation that this one would become his bride.

Diana's mother wrote to *The Times* appealing for an end to it all. 'In recent weeks,' she wrote, 'many articles have been labelled "exclusive quotes", when the plain truth is that my daughter has not spoken the words attributed to her. Fanciful speculation, if it is in good taste, is one thing, but this can be embarrassing. Lies are quite another matter, and by their very nature, hurtful and inexcusable … May I ask the editors of Fleet Street, whether, in the execution of their jobs, they consider it necessary or fair to harass my daughter daily from dawn until well after dusk? Is it fair to ask any human being, regardless of circumstances, to be treated in this way? The freedom of the press was granted by law, by public demand, for very good reasons. But when these privileges are abused, can the press command any respect, or expect to be shown any respect?'

Sixty MPs tabled a motion in the House of Commons 'deploring the manner in which Lady Diana Spencer is treated by the media' and 'calling upon those responsible to have more concern for individual privacy'. Fleet Street editors met senior members of the Press Council to discuss the situation. It was the first time in its twenty-seven-year history that such an extraordinary meeting had been convened, but it did nothing to stop the harassment.

It was against this background that the Duke of Edinburgh wrote to his son saying that he must make up his mind about Diana. In all the media madness, it was not fair to keep the girl dangling on a string. She had been seen without a chaperone at Balmoral and her reputation was in danger of being tarnished. If he was going to marry her, he should get on and do it; if not, he must end it. The Prince of Wales read the letter as an ultimatum from his father to marry Diana.

Others to whom he has shown the letter believe that the Prince misinterpreted what his father wrote, and that to have laid the ultimate blame for his failed marriage on his bullying father is unfair. There was obviously an ambiguity that was never resolved verbally. The two men did not sit down and talk – indeed, they cannot sit down and talk, which is a great sadness to both.

The Prince was faced with an impossible choice. To ask Diana to marry him before he was quite sure she was the right girl, or to risk letting her go when she was so perfect in so many ways and things were looking so promising.

'It all seems so ridiculous because I do very much want to do the right thing for this country and for my family – but I'm terrified sometimes of making a promise and then perhaps living to regret it.'

He allowed himself to be pushed into a marriage that he was uncertain in his own mind was a good idea. He confessed to one friend that he was in a 'confused and anxious state of mind'. To another he said, 'It is just a matter of taking an unusual plunge into some rather unknown circumstances that inevitably disturbs me but I expect it will be the right thing in the end.'

He knew he wasn't in love with her, but he liked her very much, and he knew there was a good chance he would grow to love her.

Mountbatten had told him to find a young girl and mould her to his way of life. Wasn't someone like Diana precisely what he meant? More importantly, given the hysteria that Diana had caused in the media, what other girl would ever dare be seen with him, if this was the likely consequence? Convinced that his father was telling him to marry Diana, he decided to go with that decision and hope for the best.

Had Lord Mountbatten been alive Charles would have turned to him for help; and Mountbatten would in all probability have told him not to marry Diana. Yes, he had a duty to marry, but it was imperative for the Prince of Wales above all people, who could not contemplate divorce, to be quite certain he had found the right woman.

In Mountbatten's absence, Charles consulted his official advisers, friends and family, most of whom were eager to approve. It is the curse of the Prince of Wales to be surrounded by friends and advisers, most of whom tell him what they think he wants to hear. Few have the courage to say what they think he needs to be told for fear that it might put an end to their friendship or employment. The Queen offered no opinion whatsoever. The Queen Mother, a hugely influential figure within the Royal Family to this day, was strongly in favour of the match. Lady Diana was, after all, the granddaughter of her good friend and lady-in-waiting, Ruth, Lady Fermoy. And Ruth, Lady Fermoy, who knew that Diana had emotional problems, which would make the match extremely unwise, failed to speak up.

Two of Charles's close friends, Nicholas Soames and Penny Romsey, advised against marriage. Soames thought that the pair had too little in common, and saw an intellectual gap of giant proportions. Penny Romsey was similarly worried about the intellectual mismatch, but she was also very concerned that Diana was in love with the notion of being Princess of Wales without any real understanding of what it would involve. Penny told the Prince of her worries some weeks before the engagement, and persuaded her husband Norton, the Prince's cousin, to do the same. Norton's principal concern, like that of Nicholas Soames, was the intellectual gulf, which he predicted would lead to silent evenings, resentment and friction. All three were deeply suspicious about the way in which Diana had gone after the Prince so single-mindedly. They had seen how she controlled the relationship. She had wanted the Prince of Wales, she had flirted and flattered and been everything that he wanted, and she had got him. Romsey tackled the Prince on more than one occasion, becoming blunter with every attempt. The Prince didn't want to hear, and he was angrily told to mind his own business.

Although he often seeks solitude, the Prince has a network of close friends upon whom he is very dependent and confides in, as they do in him. He is a tactile man, and he pours out love and affection to them, both male and female, although he has always tended to be closer to women. He speaks to them on the phone, writes long, soul-baring letters, and asks their opinion on every subject that interests or worries him. He confides far more than is probably wise, and is completely open and honest with them. In return they protect his trust absolutely. It is a tightly knit bunch, mostly older than him, and includes the Palmer-Tomkinsons, the van Cutsems, the Keswicks, the Paravicinis, the Wards, the Romseys, the Brabournes, the Devonshires, the Shelburnes and Nicholas Soames. They wield great influence with the Prince and are fiercely jealous of their friendship. Most of them have plenty of money, which is inherited, and not a great deal of sensitivity about how the other half lives. None of them shares the Prince's enthusiasm for hunting but they indulge in all the other sporting activities of the British upper classes. They shoot grouse in either Yorkshire or Scotland, from 12 August through to December; shoot pheasant and partridge from October to February, and duck from a month earlier. They fish for salmon on any of the great rivers, mostly in Scotland or Iceland. They have large country houses, which the Prince visits, and in return they enjoy invitations to his family homes, to weekend shooting parties at Sandringham, and stalking and fishing holidays at Balmoral.

The Prince of Wales thought he had found the girl of his dreams, the girl whom the country would find acceptable, and who would be able to share his job and his life. He had not reached this judgement alone. He was not a normal man wanting a normal wife to live a normal life. He had waited a long time to find the right person, and he was now thirty-two years old. It was important for the country that he make the right decision, and he wanted to be reassured by his friends and advisers that he was correct in his selection. But though he canvassed opinion about Diana before he asked her to marry him, and he relied upon friends to bolster his resolve, once she had accepted his proposal, the subject was closed. He had made his decision, and was not receptive to advice, warning or criticism. He was determined that the decision to marry Diana was the right one, and when doubts began to creep into his mind during the five months before the wedding, he kept them to himself.

'I do believe I am very lucky that someone as special as Diana seems to love me so much,' he wrote to two of his friends. 'I am already discovering how nice it is to have someone round to share things with ... Other people's happiness and enthusiasm at the whole thing is also a most "encouraging" element and it makes me so proud that so many people have such admiration and affection for Diana.'

The truth was rather different; but when his friends told him they had serious doubts about the suitability of the match, he refused to listen. When he himself began to have serious doubts about Diana, he refused to talk about it. He went ahead knowing that there was a question mark over the future. To have called off the wedding would have been horrendous and humiliating for everyone, and the headlines and public castigation could only be imagined, but with hindsight, it would have been infinitely less painful and less damaging to everyone concerned, particularly the monarchy, if he had had the courage to do it.

There are some close to the Prince who believe he had a duty at least to have discussed it. A relative goes so far as to say that his failure to do so was his big mistake.

'In his position he bloody well should have spoken to people because he had to think of the constitutional side as well as the private side. He had chosen Diana with both sides in mind, but equally he needed to think of the consequences for both, if it was going to go wrong.'

FIVE

The Fairytale Fiancée

'Such exciting news …'
Camilla

The Prince of Wales proposed in early February, just after his annual skiing holiday with the Palmer-Tomkinsons in the Swiss resort of Klosters. He had phoned Diana from Switzerland and told her he had something to ask her when he got back the next day. Knowing full well what the question was likely to be, she laughed when he said, 'Will you marry me?' But was not slow to reply, 'Yeah, okay.'

Then she laughed some more. He was thrilled.

'You do realise that one day you will be Queen,' he said.

'Yes,' she said. 'I love you so much, I love you so much.'

According to Diana, he then coined that most memorable phrase, 'Whatever love is', and ran upstairs to telephone his mother with the news.

Diana rushed back home to tell her flatmates, and they screamed and howled and went for a drive around London with their secret. Meanwhile, the Prince rang a few of his closest confidants to let them know how he had got on, one of whom was Camilla Parker Bowles. Not because she was his lover – that had ended when he started to fall for Diana's charms – but because she was his best friend, as she is today. She had played a key role in helping and advising Charles in his relationship with Diana. She and Andrew had been at Balmoral in September, and he had taken Diana to spend weekends at their house in Wiltshire several times. They had been racing at Ludlow together from there, when Charles was riding his racehorse, Allibar; he had first taken Diana to see Highgrove while staying with the Parker Bowles; and he and Andrew had been hunting together on a couple of occasions, leaving Diana and Camilla together at home. Camilla had known he was planning to propose to Diana that day and, like so many others, was eager to have a progress report.

The Prince had also told Michael Colborne, secretary to the Prince of Wales's office, about his marriage plans the day after the proposal. He had come into Colborne's office in Buckingham Palace, sat down in an armchair and told Michael to shut the door.

'I've got something to tell you,' he said. 'Other than Her Majesty, and Papa and a few others, nobody knows. This is between you and me. I've asked Lady Diana to marry me, and she said yes straight away, but I've asked her to think about it and she's going to Australia to stay with the Shand Kydds. We've got a very busy period in front of us and we've got a tour coming up ...'

Michael was thunderstruck. 'Congratulations, sir,' he said.

The Prince smiled. 'Well, we'll see what happens.'

Michael Colborne knew the Prince better than most, and was to play an important part in Diana's early years at court. The two men had met aboard HMS *Norfolk* when the Prince was a sub-lieutenant and Colborne a non-commissioned officer, and he was one of the few people who were not afraid to tell the Prince what he thought. They struck up a good friendship and, when the Prince left the Navy and needed to set up an office in London, he invited Colborne to join it. Officially in charge of his financial affairs, he became the Prince's right-hand man, and remained with him for ten years, providing many valuable lessons about what life was like beyond the ocean of privilege in which the Prince swam. He was the only member of his staff at the time who was not in the public school, officer training college or Foreign Office mould, and he viewed all those who were with a healthy disdain. The Prince liked his straightforward approach. In offering Colborne the job he had made him promise that he would never change. 'If you don't agree with something, you say so,' he had said, and over the years Michael had spoken his mind. Charles didn't always like what he heard and became extremely angry on several memorable occasions, but it was an exceptionally warm relationship nonetheless.

That same day, Diana went to Australia for a holiday with her mother and stepfather, Peter Shand Kydd. As Charles put it, 'to think if it was all going to be too awful'. For three weeks they hid from the press and kept Diana's whereabouts such a guarded secret that even the Prince of Wales had difficulty getting through to her when he telephoned.

'I rang up on one occasion,' he said in a television interview after the engagement had been announced, and I said, "Can I speak?" And they said, "No, we're not taking any calls." So I said, "It's the Prince of Wales speaking." "How do I know it's the Prince of Wales?" was the reply. I said, "You don't. But I am," in a rage. And eventually … I mean, I got the number because they were staying somewhere else. They said the phones were tapped or something – which I found highly unlikely …'

When Diana arrived back in London the Prince told Michael Colborne that he wanted the biggest, smelliest bunch of flowers possible delivered to Diana's flat, and gave him a hand-written note to be delivered with the flowers. Knowing that her flat would be under siege, Colborne telephoned ahead to warn Diana that some flowers were on their way and a very sleepy voice answered the phone. 'Okay,' she said, 'I'll look out for them.'

Sergeant Ron Lewis was duly dispatched to deliver the flowers and note to Coleherne Court that morning, but Diana's memory of the incident was sadly different from the facts. Ten years later she said, 'I came back from Australia, someone knocks on my door – someone from his office with a bunch of flowers and I knew that they hadn't come from Charles because there was no note. It was just somebody being very tactful in the office.'

Michael didn't meet Diana until shortly after she returned from Australia, when the Prince asked him to look after her for the afternoon. She had been to watch Charles ride out his racehorse, Allibar, along the gallops at Lamborne early one morning. He was in training for a race at Chepstow the following weekend, and having completed seven furlongs, they were walking quietly home for breakfast, when Allibar had suddenly collapsed with a massive heart attack and died in his arms. The Prince refused to leave the horse until a vet arrived, and was so distraught that he couldn't drive. It was his detective, unusually, who drove them back to Highgrove.

It was obvious as soon as the car arrived back at the house that something was wrong, and Diana went into the kitchen with Michael to explain what had happened, while the Prince went off to be alone for a moment. But the treadmill of his life pauses for neither courtship nor grief. That afternoon, a helicopter arrived at two o'clock sharp to take him to an engagement in Swansea. Meanwhile Diana and Michael Colborne went into the drawing room for the first of many lengthy heart-to-hearts. Later, as they wandered around the garden together, Diana told him all about herself, her family, her parents' divorce, her father's illness and her stepmother. The relationship between them was cemented. He was struck by how young she was – she had puppy fat and quite ruddy cheeks – and how badly educated. He also realised how little discipline she had had in her life, and wondered if she had any idea what she was taking on. Twenty-seven years her senior, he felt like a father to her and became one of her closest friends in the Palace. They shared an office in the run-up to the wedding and he tried hard to help her understand and prepare her for what lay ahead, but knew it was going to be difficult.

'Is it all right if I call you Michael, like His Royal Highness does?' she asked, to which he said, 'Of course.'

'Will you call me "Diana"?'

'No,' said Colborne. 'Certainly not. I appreciate what you've just said, but if it all works out you're going to be the Princess of Wales and I'll have to call you Ma'am then, so we might as well start now.'

Two days later the engagement was officially announced and Diana was swept into the royal system. The idea was to rescue her from the media that had made her life so impossible. She had certainly found the attention extremely frightening at times and was pleased to be rescued. But the effect was to make her lonely and insecure. Buckingham Palace is not a home by any normal standards, and not even members of the Royal Family would describe it as such. Over 200 people work there, from the Lord Chamberlain to the telephone operators who man the switchboard. There was no alternative place to take her, but with hindsight, nobody – least of all her fiancé – had thought through the implications of removing a nineteen-year-old from a flat full of jolly giggly girls and setting her down in a suite of impersonal rooms with no one of her own age for company, and a fiancé who was always busy.

Diana told Andrew Morton that it was during the first week of her engagement that her bulimia started. One of Diana's flatmates said, 'She went to live at Buckingham Palace and then the tears started. This little thing got so thin. She wasn't happy, she was suddenly plunged into all this pressure and it was a nightmare for her.'

In fact she was initially treated not for bulimia but for anorexia nervosa, which was the same eating disorder that her sister Sarah had when she first met the Prince of Wales in 1977, shortly after breaking up with a previous boyfriend. Desperate to find ways of encouraging Sarah to eat, her family would refuse to let her speak to the Prince on the telephone unless she put on weight. In the end she sought professional help in a London nursing home, and she recovered.

The two conditions are similar in that the root cause of both disorders is an upset in childhood, but the trigger is some sort of emotional stress in the present, and teenage girls are the most commonly affected. Bulimia involves binge eating followed by self-induced vomiting, whereas anorexics go to ingenious lengths to avoid food. Secrecy is a key element, and also denial. Both result in dangerous weight loss, and a host of related medical problems, and both can be fatal.

Shortly before the engagement Diana started taking the contraceptive pill and, as so many women do, put on a lot of weight. Her reaction was to stop eating, and her weight loss was dramatic. The blue Harrods suit she wore for the engagement photograph was a size fourteen. In the five months to the wedding in July, her waist measurement fell from twenty-nine inches to twenty-three and a half, and it continued to diminish.

Diana's memory of the events as told to Andrew Morton are repeatedly at odds with what others remember. Her first night at Clarence House, the Queen Mother's London home, is a case in point. She told Morton that there was no one there to welcome her. In fact, she had dinner that evening with both the Queen Mother and the Prince of Wales, and the next day moved to Buckingham Palace, where she was greeted with open arms by many of the Queen's household who had known Diana and her family for years. A particular friend was Lady Susan Hussey, a lady-in-waiting, who had known Diana all her life, and in the coming months spent hour upon hour with her. She had a son almost exactly the same age as Diana, and was like a mother to her. She thought Diana was quite adorable, and was thrilled for the Prince whom she also adored. She and Diana went shopping for clothes together and prepared for the wedding and talked about all Diana's hopes and fears.

There were others in the Palace whom Diana loved in those early days and who were deeply fond of her. Lt.Col. Blair Stewart-Wilson, the deputy master of the household, was one, whom Diana kissed on the station platform on her wedding day to his utter confusion; Sir Johnny Johnston in the Lord Chamberlain's office another, and Sir William Heseltine, the Queen's deputy private secretary. She used to go into their offices and sit on their desks and talk to them, or invite them to lunch or to drinks. And she was forever popping in to see the ladies-in-waiting and the helpers who had been taken on to deal with everything that needed to be organised for the wedding. She would pop in to chat or to giggle about some extraordinary present that had arrived, or to show off clothes that she had bought. Her sister Jane was with her a lot, her mother too, and she frequently met friends for lunch. Yet she said she was unhappy and lonely.

One of Diana's fears at that time, which she often talked about, was the Prince's former girlfriends. Charles had made no secret to Diana of his previous love affairs, and possibly with his fatal compulsion to tell the whole truth when half would be kinder or more sensible, he told Diana everything. He had never experienced jealousy himself, and had no understanding of how a young girl might feel, knowing that he had loved other women, particularly those who were still friends that he saw regularly. It didn't cross his mind that there might be a problem. From her perspective, at nineteen with precious little education, no accomplishments, no sense of style and no knowledge of the world, they were grown up, clever, smart and sophisticated, and they made Diana feel desperately insecure. One of the Queen's ladies-in-waiting had also married a man much older than herself when she was nineteen, and she and others repeatedly told Diana she must forget about these other women. Yes, of course the Prince had had girlfriends and some quite serious relationships in his time, which at thirty-two years old was to be expected; and yes, they were older and more sophisticated than she was, but the Prince hadn't married any of *them* – the one he wanted to marry was *her*.

Jealousy and insecurity nonetheless gnawed away at her. She was even jealous of the Prince's relationship with his mother. He put letters and memos that came from the Queen into a safe to ensure no one could copy or steal them. He had always done it as a matter of course, but Diana was suspicious that the Queen was writing about her and that Charles was deliberately keeping it from her. 'Why don't you just ask me about the things that are worrying you?' Charles would say, but she never would. When she arrived at Clarence House there was a letter waiting on her bed from Camilla Parker Bowles. It was dated two days previously and said, 'Such exciting news about the engagement. Do let's have lunch soon when the Prince of Wales goes to Australia and New Zealand. He's going to be away for three weeks. I'd love to see the ring. Lots of love, Camilla.' It was a friendly note sent with the best of intentions. She and Diana had seen a lot of each other during the previous few months, and Camilla thought they were friends. She thought Diana was young, but good fun, as most of his friends did.

Diana told Andrew Morton she thought 'Wow' and organised

lunch, 'bearing in mind that I was so immature, I didn't know about jealousy or depressions or anything like that … So we had lunch. Very tricky indeed. She said, "You are not going to hunt, are you?" I said, "On what?" She said, "Horse. You are not going to hunt when you go and live at Highgrove, are you?" I said, "No." She said, "I just wanted to know," and I thought as far as she was concerned that was her communication route. Still too immature to understand all the messages coming my way.'

Camilla remembers the lunch as being entirely friendly. Diana was extremely excited, showed off her ring with glee.

Camilla had been one of the girlfriends the Prince of Wales had told Diana about, and Diana had made him give her a solemn promise that there was no longer anyone else in his life, and that there would never be any other women in his life. He had happily given his promise on both counts. His mistake was thinking this was all he needed to say. He was telling the truth – he intended to be entirely monogamous – and as a man of honour, he expected Diana to accept his word as the truth. Similarly, as a man of honour, when Diana asked him whether he still loved Camilla he said 'yes', which was also the truth. Camilla was very special to him, but so were a number of other women. He loved and still loves them all, and no doubt always will.

The Prince of Wales is a thinker and a philosopher, a spiritual and religious man, and love to him bears little relationship to the two-dimensional 'love' discussed on the pages of romantic novels and women's magazines. This is why he used that dreadful phrase 'whatever love means' when asked by a television reporter about his feelings for Diana on the day of his engagement. He is too honest for his own good; he can't give the simple answer that everyone is waiting for, because for him the matter is not simple.

It didn't occur to him that a white lie would have been kinder. He didn't put himself into Diana's position, didn't ask himself how this nineteen-year-old girl might be feeling or whether she might need greater reassurance. Most young people are intrinsically jealous, and the notion that someone can love more than one person without diminishing their feelings for another only comes with age and experience. For an intelligent man, there are astonishing gaps in his awareness.

What he didn't realise at the time was that Diana was a particularly vulnerable nineteen-year-old, with an abnormally pronounced sense of suspicion and insecurity, and a strong feeling that people were conspiring against her. This had not been apparent during their courtship, but immediately after the engagement was announced the Prince sensed a change in Diana which he didn't understand. Where before she had been so happy and easygoing, she became moody and wilful. She displayed a terrible temper, which he had never seen before; it came from nowhere, along with hysterical tears, and could be gone as quickly as it came. She suddenly turned against people she had appeared to like and said they were out to get her, to undermine her, or spy on her.

He was not the only one to notice the change and to be worried about her. But Charles put it down to nerves and the stress she had been under during the past few months, which he assumed would all disappear once the wedding was behind them.

Diana hated being left alone. She wanted the Prince to be with her all the time and couldn't understand why his work had to take precedence over their being together. His days then, as now, were a relentless round of public engagements, meetings, paper work and sporting commitments from early in the morning until late at night, often taking him out of London. Almost immediately after the engagement was announced, he left on a tour of Australia, which had been fixed long before, and there was a very tearful and loving farewell at the airport.

During Charles's various absences Diana was looked after by whichever members of his staff were not accompanying him. The Prince's private secretary at that time was the Hon. Edward Adeane, a brilliant barrister, Eton and Cambridge educated, whose father and grandfather had been private secretaries before him. The Prince's assistant private secretary, Francis Cornish, came from the Foreign Office. His predecessor, Oliver Everett, was also ex-Foreign

Office and had returned there in 1980, but was invited back specifically to help Diana before the wedding, and afterwards became her official private secretary. It was an intellectually high-powered team, who were all at least twice her age. Sympathetic as they might have been, and flattered by her charm and giggly girlishness, they had no idea of how to handle someone so young, whose experience and education were so severely limited. They were astonished when, for example, she asked where Dorset was, or confessed she didn't know the capital of Australia.

Diana had no inhibitions about her ignorance and laughed such moments off carelessly, but it was an awkward situation for them all. Socially, she had much in common with the private secretaries, but she found their intellect threatening. She was more comfortable with Michael Colborne, a former grammar school boy, whose office she shared. He could see how lost she was and would spend hours talking to her, which was all she wanted to do. The Prince's staff were not prepared for this. They would never have expected to sit and idly chatter with the Prince, and found it hard to do so with Diana. He was the Boss, and the relationship between employer and employees was always strictly professional. They expected it to be the same with Lady Diana Spencer.

But Diana was scarcely more than a child. She had never employed anyone in her life. She had never had much of a job, never worked in an office. She had no idea what was expected of her and no idea of what she was taking on in marrying into the Royal Family. Her concept of what lay before her was little more than a romantic notion.

Like thousands of girls of a similar age, who devoured Barbara Cartland novels and soap operas on television, she had no interest in a career. All she wanted was to be loved, looked after, have babies and live happily ever after. She thought she had found a man who would provide all of this and more. In the excitement and thrill of the chase she had visualised none of the reality.

She could be forgiven. There had been no Princess of Wales for over seventy years – when the future George V was created Prince of Wales in 1901 and his wife, Princess May of Teck, became Princess

– and there was no job specification to guide either Diana or her courtiers. There was no one she could consult who had experience of her predicament. No commoner had married into the Royal Family at such a senior level this century, not even the Queen Mother. Her husband became George VI, but at the time of their marriage he was Duke of York, and only second in line to the throne.

Several people did try to give Diana some help, Michael Colborne and Susan Hussey amongst them, but Diana was not altogether receptive. She didn't want to be told what to do and when. In the past when she had not wanted to do something, with the indulgence of divorced parents, she had never been coerced. Accepting the discipline of royal life did not come easily.

The Family and their courtiers all took what they did so much for granted, they assumed that, being a Spencer, Diana would have no problems and would know what to expect. She was, after all, a member of one of the most aristocratic families in Britain and had lived from the age of thirteen in one of the most traditionally run stately homes in England. Her brother is the Queen's godson, one of her sisters is the Duke of Kent's goddaughter. Her father had been equerry to the Queen. Both her grandmothers had been ladies-in-waiting to the Queen Mother; and both the Spencers and the Fermoys had been close friends of the Royal Family for several generations. It was not an unreasonable assumption that Diana would know what royal life was all about. That was partly why she had seemed so tailor-made for the role. But she was lost, and no one realised.

When she went to spend the weekend at Royal Lodge at Windsor, for example, no one had thought to tell her that if she wanted to go out for a walk in the Great Park she had to tell someone where she was going. She returned to find the whole place in turmoil, alarms going and her policeman on the verge of heart failure. The following Monday morning she told Colborne what had happened and said she didn't know how she was going to cope.

'This is going to be your life,' he said. 'You're never going to be on your own again. And you're going to change. In four to five years you're going to be an absolute bitch, not through any fault of your own, but because of the circumstances in which you live. If you want four boiled eggs for breakfast, you'll have them. If you want the car brought round to the front door a minute ago, you'll have it. It's going to change you. Your life is going to be organised. You open your diary now and you can put down Trooping the Colour, the Cenotaph service, Cowes Week, the Ascots. You can write your diary for five years ahead, ten years, twenty years.'

Gradually the truth began to dawn and Diana recognised that what he was saying was true, and from that moment she began to look increasingly apprehensive. But she was on a giant roller coaster with the wedding just weeks away and preparations to be made before then. There were also presents to be acknowledged and people thanked. They were pouring into Michael Colborne's office from all over the world, and Diana wrote most of the thank you letters herself, in her distinctive large, rounded hand.

One Friday afternoon, about two weeks before the wedding, a package was delivered to the Privy Purse door, which the footman brought up to Michael Colborne's office. He opened it and found a number of things he had ordered on the Prince's behalf to give as gifts to various friends. The Prince has always been a great giver of presents, particularly jewellery, as a means of thanking people. Amongst various pieces, one of which was for Dale, Lady Tryon, and another for Lady Susan Keswick, and another for Lady Cecil Cameron – all good friends – was a bracelet for Camilla Parker Bowles. It was a gold chain with a blue enamel plate, engraved with the initials GF. They stood for Girl Friday, which was the Prince's nickname for Camilla.

As Colborne was examining the contents, the buzzer went, calling him into Edward Adeane's office. He left the package on his desk and went next door. While he was out of the room Diana came in and, suspicious of everyone, must have had a look through the things on Colborne's desk. She saw everything that came into the office, and he had no reason to hide this or anything else from her. As far as he was concerned this bracelet held no special significance. Camilla, like a number of the Prince's other very close friends, had been an emotional mainstay during his bachelor years, and given him house-space on innumerable occasions, as well as advice and help during his courtship. He wanted to thank them, and saw each of them individually to hand over their presents and say goodbye to the bachelor life they had all supported him through in one way and another.

Colborne finished his conversation with Adeane and, instead of going straight back to his desk, went into the main office. Adeane, suddenly remembering there was something more he wanted to say, went into Colborne's office, thinking he would find him there, and was almost knocked clean off his feet by Diana rushing out at top speed.

'What on earth have you done to Lady Diana?' he said when he finally found Colborne. 'She nearly bowled me over and was really upset.'

When Colborne got back to his office he realised what had happened. The package had been opened up and the lid was off the box with the bracelet inside. He didn't see Diana again until Monday morning, when she confessed to having had a look at what was on his desk, but said nothing more about it. Her account of that incident appeared in *Diana – Her True Story*, but like so much of the book, with a twist that gave it a different interpretation.

'Anyway, somebody in his office told me that my husband had had a bracelet made for her which she wears to this day. It's a gold chain bracelet with a blue enamel disc. It's got "G and F" entwined in it, "Gladys" and "Fred" – they were their nicknames. I walked into this man's office one day and said: "Oh, what's in that parcel?" He said: "Oh, you shouldn't look at that." I said: "Well, I'm going to look at it." I opened it and there was a bracelet and I said: "I know where this is going." I was devastated. This was about two weeks before we got married. He said: "Well, he's going to give it to her tonight." So rage, rage, rage! "Why can't you be honest with me?" But, no, he cut me absolutely dead. It's as if he had made his decision, and if it wasn't going to work, it wasn't going to work. He'd found the virgin, the sacrificial lamb, and in a way he was obsessed with me. But it was hot and cold, hot and cold. You never knew what mood it was going to be, up and down, up and down.'

Diana later harboured another destructive fantasy about the Prince and Camilla, which ate away at her. She became convinced about ten years after their marriage that Charles and Camilla had slept together in Buckingham Palace two nights before the wedding, which took place on Wednesday 29 July. On the Monday night the Queen had given a dinner party for Diana's mother and father with their respective spouses, and family and close friends. That was followed by a huge reception and dance, to which Camilla and her husband, also her sister Annabel and her husband, Simon Elliot, were all invited. The ball went on until the small hours of the morning, when the Royal Family all had to see their guests, including most of the crowned heads of Europe, into coaches to take them to Windsor Castle, where they were staying, as there was insufficient room at Buckingham Palace. When the last coach had gone, Charles and Diana climbed into their beds in their separate suites of rooms at Buckingham Palace, both exhausted.

The Tuesday night is the only one when Diana was sleeping elsewhere, and when it might have been possible, in theory, for Charles to have seen Camilla. Diana stayed at Clarence House, in keeping with the tradition of not seeing the groom the night before the wedding, and he spent the evening along with the rest of the Royal Family and half a million of the public at a fantastic fireworks display in Hyde Park. The display was a copy of celebrations held two hundred years earlier for the Peace of Aix-la-Chapelle. Rockets whizzed into the air, multi-coloured stars burst over the city's skyline, the massed bands of the household musicians struck up, and the Morrison Orpheus Choir and the Choir of the Welsh Guards burst into song. Above the noise of it all, the Royal Horse Artillery fired salvoes from the guns of the King's Troop.

It was an extraordinary night of happiness and celebration. Beacons were alight and parties in full swing all over the country. Millions of people had arrived in the capital in preparation; hundreds had been camping along the route to St Paul's Cathedral for days, and had come equipped with sleeping bags and supplies of sandwiches, beer and Champagne. Strangers talked to strangers, there was no ugliness, no crime, and real life was suspended for a while. The weather was balmy, and the excitement was electrifying. It was to be the wedding of the decade, a glorious musical extravaganza, a gathering of most of the Kings and Queens of Europe, Africa, the Middle East and Asia, along with 160 foreign presidents and prime ministers. It truly was, as the Archbishop of Canterbury declared, 'the stuff of which fairy tales are made'.

Once the fireworks were over, the Prince went home to Buckingham Palace in a highly emotional state for his last night as a single man, to contemplate the enormity and nagging uncertainty of the step he was about to take in the morning. He sat up chatting for a while to Lady Susan Hussey, whose rooms were adjacent to his own. She had been a friend, confidante, shoulder to cry on and tower of strength to him for many years and had known him since he was twelve years old, when she became a lady-in-waiting to the Queen. She knew the whole family extremely well and there was scarcely a secret Charles had not shared with her. Soon after midnight, they said goodnight and went to their beds.

About half an hour later, Lady Susan heard a knock at her door. It was the Prince saying he couldn't sleep. She had not been able to sleep either, and so they went into her sitting room and, dressed in their night clothes, stood looking from her window down on the Mall, at all the activity going on below, and the music and the excitement, with tears streaming down both their faces. Some time after 2 a.m. she insisted he go to bed or he would be hopeless in the morning, and persuaded him to take an Aspirin to help him sleep. Camilla was a long way away.

SIX

The Honeymoon Period

'I seem to do nothing but collect flowers
these days; I know my role.'
Charles

With hindsight, the plans for the honeymoon could not have been worse. The Prince should have taken Diana to some sun-drenched island with no memories of his past, no royal connections, and no obligations to entertain others or be on duty in any way. After the stress and scrutiny they had both been under in the months leading up to the wedding, they needed time together on their own, to get to know each other better, to have some fun doing things they both enjoyed, and discover what marriage and sharing your life with someone else was all about.

Instead it was an inauspicious beginning. They spent three nights at Broadlands, Lord Mountbatten's former estate in Hampshire, now owned by his grandson, Norton Romsey, and his wife Penny. The Romseys had moved out to give them some privacy, but it was where Charles had taken most of his previous girlfriends, and by the second night, according to Diana, he had buried himself in the first of seven Laurens van der Post novels he had brought with him. Having the time to sit and read was a pleasure and a luxury for the Prince, but for Diana, who was not a great reader, it was a monumental slight. She concluded he was more interested in his books than in her. To make matters worse, when she did have his attention, he talked about what he had read: 'He read them and we had to analyse them over lunch every day.'

From Broadlands they flew to Gibraltar to join the royal yacht for a couple of weeks in the Mediterranean and Aegean seas, where they sailed, swam and sunbathed, and wrote warm letters of thanks to their staff and everyone who had helped make their wedding day such a huge success. Both of them wrote about their happiness at being together, although the Prince admitted that 'Diana dashes about chatting up all the sailors and the cooks in the galley, while I sit hermit-like on the verandah deck, sunk with pure joy into one of Laurens van der Post's books.'

But with twenty-one naval officers and a crew of 256 men, a valet, a private secretary and an equerry, it was hardly the romantic cruise either of them might have hoped for. It was a grave disappointment and a tough introduction for Diana to the very public way members of the Royal Family have to live their lives if they are not to cause offence to all and sundry. They were hardly ever alone. When they weren't entertaining dignitaries, including the President of Egypt, Anwar Sadat, and his wife in Port Said, the candle-lit dinner they sat down to at night was shared with the officers and a band of the Royal Marines. Had they borrowed some friend's private yacht things might have been different, but if a member of the family is on board *Britannia*, they cannot visit foreign soil without being met and greeted by local dignitaries. Similarly, when they travel around Britain, unless a visit is entirely private, the local Lord-Lieutenants, mayors and councillors expect to be involved when members of the Family come on to their patch.

'By then,' Diana told Morton, 'the bulimia was appalling, absolutely appalling. It was rife, four times a day on the yacht. Anything I could find I would gobble up and be sick two minutes later – very tired. So of course, that slightly got the mood swings going in the sense that one minute one would be happy, next blubbing one's eyes out.'

There were two particular incidents which Diana remembered very clearly: one when a photograph of Camilla fell out of the Prince's diary, and the second when, dressed for a white-tie dinner with the Sadats, the Prince wore a pair of gold cufflinks, engraved with interwoven Cs. 'Got it in one,' said Diana. 'Knew exactly.

"Camilla gave you those, didn't she?" He said: "Yes, so what's wrong? They're a present from a friend." And, boy, did we have a row. Jealousy, total jealousy …'

Their rows were usually very one-sided. Diana screamed and shouted and burst into tears. The Prince – though perfectly capable of losing his temper and shouting at the people who work for him and even throwing ornaments – had never experienced anyone shouting at him before, with the possible exception of his father, and was completely nonplussed. Her rage was quite terrifying, and he soon discovered that when she was in this condition, nothing he could say appeared to calm her. Indeed, trying to argue with her or justify himself only made matters worse. On these occasions he refused to engage, which made her even more furious.

The third and final stage of the honeymoon was spent at Balmoral with the in-laws and the rest of the Royal Family, which congregates there traditionally between August and October. Once again, not the most sensitive way to treat a young bride; and for Diana, it was another brutal introduction to the life she had signed up for without fully understanding what marriage to the Prince of Wales and to the job would really mean. Although they were not staying with the Queen, they dined with her and the rest of the family, also the lady-in-waiting and equerry, who always eat with the family, several times a week. This was either at the castle, when official guests like the Prime Minister came to stay, or more often in one of the lodges on the estate, built by Prince Albert, Queen Victoria's husband, for deer stalking. In a rare show of informality, they pack food for a barbecue into the cars and, dressed in slacks or jeans, and with the Queen in a tweed skirt, take off with no servants to a different lodge each night for supper. The Queen's job is to lay and then clear the table, the Duke of Edinburgh is the cook, and the Prince of Wales and the equerry between them traditionally hand round the drinks.

Balmoral is probably the Prince's favourite place in all the world. It's the one place where he can be entirely on his own – or rather, where police presence is minimal – where he can walk for miles without seeing another human being, and where he can indulge his passion for stalking and fishing, or sitting on a craggy hillside with his sketch pad and watercolours. He hoped Diana would share his enthusiasm, as she had seemed to the summer before. Then, she had joined in. She had appeared thoroughly to enjoy the place, which was one of the things that so endeared her to him and made him feel they were so compatible. But now she had hated it. Hated the countryside and hated the Royal Family's obsession with horses and dogs. She hated the rain that poured down remorselessly, and the feeling that the Prince was avoiding intimate contact. The anorexia had entirely taken hold and she was still suffering terrible mood swings and losing weight at an alarming rate. The Prince had no idea what the problem was. He couldn't understand why she wouldn't eat and did everything to try and tempt her. 'Come on, Darling,' he would say, 'try just a little bit of this, it's delicious.'

If she was disappointed by her first taste of marriage, so was he. He was a romantic. He had had visions of his life being enhanced by a wife. She would be a friend and confidante, boost his morale, massage his ego, share his bed and fit comfortably into his life. What he imagined, however, like many men perhaps, was that all this would happen without him having to change one iota of his routine.

Diana had an equally romantic view of matrimony. She had visions of a man who would devote himself to her and want to spend every minute by her side, who would love and cherish her, give her beautiful children and be there to protect and look after her, to give her confidence and a secure family unit. Both their expectations were equally unrealistic. They had married the wrong person to give them even a fraction of what they needed.

At Balmoral this conflict was polarised. Charles didn't alter the routine of his days to accommodate his wife. He slipped straight into the Balmoral lifestyle that he had adored since childhood, imagining that Diana would want to join in. But now that she was married, she wanted no part in any of it. His friends came to stay, as they always had done, and he went off for hours at a time engaged in one of his solitary or sporting pursuits. Diana, younger than his friends by far and longing to have her husband to herself, quickly became cross and bored, and her friends, summoned to Balmoral to keep her company and try to cheer her up, failed to do any good.

Amongst those asked to help was Michael Colborne, who was solid and dependable and enormously fond of both Charles and Diana. He was enjoying a weekend at home when the phone rang on the Saturday night and the Prince said he wanted him to take the sleeper train from King's Cross the next night to Aberdeen, where a car would meet him and take him to Craigowan Lodge, the small house on the estate where the Prince and Princess were staying. 'I will be out stalking that day,' he said, 'but I will see you before I go and I'd like you to spend the day with the Princess.'

On Monday morning he was sitting in the kitchen at Craigowan, eating a hearty breakfast which the chef had just prepared for him, when the Prince arrived and thanked him for coming. 'I'll see you when I get back,' he said, with no further explanation, and with that disappeared for the day along with his house guest, Norton Romsey.

A little later Penny Romsey came into the room and, seeing Michael said, 'What are you doing up here? Are you working today?'

Colborne explained that the Prince of Wales had asked him to come up. 'I think I'm going to spend the day with the Princess of Wales.'

'Oh, that's strange,' said Lady Romsey. 'The Princess and I were going out for a walk in a minute.'

A moment later Diana put her head round the door and, without a word to Penny Romsey, said, 'Oh, Michael, come on.' He followed her down the corridor into the drawing room. 'Did you have a good journey up?' she asked, but wouldn't look at him. He sensed she didn't really want to talk. He had learnt long ago with the Prince that sometimes he would not want to talk, often for very long stretches, and had become accustomed to sitting in silence. So he was not uncomfortable sitting in the room with the Princess saying nothing, and this was how they sat for about fifteen minutes. Then suddenly she began to cry, and through the tears she told him how unhappy she was, how she hated Balmoral, hated stalking, hated the rain.

Then she fell silent, and so they sat until she began again; pacing around the room this time, angrily kicking the furniture and raging furiously against everything and everybody – the place, the Royal Family, the friends, the weeks she was going to be stuck there, the boredom, the things they wanted her to do. Nothing he could say seemed to help, and then she stopped as suddenly as she had started. And so the day passed, with tears, anger and brooding silence, from ten to nine in the morning until five past four in the afternoon. He sat and watched the hands of a large clock on the wall creep slowly forward, with a plate of sandwiches brought in at lunchtime the only distraction. At five past four the Princess suddenly said, 'I'm going upstairs,' and left the room.

Shocked, distressed and utterly drained, Michael Colborne borrowed a pair of wellington boots, and despite the pouring rain, which had not let up all day, took himself off for a long walk. When he returned, there was a note from the Prince saying he wanted to see him. How had he got on? he wanted to know.

'I haven't had a very good day, sir,' said Colborne.

'I understand,' said the Prince. 'I'll see you later.'

At eight o'clock that evening they were due to drive to Aberdeen to board the royal train. The Prince had a regimental engagement in Aldershot the following day. At eight o'clock sharp Colborne, the Prince's detective, John Maclean, and valet, Ken Stronach, were standing about on the gravel outside the front door of the house, waiting for the Prince. A brand new Range Rover which had been delivered that morning was packed and ready to go. It was pitch dark outside and a single lamp hung over the door.

As they stood by the car they could hear the Prince and Princess having a fearsome row on the other side of the closed door. All of a sudden the door flew open, the Prince came shooting out, said, 'Michael!' and threw something at him. It was Diana's wedding ring, made of twenty-two carat Welsh gold, from the same nugget used to make wedding rings for the Queen Mother, the Queen, Princess Margaret and Princess Anne. By some miracle Colborne caught it before it vanished into the gravel. Diana had become so thin it no longer fitted and she wanted him to take it back to London to be made smaller.

They began to get into the car. The Prince always drives with his detective by his side. 'Sit in the front, Michael,' said the Prince. Michael ignored him purposefully and climbed into the back. They travelled down the winding road to Crathie Church in absolute silence. When they reached the main road the Prince began to attack Colborne verbally. He called him all the names under the sun because the new Range Rover was not exactly as he had specified. He had not wanted carpet in the back because he wanted to be able to put deer carcasses there, and Michael hadn't taken any notice of what he had asked. In fact, Colborne had written the Prince a note telling him that, in response to his request, Range Rover had given him a special carpet with press-studs, so that it could be very easily removed. It was clear that the Prince had not read the note. All the way to Aberdeen, the Prince laid into Colborne for one failing after another. Having just had a bloody day with his wife, Michael was not prepared to engage. He simply stared out of the window until they drove on to the station platform soon after nine o'clock. On board the train he ordered himself a treble gin and tonic.

It had not yet arrived when there was a bellow from down the corridor. 'Michael!' He ambled slowly down the train in no great hurry for once to join the Prince of Wales. The Prince offered him a drink. 'Tonight, Michael,' he said, 'you displayed the best traditions of the silent service. You didn't say a word.'

'Firstly,' said Colborne, 'you never gave me a chance to say anything because you just went on and on. And secondly, if you had read your notes you would understand that the press-studs in the back can be taken out by anyone. They are very simple to do.'

'I hear you've had a rough day,' said the Prince.

'Yes,' said Michael, 'I've had an awful day.'

For the next five hours or more, they talked about Charles's marriage to Diana. The Prince was baffled and despondent, and quite at a loss to know what had gone wrong or how to cope.

Diana came to London soon afterwards. 'All the analysts and

psychiatrists you could ever dream of came plodding in trying to sort me out. Put me on high doses of Valium and everything else. But the Diana that was still very much there had decided it was just time; patience and adapting were all that were needed. It was me telling them what I needed. They were telling me "pills"! That was going to keep them happy – they could go to bed at night and sleep, knowing the Princess of Wales wasn't going to stab anyone.'

Back in London, however, they had no home of their own to go to – another thing not properly or sensitively thought through. The Prince had bought Highgrove in 1980 but the new décor had not been completely finished and, at that stage, his office was at Buckingham Palace and all his work was done from London. Apartments in Kensington Palace had been earmarked but they were not ready until shortly before William was born the following year. And so Charles and Diana moved into the Prince's bachelor apartment at the top of Buckingham Palace. He had no household staff of his own, no butler, no footman, or chef: living in his mother's house he had not needed them. For nearly nine months of marriage, therefore, they were dependent upon the Queen. It was rather like living in a hotel above the office, with the in-laws along the corridor. It wasn't a home, and for Diana, who had been used to her own flat, where she did everything herself and was surrounded by her own things and furnishings, it wasn't a real life. She didn't need to shop or cook or even instruct the chef or talk to the housekeeper, and although there was a lot to learn and plenty going on, she felt very bored and lonely.

No one had thought through what her public role would be. All these things which seem so obvious are perhaps only obvious with the benefit of hindsight. No one had considered how she might be affected by the public's adulation, and what demands it would put upon her, although it is true to say that no one expected the adulation to continue beyond the wedding. No one was prepared for the extraordinary way in which her popularity grew over the years, not even Fleet Street. No one had reckoned on her star quality, and her unique ability to touch the hearts and minds of the people she spoke to in the crowds. She was a natural from her very first tour in October, which, fittingly, was to Wales. The Prince proudly presented her to the principality. It was a baptism by fire for both Diana and her newly appointed and only full-time lady-in-waiting, Anne Beckwith-Smith. But the people of Wales were knocked out by the Princess, and Charles was delighted.

Diana had been told how to cope if someone in the crowd grabbed or attacked her, but she had no idea about the simple logistics of accompanying her husband. How, for example, would the Prince and Princess walk into a room together? Would she walk beside or behind her husband? The Prince of Wales had had a mother, father and grandmother to watch over the years, and had grown up with the cameras and the crowds; but even he at almost thirty-three was unsure of his role in life. Diana came to it completely cold, and at twenty had to make up the rules as she went along. Charles was very worried about how she would cope with the crowds and the cameras, particularly given her state of health, and he was very encouraging in the early days when, sick with fear, she had to be cajoled out of the car at each stop.

But it was virgin territory, and no one knew quite what a modern day Princess of Wales should do. If anyone had thought to try and help, the title HRH had elevated Diana to such a level of seniority that friendly words of advice, unless she was in a particularly receptive mood, were difficult to deliver. Certain members of the Queen's household did try to make suggestions, but Diana was suspicious of everyone's motives.

Like every member of the Royal Family Charles was accustomed to being the star and the focus of attention at home as well as out and about. They operate in isolation from one another and they don't like being upstaged by anyone else. They now have what is called a Way Ahead Group, which the Duke of Edinburgh suggested. Senior members of the family get together with their private secretaries to discuss what they are all doing, so they don't double up, but this is an innovation. There is no mutual support, no thrashing out of ideas, no discussing problems, no real interest in one another's work, and no handing out of praise. Because of who they are and how they have been brought up, surrounded by deferential courtiers and deferential friends, they are all intrin-sically selfish. They are also all fundamentally jealous of one another's success. One of the accepted wisdoms passed on to new members of the household is that they should never try to get members of the Royal Family to appear at the same event. Apart from the traditional events like Trooping the Colour and the remembrance ceremony at the Cenotaph, they very seldom appear together.

As his wife, Diana was the Prince's equal, but he was very set in his ways and it didn't come easily to have to consider someone else when planning his day. Diana, in her youthful naiveté, was equally unprepared to accommodate someone else's needs. She had no better idea of what the give and take of married life involved than he did. Her vague, traditional vision of marriage was gleaned mostly from novels and magazines and, in her determination to become Charles's wife, she had not wanted to see or be told that the Prince was by no means a normal man. She could never have done the cooking, shopping and ironing, and been the epicentre of his existence. He was already committed from birth to a life of courtiers, butlers, valets and, above all, duty. He belonged to his country, to the people who would one day be his subjects, who already felt an ownership of him in some small way, and the right to his time. His life was not his own to give wholeheartedly to any woman, and could never have accommodated the kind of marriage Diana, in her girlish, idealistic way, dreamed of.

She didn't understand why he flirted so brazenly with danger, worked himself so hard, or in idle moments took such pleasure in being entirely by himself, away from everyone. She wasn't interested in his needs. She wanted him to pay attention to her one hundred per cent of the time, and couldn't bear it if he was wrapped up in a book, even if he was by her side the while.

Yet the marriage was not all disaster. There were certainly occasions when they had a wonderful time together, and made each other roar with laughter, and their happiness was a pleasure to see.

There were moments of pure unalloyed joy when she was feeling happy, and some very vigorous and enthusiastic sex. Their mutual love of Highgrove in the very early years, and of William and Harry, brought them significantly closer for a while. Friends remember going to lunches with them at Kensington Palace where they would giggle and joke throughout. They remember arriving to go to the theatre with them in the evening, and Diana saying to Charles, 'Come on, let's go and say goodnight to the children – I'll race you to the top of the stairs!' The pair of them would run up the stairs and collapse at the top in a heap of laughter.

But it was all froth. There was never any depth to the relationship or to their understanding of each other. Diana couldn't be the soul mate he wanted in a wife. She didn't share his enthusiasm for books or horses or gardening, or opera or any of the dozens of things which she had pretended to be so interested in at the outset. She was not the one to cure the loneliness and uncertainty of his life, or give him the unconditional love and support and reassurance he needed to make him a confident and happy man – because she desperately needed all of those things herself. Diana was yet another example in the long list of characters he had misjudged.

Charles is no great intellectual, and some people would say he doesn't always use the intellect he has to full capacity, but he does know a huge amount about a vast number of different subjects. He reads extensively, listens to experts in every field and soaks up what he hears. He has a curiosity about everything that goes on around him. Diana had none of that, and if they had had more time together before Charles was rushed into becoming engaged, he might have discovered this.

What Diana did have was an extraordinary instinct for what made people tick; she always knew what to say to make them feel on top of the world, and a warmth and compassion and sense of fun. She was also extremely sexy. It was an irresistible combination for a brief encounter, as so many of the people who fell under her spell discovered, but not for life. The pity was that the Prince of Wales did not discover this until the ring was on her finger.

At Diana's funeral, nothing was more heartbreaking than the hand-written note to 'Mummy'.

It was the Duke of Edinburgh who settled the argument between the Prince of Wales and Charles Spencer about who should walk behind Diana's cortege. In the end, they all did.

Diana and Charles met for the very first time on a shoot at Althorp in November 1977.

To begin with Diana was perfectly friendly towards Camilla. But later, to use Camilla's words, 'Diana went Tonto'.

Diana outside the kindergarten where she worked. The photograph caused a huge stir, and made Diana realise just how effectively she could use the cameras.

Charles couldn't believe his luck. Here was a gorgeous, funny, delightful girl whom everyone seemed to adore and approve of, and she loved *him*.

'Here is the stuff of which fairytales are made,' declared the Archbishop of Canterbury as he made them man and wife. The crowds basked in the romance of it all, but the fairytale was already in question.

In retrospect, Balmoral was not the best place to choose for such a large part of the honeymoon.

Diana's first walkabout in Wales, in October 1981. Although Charles was proud of the way she handled the crowds and the cameras, it was the first time he had had to share the limelight, and it was uncomfortable for him.

Leaving hospital with Prince William, June 1982. For Diana, already debilitated with anorexia, it was the start of crippling post-natal depression.

Diana made Charles laugh and when times were good, they were very, very good – as they were on a visit to Pinewood film studios when she hit him over the head with a fake bottle.

Mother and son, sovereign and heir. There is great love, but no real communication.

An exuberant Diana running to win the mothers' race at William and Harry's school sports day.

Charles and Camilla Parker Bowles in 1979. She had been his first real love and his best friend. There was an intimacy and an easiness which made them enjoy each other's company.

Diana with James Hewitt in 1987. Their affair lasted many years and she admitted she had adored him, but he let her down. He felt that Diana had discarded him.

The family at Highgrove, in the wild flower meadow Charles created. They were already leading separate lives, but put on a show of togetherness for the sake of the children, the country and the cameras.

In marrying, the Prince would have to share the stage, on which he had been a solo player for all his adult life, with his bride, and initially he was proud to do so, and delighted by the public's enthusiasm. In Wales thousands upon thousands of people turned out to catch a glimpse of her, undaunted by the pouring rain, and he was touched. He was even quite amused when people handed him bunches of flowers to give to his wife. 'I seem to do nothing but collect flowers these days,' he said. 'I know my role.'

What he had not bargained on, however, was this role becoming permanent. As time passed, it became increasingly obvious that in their enthusiasm for Diana, the public was losing interest in him. It had been amusing for three days in Wales but when he realised that this was his future, always to be eclipsed by his wife – albeit at that time quite unintentionally – he became distinctly humourless. The Princess of Wales was supposed to be his consort, not his leading lady.

The public's fascination with Diana grew and grew. She was photogenic, she began to wear glamorous clothes and dazzling jewellery. Gone were the borrowed skirts that had made everyone laugh and love her so much in the early days. She was young and modern, and she was a Princess who loved to spend money and dress the part. Newspapers sold millions more copies than usual if they had a photograph of Diana on the front page, so the pressure was on to get those pictures. Photographers besieged her wherever she went; long lenses sought her out even in what she had assumed was the privacy of her own home. There was no distinction between the public and private Princess. They even followed her to a private beach on the island of Eleuthera in the Bahamas where, unknown to her, they took photographs of her five months pregnant wearing a bikini. And with the photographs went commentary, acres of newsprint devoted to analysing every look and gesture she made, to speculating on her state of health, or possible pregnancy, her hairstyle, her clothes and which designer was in the ascendant. The Prince was scarcely mentioned and when he was it was usually to congratulate Diana on having successfully changed his hairstyle or his wardrobe.

When he delivered speeches on matters which he thought important and had put time and effort into preparing, his words were largely dismissed, and the focus fell instead on his wife. Diana had not sought the coverage and at that time was quite intimidated by the attentions of the press; but at the same time she loved to read about herself in the newspapers, and as the media obsession with her grew, so too did her obsession with the media.

In November 1981, Diana announced she was pregnant and they were both thrilled. The Prince rang all his friends, including Camilla Parker Bowles, to tell them the good news. He was overjoyed, not because Diana might be carrying his heir but because for years he had longed for children, as his friends well knew. He had lots of godchildren, whom he loved visiting and playing with, and whenever friends of his had babies he always wrote effusive letters. He had heard the news about one baby while he was confined to his bunk on board HMS *Minerva*.

'For some time I *entirely* forgot that I was meant to be feeling sick and had a headache, and leapt about in my bunk with joy and squeaks feeling incredibly happy for you both … By the time you receive this I expect you will be out of hospital and beginning to wonder how on earth you're going to cope with a small screaming thing that requires feeding every four hours.'

He had thoroughly enjoyed his brothers, Andrew and Edward, eleven and fifteen years younger than him, and at the age of twenty sat down and wrote a book for their bedtime reading called *The Old Man of Lochnagar*.

It was a difficult pregnancy. Diana suffered from morning sickness. She was tired, though she was still carrying out engagements. She was under pressure, and the anorexia was a constant factor. She said she felt that she was 'a nuisance to the set up'. They spent their first Christmas together at Sandringham.

'We've had such a lovely Christmas – the two of us,' wrote Charles to a friend on Boxing Day. 'It has been extraordinarily happy and cosy and being able to share it together … Next year will, I feel sure, be even nicer with a small one to join in as well.'

Days later Diana fell down the stairs in what she later claimed was the first of a series of cries for help. 'I threw myself down the stairs. I said I felt so desperate and I was crying my eyes out and he said: "I'm not going to listen. You're always doing this to me. I'm going riding now." So I threw myself down the stairs. The Queen comes out, absolutely horrified, shaking – she was so frightened ... Charles went out riding and when he came back, you know, it was just dismissal, total dismissal. He just carried on out of the door.'

Other witnesses to that particular incident believe that the Princess fell by accident, and are convinced that she would have done nothing to endanger the baby she was carrying. But there were other 'cries for help', which are not so open to interpretation. On one occasion, she told Morton, 'I wanted to talk to Charles about something. He wouldn't listen to me, he said I was crying wolf. So I picked up his penknife off his dressing table and scratched myself heavily down my chest and both thighs. There was a lot of blood and he hadn't made any reaction whatsoever.' Another time she hurled herself at a glass cabinet, and on yet another occasion she cut herself with a serrated lemon knife.

These were not the actions of a rational mind. In her desperation to make the Prince pay her more attention, she was doing the very things that were guaranteed to drive him away. The first few times she had become hysterical, he had been very seriously alarmed. However, as he heard the threats again and again, as he listened to the hysterics and the screaming, the shouting and the tears, and as time passed, he did just walk away when it happened. He was baffled and frightened by the strength of her emotion; he didn't understand what caused it, nor did he know how to help. It was like being with a complete stranger, a different woman entirely from the sweet gentle girl he had fallen in love with, and his instinct was to turn and run.

Diana said Camilla Parker Bowles was responsible for all her years of unhappiness. It was her husband's obsession with his friend from the beginning that had destroyed their marriage. This is what she told Andrew Morton in 1992, and repeated on television in 1994. But it is not what those people who were around at the time remember. In the early years of the marriage, Diana did not make particular mention of Camilla's name at all. Her constant complaint at that time was that she was not getting enough attention, not being taken seriously, that the Prince seemed more interested in his work than dealing with her problems, and that she was bored and lonely.

After 1986, however, when the Prince had started seeing Camilla again, her name was very much on the Princess's lips, and it was very clear that she hated and resented Camilla. She knew that her husband was in love with her, and that they were having an affair. She would rant and rave about her and kick the furniture, and call her 'that woman' through clenched teeth. But this was not the case in the early part of their marriage. Her tantrums then were not about Camilla – they were about her life.

It was true that the Prince did have a very heavy workload, more than most men. He was the Queen's representative, the Colonel-in-Chief of seven British regiments, the patron or president of innumerable charities and organisations, and as heir to the throne, had a duty not only to attend receptions, investitures, banquets for visiting foreign dignitaries, but to keep himself abreast of affairs of state, and in addition, take part in ceremonial occasions. He had always taken his duties as Prince of Wales seriously, always worked long hours, and always worked his staff hard. He had also always played hard, hunting in the winter months, playing polo in the summer. They were both a valuable release from the stress and frustrations of his work, and with polo there was often the added bonus of making money for charity in the process – he has raised millions of pounds this way over the years. In between times, he had great need for solitude, which he found walking in the countryside, settling down for a couple of hours in a lonely spot with his watercolours or standing thigh deep in a cold river, fishing. Apart from socialising as a couple in future, he had imagined life would go on very much as before. His friends had also been an important part of his life, and it never occurred to him that he might have to stop seeing them so much after his marriage. He imagined Diana would enjoy seeing them as much as he did. But the Princess resented the time he spent working, resented the horsy activities for which she had no love, resented the time Charles spent on his own, and resented his friends who were always around. She wanted him to concentrate on her.

Despite having appeared to get on so well with the Prince's friends when they first met, in reality she disliked and mistrusted most of them. In some cases, not without some justification. He listens to their advice, which is not always what his official advisers over the years have considered the wisest, and they enjoy the power they have. They did not want it diluted by a wife. Some were wonderful and went out of their way to help and to make Diana feel at ease. Emilie van Cutsem was one in particular, and the Princess was touched by her kindness. She wrote to thank her on one occasion, saying that she was like the mother she had never had. Lady Susan Hussey was another who was thanked in the most loving tones.

There were polo friends too, not so close, but whose company the Prince enjoyed from time to time. They were a highly sexed lot, loud and vulgar and after one dinner party with them all, Diana refused to go to another. Another group that he partied with occasionally were members of the Beaufort Hunt, less brash than the polo crowd, but still highly-sexed, loud and horsy. Diana felt very uncomfortable and out of her depth in their company. She made it clear that she did not want anything to do with them.

But as time passed, Diana turned against all of the Prince's friends, including the two who had been so solicitous and to whom she had initially been so grateful. While writing warm and tender letters to them, she would in the same breath be saying terrible things about them behind their backs and sowing seeds of dissension amongst friends and colleagues. 'You wouldn't say that about so and so, if you knew what she told me about you,' she would say, and then repeat a conversation which would turn out to be complete fabrication but which sounded plausible. She accused friends of disloyalty, staff of dishonesty, and caused a lot of harm and uncertainty amongst people who no longer knew whom to trust.

When friends started to realise that something was amiss, they dropped discreet hints, which the Prince did not want to hear. His parents also made it clear that they thought Diana was less than perfect, but he was not prepared to listen to criticism, even from the Queen. He was fiercely loyal to Diana – he wouldn't discuss her moods or her tantrums with anyone – and he was desperate to make her happy, desperate to make her well. At one time she was so thin and ill he was afraid she was going to die. And he thought he was responsible. He thought maybe he had done something to make her like this, that maybe marriage to him was just too awful, and he had destroyed her by bringing her into this bizarre way of life. He was thoroughly depressed and despondent.

In an attempt to please her, and to try and bring back the lovely girl he had fallen in love with, he did everything she asked. He reluctantly cut his friends out of his life. One by one he stopped all contact with them. He didn't telephone, didn't write and didn't visit. He said nothing to explain to them what had happened and they were all too reticent to telephone and ask why they had not heard from him. They had valued their friendship with the Prince; they had protected him, been there for him when he needed them, and were very deeply hurt. Some went earlier than others. The Romseys were one of the last to go. In the midst of an ornament-throwing, screaming match one day, the Prince lost his cool with Diana and said, 'I should have listened to Norton. He said I should never have married you.' That was the end of the Romseys. They were no longer allowed in the house, banished like all his other friends.

Charles not only gave up his friends in an effort to please Diana, he also gave up his dog at her behest. Harvey was a big yellow Labrador, whom he had had for many years. He travelled everywhere with him, living in Kensington Palace during the week and at Highgrove at weekends. When he went shooting at Sandringham, Harvey went too, as he did to Balmoral for the summer. Diana said the dog was associated with his past and with his friends and she couldn't have him around. Sadly, Harvey was sent off to live with the Prince's comptroller, Lt.Col. Philip Creasey, who had a house in Kent. Diana was never particularly moved by animals, despite having had pets as a child. Animal charities always left her cold and, when presented with an animal, as she occasionally was, she would never reach out and touch it as she would a child. But the Prince loved dogs, having grown up with them, and in time filled the space in his life left by Harvey with a Jack Russell terrier from Lady Salisbury, an old friend who had known the Prince since he was a child and helped create the garden at Highgrove.

By the summer of 1982 Charles and Diana were using Highgrove on a regular basis. At the Prince's instigation, Diana had overseen the interior, employing a designer called Dudley Poplak, whom her mother had used in the past and who had also decorated Kensington Palace. Both interiors were pretty, bright and colourful, quite unlike anything the Prince had known before. The Prince loved Highgrove. It was not overly grand or ostentatious, although it boasted nine bedrooms and domestic quarters. It was a comfortable family home, with a garden into which, over the years, the Prince poured heart and soul – with enthusiastic support in the early days from Diana. It had originally belonged to the Colonel Mitchell who founded a famous arboretum at Westonbirt just down the road. It was planted with magnificent trees, and it was this, principally, which attracted the Prince immediately. More recently the house had belonged to the Macmillan family and, when the Prince took it over, he kept on the couple who had looked after the Macmillans, Nesta Whiteland, who had been cook come housekeeper, and her Irish husband, Paddy, who worked as general factotum.

Mrs Paddy, as she was known, and the Princess didn't hit it off together. The housekeeper was frankly at a loss to understand what the Prince had seen in Diana. Having been used to aristocrats who understood their place in the house, she was disturbed to have Diana rushing into the kitchen to raid the fridge or to arrange flowers for the house, when there was a woman employed to do the flowers. Nesta was a shrewd judge of character and, although she never said anything, the Princess began to feel the vibrations. Paddy, meanwhile, kept out of it and devoted himself wholeheartedly to the Prince.

On 21 June 1982, soon after they had moved into Highgrove, Prince William was born in the private Lindo Wing of St Mary's Hospital in Paddington, London. Her obstetrician, George Pinker, had decided to induce the birth because he was concerned for Diana's health, and William Arthur Philip Louis came into the world at 9.03 p.m., after a sixteen-hour labour.

'Thrilled, everyone absolutely high as a kite – we had found a date where Charles could get off his polo pony for me to give birth. That was very nice, felt very grateful about that!' said Diana.

Her rancorous account was written ten years after the event. The Prince's letter to Patricia Brabourne, Lord Mountbatten's daughter, written days afterwards, indicates a very different attitude. 'The arrival of our small son has been an astonishing experience and one that has meant more to me than I could ever have imagined. As so often happens in this life, you have to experience something before you are in a true position to understand or appreciate the full meaning of the whole thing. I am *so* thankful I was beside Diana's bedside the whole time because by the end of the day I really felt as though I'd shared deeply in the process of birth and as a result was rewarded by seeing a small creature which belonged to *us* even though he seemed to belong to everyone else as well! I have never seen such scenes as there were outside the hospital when I left that night – everyone had gone berserk with excitement ... Since then we've been over-whelmed by people's reactions and thoroughly humbled. It really is quite extraordinary ... I am so pleased that you like the idea of Louis being one of William's names. Oh! How I wish your papa could have lived to see him, but he probably knows anyway ...'

The Prince was overwhelmed by the experience of becoming a father and watching his son being born was something he enthused about for long afterwards; but it brought no let up in Diana's condition, and only the briefest respite to the misery of their situation. After the initial elation, the Princess sank into severe post-natal depression, which she described herself. 'Boy, was I troubled. If he didn't come home when he said he was coming home I thought something dreadful had happened to him. Tears, panic, all the rest of it.'

The Prince was seriously worried, and that autumn he arranged for her to see a behavioural psychiatrist. He saw her for about six months at which point she signed herself off and refused to go back. He said she was not well, but no one could force Diana to be treated, and there was obviously nothing further he could do.

Friends in the Queen's household suggested Diana take it easy after William's birth and simply enjoy being a mother, cutting out the public side of her life for a while. But she wanted to work. Early in 1983, she and the Prince took William, then nine months old, on a six-week tour of Australia and New Zealand, which she found completely gruelling. The crowds and the fascination with Diana was unprecedented, and the Prince was hurt and depressed by the comments he couldn't help hearing, from people disappointed when they found he was taking their side of the street on their walkabouts rather than her. He was also desperately worried about her health again and the effect the stress of the cameras and the crowds was having on her, combined with his inability to persuade her to eat.

While they were away William learned to crawl. Charles wrote excitedly to Lady Susan Hussey, 'Your godson couldn't be in better form. Today he actually crawled for the first time. We laughed and laughed with sheer, hysterical pleasure and now we can't stop him crawling everywhere.' And to the van Cutsems he wrote, 'William now crawls over Government House at high speed knocking everything off the tables and causing unbelievable destruction.'

By 1983, before moving on to his friends and dog, Diana had seen off a number of the Prince's staff. The first to go was a policeman called Paul Officer, who had once saved the Prince's life and to whom he was as a result very close; Diana took against him for no apparent reason. Next went his valet, Stephen Barry, who had also been very close for many years, and was too intimately associated with the Prince's past sexual liaisons. He had cared for the Prince like a wife, and doubtless he resented the intrusion of a real wife who wanted her husband to herself, as much as she resented him. It was he who some years after his departure, bitter at the way life had treated him, started the rumour that the Prince had slept with Camilla Parker Bowles two nights before the Royal Wedding.

Saddest by far was the departure of Oliver Everett, Diana's private secretary, who left in December of that year. Oliver Everett was a charming, intelligent and sensitive man who had served the Prince well as an assistant private secretary between 1978 and 1980, and who had been recalled as the perfect person to look after Diana. It was he who had taken her down to join *Britannia* for Cowes Week in the summer of 1980, and reported back to the office that this one looked serious. He was married with a young family and lived in Oxford and, having to commute, was never in the office quite as early as the Princess would have liked. She was an early riser, and after a swim in the Buckingham Palace pool and breakfast at whatever time it was brought, she sat impatiently awaiting his arrival. Initially this was not a problem – nothing was a problem, he could do no wrong. They got on very well together, and the relationship was warm and friendly. She was always popping into his office for a chat. They were even described as being more like conspirators and friends than private secretary and Princess. Then quite suddenly and for no reason that anyone could fathom, she went off him. She said she didn't like him fussing over her, it drove her demented. She completely cut him out of her life. She wouldn't speak to him, didn't return his phone calls, and if they were in a room together, ignored him. She talked to other people in the office who said that if she felt that strongly about Oliver Everett, she must talk to the Prince. The Prince was mortified. Everett had given up his career at the Foreign Office to join his office at the Prince's request, and although a job was found for him as Librarian at Windsor Castle, many regard it as a shocking waste of talent; and the whole episode offended the Prince's sense of justice. But yet again, he went along with what Diana wanted.

Instead of bringing in a replacement, Anne Beckwith-Smith and Michael Colborne both took over Everett's responsibilities. It was a good solution. Anne, slightly older than the Princess, and a motherly figure, was much more informal; and Colborne – so Diana told the

Prince – was the only person she could really get on with. But it was not long before he grew tired of being caught in the cross-fire between the Prince and Princess. Matters reached a head on their tour of Canada in 1983.

The Prince by this time had become uncharacteristically moody. Gone was the man Colborne had known in his bachelor years, a man thirsty for life, who was ready to have a go at anything and everything, who worked hard and drove himself hard, but who was fun to be with. The joy seemed to have gone out of his life, and the serious side to his nature, which had always been there, appeared to have taken over.

They were on board *Britannia* in Canada. It was a beautiful afternoon and the Prince had gone off to visit his regiments. Colborne had just gone into the office to prepare for a reception that evening for President Trudeau, when he was told that the Princess wanted to see him up on the sun deck. She told him to get a chair and, as the afternoon passed, it became clear all she wanted was someone to talk to. The Prince wanted to speak to the editor of *The Times* when he came back, which Colborne organised for him via satellite. All went well, the Prince made the phone call and the two men then went into the Duke of Edinburgh's cabin for a drink, as they always did on board the royal yacht if they had a chance. The moment the cabin door was closed, the Prince went berserk. He paced round and round the cabin, kicking the furniture and shouting at Colborne. He said he had upset him greatly recently by spending more of his time looking after the Princess than after him. Colborne struggled to explain that he thought he had been helping the Prince by looking after Diana, but the boss was not in the mood to listen. After about fifteen minutes of ranting and raving the Prince suddenly looked at his watch and said, 'We'd better go and get changed.' He flung open the door, and there standing in the doorway was the Princess, who had been listening to everything that had been said, and was in tears. Charles wrapped her in his arms and, after a few moments, the two of them disappeared to their cabin to change into evening dress and be ready to greet the President.

Such was the pace of life that there was never any time for either of them to deal with problems properly. Duty dictated they were always on to the next engagement, the next photo call, the next handshake and, ever professional, they stitched the smiles on to their faces and tucked the inner turmoil away.

Michael Colborne had had enough. He was tired of being piggy in the middle. He recognised there was some truth in what the Prince had said. He had recently been devoting more attention to the Princess but because he felt so sorry for her. She was becoming quietly intoxicated with the extraordinary effect she was having. She was operating too much on impulse, enjoying the glitter more than she ought and beginning to flirt. Wherever she went, whatever room she walked into she was the centre of attention and she could see men fall like ninepins in her thrall, with no more than a coquettish tilt of the head or a teasing laugh. It would have been enough to turn even the strongest head, let alone a girl who was still only twenty-two. She was, he felt, in danger of becoming an unguided missile.

That evening he sat down and wrote a note to the Prince. He said that the one thing he had always tried to do during his ten years of service was look after the Prince. It was something which Lord Mountbatten had asked him to do. And he felt the Prince had been unfair to accuse him of looking after the Princess more than him because he thought that by helping her he would be helping him.

That was the Tuesday and the Prince didn't speak to him again until the Friday, their last day in Canada. That night the Prince and Princess went along to the mess to say goodbye and thank you to the crew, as they always did at the end of a stay on *Britannia*. As they were walking along, the Prince dropped back and said, 'Thanks for your note, Michael. I realise what you meant and I'm sorry for that evening.'

It was too late. Those fifteen minutes on the receiving end of the Prince's blistering wrath, unable to do anything but stand and take it, sowed the seeds that would mark the end of their relationship – the longest the Prince has had with anyone in his office. Colborne had had one earful too many. He had given the Prince ten years of his life. He had loved most of it, and he loved the man – he would have walked through fire for the Prince – but the man he knew had changed and he couldn't see how the situation was going to improve. The Princess was becoming more and more demanding and he was being pulled in two directions at once and couldn't go on.

The Prince was shocked when he read Colborne's letter of resignation. Colborne was important to him: he was a link with the real world, in tune with his thinking, and where the more traditional courtiers were cautious about the areas he was becoming involved in, like inner city deprivation and young people, Colborne was encouraging. He understood the man in the street in a way that the establishment around him couldn't begin to. The Prince tried repeatedly to persuade Michael to change his mind, and even telephoned his wife, Shirley, several times at home to try and get her to persuade him. Several other people tried, including the Queen's former private secretary, Sir Martin Charteris, and Colborne finally agreed to stay on until the end of 1984, having handed in his notice in the spring, but that was it.

He was still a member of the household when Prince Henry, known as Harry, was born on 15 September 1984 – like his brother in St Mary's Hospital, Paddington. The Princess later said that six weeks before his birth she and the Prince were closer than they had ever been, or ever would be. 'Then suddenly as Harry was born it just went bang, our marriage, the whole thing went down the drain.' She had known her second child was a boy from the scan, but had not told her husband because she knew he had been hoping for a girl. 'Harry arrived, Harry had red hair, Harry was a boy. First comment was "Oh, God, it's a boy", second comment "and he's even got red hair". Something inside me closed off.'

Those around them at the time knew Diana had been worried that the Prince would be disappointed; however, they say that if he was, he certainly showed no trace of it. In fact he appeared to be thrilled to have a second son, and was once again overwhelmed by the miracle of childbirth. It put life into perspective again.

But Harry's birth was no miracle cure for the relationship. The Prince's moodiness and temper were getting worse, and although Diana didn't go through the same terrifying post-natal depression that she had suffered after William was born, she was by now in the grip of bulimia, and still experienced frighteningly violent mood swings. She was also growing ever more demanding, and the Prince continued to do what she wanted in a desperate effort to make her happy. One of the things she insisted upon was that he spend more time with the children. Diana sent a note to Edward Adeane saying that in future her husband would not be available for meetings in the early mornings or evenings because he would be upstairs in the nursery. Adeane could not believe it. He was a bachelor. He had no children and no understanding of what it was like to change a nappy, bath a baby, or read a little boy a bedtime story. He was a courtier in the best old school tradition. New man he certainly was not, and he was not happy for his boss to become one either. His best times of day with the Prince were first thing in the morning and last thing at night. They were the two moments in a normally very busy day when there was some peace in which to talk and to go through vital briefings for the day ahead. It was yet another of the irritants which made his departure at the end of the year inevitable.

They had also clashed over the Prince's plans to deliver a damning speech to the Royal Institute of British Architecture earlier in the year, and put a bomb under an institution which had enjoyed uncritical royal approval for 150 years. When Adeane saw what Charles had drafted in cahoots with one or two architectural advisers, including an art historian called Jules Lubbock, he tried hard to persuade the Prince to tone the speech down. Even as they drove to Hampton Court for the dinner he was still suggesting amendments; but the Prince was not to be moved. The speech was delivered as written and, predictably, caused an almighty row.

It offended many of the architects present at the dinner that night, and delighted a small minority of highly unfashionable community architects and, as a result, quite unintentionally, launched a crusade, which is still just about alive today. It is widely known in the Prince's office as 'the nightmare brief', the one that no private secretary wholly enjoys dealing with. And of all the issues that the Prince has taken to heart, architecture is the one which even his greatest fans question.

Sir Edward Adeane, the Prince's private secretary, was shocked when he heard that Michael Colborne was leaving, but Colborne had failed to realise how much Adeane had also been suffering. He was particularly unaware of how much he had been affected by the tension between the Prince and Princess. During a farewell lunch on the Friday of Michael's departure, Adeane was clearly very depressed. Shirley Colborne asked him if he was all right. 'I'm going to really miss Michael,' he said. 'He's been taking the personal things off my shoulders, he's been looking after everybody.'

The following day, Adeane went down to Windsor where he and the Prince had a blazing row, very similar to the one the Prince had had with Colborne. Right there and then, Adeane resigned.

SEVEN

A State of Mind

'Almost any human being would have found
[being the Princess of Wales] absolutely intolerable.'
Aide to Prince Charles

The Princess of Wales saw a great many doctors and psychiatrists as well as holistic and alternative practitioners during the course of her marriage. Most of them she dismissed after a while when it became apparent that they could do nothing for her. The condition she talked about openly was bulimia, but most experts agree that the bulimia was merely a symptom of a far greater problem. Psychiatrists are generally loath to put labels on patients, understanding that the mind is a very inexact science. Individuals vary in the symptoms they display, and no two doctors are likely to come up with the same diagnosis, far less agree on a treatment. It is reasonably safe to say, however, that Diana had severe, clinical depression. Given her childhood history and the behaviour patterns, several experts suggest that she was suffering from a well-recognised, if controversial, condition called Borderline Personality Disorder.

The condition was first described by an American psychiatrist, Adolf Stern, in 1938. He used it to categorise patients who had low self-esteem and difficulty in sustaining relationships. According to the manual of mental disorders, published by the American Psychiatric Association for diagnostic purposes, these were patients who showed 'a pervasive pattern of instability of mood, inter-personal relationships, and self-image, beginning in early adulthood and present in a variety of contexts, as indicated by at least five of the following:

(1) a pattern of unstable and intense interpersonal relationships characterised by alternating between extremes of over-idealisation and devaluation

(2) impulsiveness in at least two areas that are potentially self-damaging, e.g., spending, sex, substance use, shoplifting, reckless driving, binge eating

(3) affective instability: marked shifts from baseline mood to depression, irritability, or anxiety, usually lasting a few hours and only rarely more than a few days

(4) inappropriate, intense anger or lack of control of anger, e.g. frequent displays of temper, constant anger, recurrent physical fights

(5) recurrent suicidal threats, gestures, or behaviour, or self-mutilating behaviour

(6) marked and persistent identity disturbance manifested by uncertainty about at least two of the following: self-image, sexual orientation, long-term goals or career choice, type of friends desired, preferred values

(7) chronic feelings of emptiness or boredom

(8) frantic efforts to avoid real or imagined abandonment.'

It was several years before anyone around the Princess realised that she had a serious problem. They all thought for a very long time that the incidents of strange behaviour were unconnected, and that stress was the main factor. Stress certainly can't have helped and it is impossible for anyone who has never been with the Princess when she was in public or on tour to understand how stressful it was. As one of the Prince's private secretaries says, 'I've never succeeded in describing to anybody, who wasn't in the middle of it, the pressures of that life and that relationship, and looking as she looked and being who she was. Almost any human being would have found it absolutely intolerable. Wherever you happened to be, every look, every gaze, every smile, every scowl, every hand you held or touched, under the microscope every time, front page news in the tabloids day after day, sometimes of your own volition, I know, but everybody after you. It was the most extraordinary pressure. I did the same sort of work for politicians. It was utterly different. There was a clearish divide between public and private life, and I didn't need to cross any of those dividing lines.

'Here the whole thing was a great big ball of wax, the job, the public life, the private life, it was all indistinguishable, not just for them, but for us too. The phone calls would come at any time of the day or night, wherever you were in the world, your involvement with them was twenty-four hours a day and you couldn't distinguish because they didn't distinguish. How could they distinguish between what was public and private, what was work and what was play? It was all part of the same thing. There wasn't much respite and that clearly took its toll on her. It takes its toll on him too, but he's been brought up to it and developed his own defence mechanisms, his own thick skin.'

Charles and Diana had scarcely been married six months before everyone was so worried about Diana's state of mind that the Queen called in Fleet Street editors to Buckingham Palace, as she had only done once in her reign before – at the end of Prince Charles's first term at Cheam preparatory school in 1957 – to appeal for privacy. On this occasion she asked the editors to give Diana a break. The poor girl couldn't even go into the local Gloucestershire town of Tetbury to buy a packet of wine gums without being on the front page of the newspapers, and the strain was having a very bad effect on her. They had assumed the Palace was worried she might be in danger of a miscarriage. That was not the worry. The then editor of the *News of the World*, Barry Askew, said that if the Princess had a craving for wine gums, she ought to send a servant out to get them.

'That,' retorted the Queen famously, 'is the most pompous thing I've ever heard.'

For many of the people who worked most closely with the Princess, the discovery that she had some kind of psychiatric disorder made it easier to handle. As the Prince of Wales said about schizophrenia, when launching the SANE Appeal in 1991, 'Physical disability, illness, accidents which break bones or upset the functions of the body are painful, yet can be overcome by strength of personality, good medical care and will-power. Schizophrenia is different: we are talking about an illness which changes the way people think, understand and perceive the world around them and relate to others – the very essence of their personality – so that they are isolated from all sources of comfort and reason. I believe we have to accept that accidents can happen to the mind as they can to the body, and that the consequences can sometimes be even more devastating.'

Charles was not interested in labels. He knew what symptoms Diana displayed and sought out the best doctors and psychiatrists to relieve them. He was angered by her behaviour at times, and thoroughly depressed by it, but deep down he felt desperately sorry for her, and although it didn't making coping any easier, he was eventually convinced that Diana had an illness and could no more be blamed for her actions than she could be blamed had she bled all over the carpet from an open wound.

What puzzles some experts who knew her is that she never crashed or had a breakdown. She came close to it, they reckon, one day when, leaving therapist Susie Orbach's north London home, she burst into tears in front of waiting photographers and ran away. She also cried in public during her first engagement after Andrew Morton's book was published, when someone stroked her cheek. As one expert in psychiatric disorders said, 'If all sufferers were royal there might be no more mental illness, because if you are in control you have power and can use your fantasies and manipulations.'

What is universally acknowledged is that Borderline Personality Disorder is one of the most difficult conditions to cure. It is treated with anti-depressants, tranquillisers and intensive care and support, but the success rate is not encouraging. A recent Canadian study suggested that ten per cent of sufferers would, ultimately, commit suicide. It also takes its toll on the relatives who attempt to care and support, also on the psychiatrists who attempt to treat it, partly because the symptoms are only displayed in private. In public, sufferers are cheerful, outgoing, attractive, successful and often highly charismatic people, who give every indication of being quite well balanced. These people are generally so mesmerising that even the professionals, who are trained to keep a distance from the patients they treat, find themselves becoming sucked into their orbit and emotionally engulfed. When they fail to solve the problem, and are spewed out – as friends and relatives are too – they feel a colossal sense of failure and dejection. Many of them say that, although evil is not a word that should ever enter their vocabulary, they are tempted to use it in relation to these patients. It is because they feel frustrated that despite all their professionalism and understanding of the condition, they are allowing themselves to be so successfully manipulated by someone who on the face of it appears so rational.

A mental illness can, in theory, be treated with chemicals, as it is commonly the result of a chemical imbalance. A disorder is different. It is like a jigsaw puzzle that has had some of the pieces mixed up: the personality traits which go together to make up every individual are put together in a way that is abnormally balanced. Minor personality disorders are common, seen in people who need attention or adoration. Provided they can keep them under control there is no problem. The people who have them very often find their way into politics or on to the stage. Indeed most people don't begin to know there is any kind of abnormality. When the disorder is serious, it is particularly difficult for everyone concerned because sufferers need attention, but at the same time repel and repudiate anyone who offers it. They are unable to engage in proper relationships or feel any real emotion. It is all copied from watching others, as if through glass. The only emotion which is genuine is the sense of despair and frustration at being unable to have the relationships that they see others having.

Quite unprompted, one of Diana's closest friends at the end of her life described her as having terrible problems exactly fitting the medical description of Borderline Personality Disorder. 'She is like someone who has her nose pressed to the glass looking at the world outside, but never feeling that she is part of it. She can't emotionally, psychologically cope with it.'

Did Diana have this disorder before she became engaged to the

Prince of Wales, or was it what she called his uncaring and indifferent attitude towards her which brought it on? One of the most common causes of Borderline Personality Disorder is said to be 'unstable or disruptive early childhood relationships', which Diana was certainly not short of; and there are indications that she was showing signs of being difficult and manipulative when she was quite young.

A very senior member of the royal household, who had a daughter at Riddlesworth Hall prep school with Diana until the age of twelve, volunteered long before things became bad with the Princess that he had made specific enquiries about where Diana would next be going to school, so that he could choose somewhere different for his daughter. They were a local family and he didn't think his daughter's friendship with Diana Spencer was having a good effect on her.

Diana's grandmother, Ruth, Lady Fermoy, described her as 'a dishonest and difficult girl' and, less than a month before she died, in July 1993, said that she could have kicked herself for not screwing up her courage to warn the Prince of Wales about Diana before he married her. Diana's father, who died in March 1991, also said he had been wrong not to say something. The Prince therefore went into the marriage wholly unprepared. It is doubtful that any man could have helped Diana, and probable that Charles stuck with it longer than most husbands would have, because of the man he is and because of the position he holds.

The Prince behaved as best he knew how, unaware until the relationship had very nearly destroyed him that he had been handed an almost impossible task.

EIGHT

The Offices of a Prince

'The day you think I'm not useful, tell me.'
Charles

The mid-eighties were difficult for the Prince. He felt that Michael Colborne had deserted him – and he found his departure particularly tough; Edward Adeane had also left him; his marriage was not working; the press was critical; his father was unsympathetic; he was uncertain about what he should be doing with his life and torn about whether he should be following his instinct or listening to his cautious courtiers.

His friends were reaching senior position in their chosen professions while he was still waiting in the wings to fulfil the role he had trained for since birth. As a sensitive man, he knew he had no business feeling sorry for himself. Looking at the shattered and demoralised young people he met in the inner cities, he knew he had more than they could ever hope for. But knowing this didn't help. People listened to him, did what he asked, and came to see him when he opened a building or visited a factory. Yet it was not because of *who* he was, but because of *what* he was. He had been born with a silver spoon in his mouth and had never been able to do any real job that made him feel he had earned respect and admiration. He was desperate to be of some use, and to understand the purpose of life and his role within it.

He became temperamental and depressed and hugely demanding of everyone around him. He cut back on his engagements and spent many a contemplative hour digging the garden at Highgrove or riding hard, pushing himself physically to the limits.

Diana, trying to come to terms with her own problems, was the last person who could help. She was too young to understand the tortuous soul-searching Charles was going through; too pre-occupied with the maelstrom of her own life. In the last four years it had been turned completely upside down. She had shot from unremarkable teenager to international superstar, recognised in every corner of the globe, watched and photographed everywhere she went. She had married into the most extraordinary family in Britain – one of the most extraordinary families in the world – and in doing so taken on a title that set her apart from everyone she had ever known. She had a job and a life she had had no training for. And to top it all she had become a mother of two small boys. Even the most well-balanced, level-headed, secure and self-confident young woman would have found it difficult to cope. For Diana it was impossible.

The press began to notice that all was not well. They calculated that in a three-month period, Charles had carried out just fifteen engagements, compared with his sister's fifty-six, Prince Philip's forty-five, and the Queen's twenty-eight. Meanwhile he seemed to have plenty of time for polo. The criticism stung, but polo was one of the few things that was keeping him sane. He once said, 'If I can have a game of polo I feel five hundred times better in my mental outlook. But without some form of exercise I'm afraid to say I get terribly jaded and, well, not depressed, but below par.'

By 1985 he was not just below par, he was seriously, chronically depressed, almost suicidal, and his friends were so worried about him they decided something had to be done to restore his spirits. They knew he had always got on well with Camilla Parker Bowles; they knew she was sitting at home while her charming husband philandered his way around London and Wiltshire, and they suggested the two of them contact one another.

Charles and Camilla had had virtually no contact since 1981. They had been at the same social gathering from time to time, but had not met to talk since the time of his engagement, with one exception, when he gave Camilla the bracelet. They had spoken on the telephone a few times during his engagement, but since then he had only telephoned once to tell Camilla that Diana was expecting a baby.

It was Patti Palmer-Tomkinson who organised it, and at first they wrote long letters to each other. Then they started to speak on the telephone, and this went on for several months. Finally they met at Patti's house in Hampshire. The Prince was enormously relieved to have someone to talk to whom he trusted and who was so sympathetic. Camilla took him out of his gloom and despondency, listened to his worries and concerns, understood him and cared in a way that is only possible when two people have once been lovers. For years he had spoken to no one about the difficulties of his life with Diana for fear that to do so would be disloyal. But their former intimacy meant that Camilla was someone from whom he needed to keep no secrets, someone who he knew beyond doubt would keep his confidence. Gradually their friendship turned into something deeper and more physical. The Prince always felt guilty about this but, to his astonishment, discovered years later that while he had been feeling so guilty about Camilla, the Princess had been having an affair many months before he and Camilla had even made contact.

Camilla's friendship brought Charles back from the brink of the abyss, but it was a long climb back, and many of his friends think that he was irreparably damaged by the experiences of his marriage. Camilla bolstered his confidence, took an interest in his work and encouraged him to believe that he had a contribution to make.

One of the areas in which no one can deny his contribution to society is the Prince's Trust. It began with a few ideas scribbled on the back of an envelope in 1972, and since then all of the ideas that have driven the Trust, in outline if not in detail, have been the Prince's. He has taken enormous pleasure and pride in watching it grow and become a success. He was originally moved by hearing a probation officer talking on the radio about young offenders, and felt the urge to try and help. If young people could be given something positive to do with their time and energy, he reasoned, it might keep them out of trouble. And so he gave his naval allowance of £3,000 a year, in its entirety and quite anonymously, to young people. In the early days that was how the Trust was funded.

The facts and figures that drive the Prince's Trust today are simple. There are nearly 120,000 young people unemployed long-term in Britain, and many of them have no skills to take up jobs even if they could find them. More and more children are being ex-cluded from school, particularly amongst the ethnic minorities. Young black men are twice as likely to be unemployed as their white counterparts. And, according to studies commissioned by the Prince's Trust, crime committed by unemployed youth costs the nation over £7 billion a year. So the three areas the Trust now focuses on are targeted directly at those people. It helps children do their homework outside school hours, by way of Study Support Centres, of which there are now 800. It sets up young people in their own small businesses: 4,618 were launched last year, and a total of 44,000 since the Trust began. Sixty per cent of those people the Trust helps are still trading three years later; the top ten now turn over £38.7 million per annum; the top 100 turn over a total of £80 million per annum, and employ 1,600 people between them. The Trust's third activity is training the unemployed in the community on a mixture of courses, some of them residential, some of them dedicated to particular skills, all of them involving teamwork in the community. Seventy per cent of those people who take part move from unemployment to either work or training within three months of completing the programme.

Charles has employed some unfortunate people over the years. Equally, there have been some very remarkable people in his orbit. Tom Shebbeare, who runs the Prince's Trust, was one of his best appointments. He is an ex eurocrat and, since his arrival in 1987, has turned it from an amateurish charity with plenty of good ideas into an organisation that will spend £30 million on young people this year. As a consequence it is rapidly having its clothes stolen by the government. While the general public may still think all the Trust does is hold pop concerts, they are beginning to recognise the

Prince's part in all of it. When he arrived at a Prince's Trust concert in London's Hyde Park in the summer of 1998 and made his way to the grandstand, the crowd of over 100,000 people turned to face him, clapping and cheering for five minutes, before singing an early 'Happy Birthday'. For a while, actor Stephen Fry, who was on stage trying to introduce the Prince, seemed almost lost for words.

There have been a number of figures in the Prince's life who have played a central role for a while, and by whom he has been impressed and influenced. The South African born writer, explorer and philosopher Laurens van der Post was one, who first entranced the Prince in the mid-seventies, and encouraged him to listen to his instincts and explore the 'old world of the spirit'.

'We suffer from a hubris of the mind,' he wrote in one of his books, every one of which the Prince devoured with a passion. 'We have abolished superstition of the heart only to install a superstition of the intellect in its place.'

Another more down to earth influence, and one about whom no one had any qualms, was Stephen O'Brien, who in late 1984 brought the Prince into an organisation called Business in the Community (BitC). The combination of the man and the mission he was engaged in, which immediately struck a chord with the Prince of Wales, unleashed a whole new interest in life. BitC is now one of his principal interests, and although Stephen O'Brien has moved on, his successor, Julia Cleverdon, is another remarkable and inspirational individual, who works very closely with the Prince. The idea that drives BitC is simple: involve companies in the communities in which they operate, persuade them to invest, train and recruit from within those communities, and you solve unemployment, thereby improving the whole depressed inner city environment.

O'Brien had initially approached the Prince for support with a project for young unemployed black people in the inner cities called Fullemploy, knowing of the Prince's Trust work in that area. Out of their meeting came a daring event, known as the Windsor Conference, which people involved in race relations still talk about today. For two days the chairmen of sixty major companies in the UK were brought face to face with a crowd of bright, articulate members of the black community in a hotel in Windsor. They mixed, talked and ate together, and discussed the problems of unemployment among black youths. Racism, Charles told the assembled gathering, was a problem of the white society and not the black. It was a failure to recognise the potential of the black community and a failure to use it. By the end of the conference both black and white participants had discovered that their preconceptions about each other were entirely false. The exercise was widely regarded as one of the most significant advances ever made in race relations. Nothing of the kind had ever been done before and without the Prince of Wales it would almost certainly never have happened. But there is no doubt it was a highly risky experiment, which could have gone badly wrong.

His courage was not lost on Stephen O'Brien; and the following year, 1985, the Prince was invited to become President of BitC. He accepted with alacrity. Here was a man and a group of people with a real determination to make things happen, who appeared to share his concerns about society and his ideals, who had the financial support of government and industry, unlike his own endeavours which were so reliant on the begging bowl. Also, it was young enough, having been in existence for just four years, for him to be able to make a positive contribution.

'The day you think I am not useful,' he told one of BitC's directors, 'tell me. I want to be involved in the growth of something. I don't just want to open things and be seen trundling around. I can go to all the dinners and banquets on earth, but it's not going to make any difference to the world. What I want to do is be part of something that does.'

This was exactly what he needed to stop him brooding about his marital problems, and the Prince threw himself into what was the closest he had yet come to a real job. He quickly realised that his presence made an impact on BitC, that he was adding real value, and he found in Stephen O'Brien a man off whom he could bounce ideas that were not immediately condemned as ill advised, as they would have been by the cautious courtiers.

Whatever else may be said of the Prince of Wales, courage is never something that he has lacked. He has seldom listened to the advice of worried courtiers or royal protection officers who would wrap him up in cotton wool. Physically he has always pushed himself to the limit – he rides fast and fearlessly, he skis dangerously off piste, and has brushed with death on many occasions. He courts danger and thrives on the adrenalin of living close to the edge.

He constantly needs to push himself to the limit to prove that he in some way merits the position he was born to. During his Action Man days in the Navy he chose to do a Royal Marine commando training programme, including the drill for escaping from a sunken vessel, which in the following two years killed two men, and which he admitted he found quite terrifying. During his spell in the RAF, he made a parachute jump and got his legs caught in the rigging. And when he was later appointed Colonel-in-Chief of the Parachute Regiment, he insisted on doing the notoriously testing training course, on the grounds that he should 'be able to do some of the things one expects others to do for the country'. It enabled him, he said, to look the other men in the eye.

It was for much the same reason that during the year of the Queen's Silver Jubilee, against all advice, he stepped out of the security of his crested limousine, to find out what demonstrators corralled inside police barricades in Lewisham were so angry about. The answer, he discovered from one, sporting a badge saying, 'Stuff the Jubilee', was police harassment of the black community. Twenty-four black youths had recently been arrested for mugging and it was felt that the police were randomly, without due evidence, picking black men in particular from the street to take the rap. The Prince called over the police commander responsible and suggested the two groups should get together to sort out the matter. Eight days later, under the auspices of the Prince's Trust, the Prince invited both groups to Buckingham Palace. As a result the situation was defused, but not before the Prince was roundly rebuked by the press for having interfered in a matter which was none of his business, an opinion his father reinforced. He retired hurt, but not defeated; and through the Prince's Trust continued to work towards improving relations between police forces and minority communities in Britain 'to dampen down a potentially disastrous situation'. His instincts were right about the mounting tensions. A year later violent race riots broke out in inner cities all over the country.

It takes nerve to go ahead when the whole of Fleet Street, your father and your most senior advisers are telling you that what you have said or done is stupid. But since then, the Prince has continued to say what he believes, sticking his head recklessly above the parapet, when he has felt something needed to be done, and he has continued to be battered by the press for doing so. He has attacked architecture, medicine, farming, industry, education, religion – not one of our hallowed institutions has escaped a princely swipe – and he has been roundly criticised for meddling in things his critics claim he knows nothing about. Sometimes his critics have been right; he hasn't had the facts to support him, and has followed nothing more scientific than instinct. Yet after each and every assault, he has been flooded with mail from ordinary people thanking him for what he has said.

Time has shown, again and again, that the wacky, crackpot Prince, who went tilting at windmills, has become a man of vision, ahead of his time. And those issues that he spoke out about when no one else would, those causes which seemed obscure and unfashionable at the time, have all, several years down the line, become mainstream.

It was pure intuition that drove Charles to attack the medical establishment fifteen years ago. He caused outrage by suggesting that drugs were becoming 'the universal panacea for all our ills', and that in dismissing complementary medicine the British Medical Association was, 'like the celebrated Tower of Pisa, slightly off-balance'. The BMA immediately set up an inquiry into alternative medicine, which concluded that there was no scientific proof that any of the treatments worked. Today, however, alternative medicine is widely recognised and used by doctors as enthusiastically as the rest of the population. There is a growing mistrust of drugs; and some general practices even offer alternative treatments on the National Health Service.

It was also fifteen years ago that he horrified the farming establishment by condemning conventional high-yield methods of agriculture which relied on chemicals. In supporting the National Organic Food Production conference, he said he was 'convinced that any steps that can be taken to explore methods of production which make better and more effective use of renewable resources are extremely important'. The hugely powerful agrochemical industry thought it could ignore him, and was delighted when he apparently shot himself in the foot shortly afterwards. He confessed in an ITN documentary that he talked to his plants, and was mercilessly ridiculed by the press as 'the loony prince' who had clearly joined the beard and beads brigade. Yet today, not only are the major supermarkets stocking organic produce, they are in fierce competition with one another to find more lines and bigger and better suppliers. Farmers all over the world are converting to organic methods as they discover that the public is prepared to pay a premium price for purer food.

But nothing made him more unpopular with the powers-that-be than his attack on the architectural establishment in the famous Hampton Court speech in the summer of 1984, when he talked of 'monstrous carbuncles' and 'giant glass stumps'. Yet he seemed to be articulating what thousands of ordinary people felt. He accused architects of building houses for the approval of fellow architects and critics, not for the people who have to live in them. Community architecture was the way forward, in his view, and housing co-operatives where the tenants were consulted about the sort of environment they wanted to live in. '... Architects and planners do not necessarily have the monopoly of knowing what is best about taste, style and planning ...' he said, and ordinary people 'need not be made to feel guilty or ignorant if their natural preference is for the more "traditional designs" – for a small garden, for courtyards, arches and porches ...' There was a growing number of architects prepared to listen and to offer imaginative ideas.

The Prince still has some serious detractors about his views on modern architecture, and with some justification. Many people believe his interference in this area is an abuse of his power on a matter which is nothing more than personal preference. 'It has taken fifty years to destroy the accumulated architectural wisdom of thousands of years. I am quite prepared for it to take at least as long to rebuild it – even if I have to be sent to a taxidermist in order to see it through,' he once declared. But on the subject of urban design and development, which he put into practice with Poundbury, his model village on Duchy land outside the town of Dorchester, today even his harshest critics appear to be singing a remarkably similar tune.

Of all the areas in which the Prince has taken a stand, architecture has always been the most difficult, not least because housing is a highly political issue. He plunged in not just because of his preference for classical buildings, but because he was convinced that insensitive design, and ugly high-rise tower-blocks were responsible for a great deal of inner-city despair, and that if you design a community as opposed to a series of rabbit hutches, a happier, more civilised society will follow. Once drawn in, he was encouraged by those architects whose ideas he championed to get more and more involved. It is the curse of the Prince to be used by people who see him as a vehicle for their own advancement, and he is usually the last person to see what is going on. In challenging the development and construction industry he was challenging one of the major players in the British economy, an area riven by vested interest where vast sums of money are at stake. The classicists and community architects very much enjoyed their royal patronage, while the modernists likened him to Stalin, Hitler and Pol Pot. The architectural practice responsible for designing the National Gallery extension – which the Prince had denounced in that first speech as 'a monstrous carbuncle on the face of a much loved and elegant friend' – went to the wall.

He relishes his role as David against Goliath. When a small cheese maker in Scotland was prosecuted by his local health authority because tiny traces of listeria had been found in his cheese, the Prince, as patron of the Specialist Cheese Makers, came racing to the rescue. He brought together the cheese makers with the Ministry of Agriculture, Fisheries and Food, the Department of Health and the Department of Trade and Industry – not just officials but the ministers from each department – so they could hear at first hand the problems that the small producers faced. As he said, 'Every French farmer would go to prison if they enforced those rules in France.' They are EC rules, he said, which only the British appear to be concerned about.

When Charles opened the new Dyson vacuum cleaner factory in the Wiltshire town of Malmesbury, he learned that James Dyson had been forced to take his first invention, the ball barrow, to Japan because he couldn't get the funding he needed in the UK. The local MP, Richard Needham, was in tow the day Charles opened the factory. 'This is a marvellous example of government supporting industry,' Needham said as they left.

'Richard,' said the Prince, 'this has got nothing to do with government. All government has done is put obstacles in the way.'

During the visit, Needham had tried to get the Prince photographed pushing a vacuum cleaner, but he wasn't have any of it, knowing what the headlines would be. 'Richard, I'm sure you're much more used to doing this than I am.'

Rules, regulations and red tape are the plague of the Prince's life: a life that is inevitably bound by all three. He longs for people who will say 'yes' and not give him a hundred and one reasons why something cannot be done. Edward Adeane was conservative, in the mould of old-style courtiers who understood perfectly the purpose and role of monarchy, and did everything in their power to discourage enterprise. The Prince felt shackled by him, partly, no doubt, because while Adeane was advising caution, Michael Colborne was telling him to listen to his instincts, to look about him and see how the world was changing, and how he, the Prince of Wales, could provide some badly needed leadership and make a difference.

The man he found to replace Edward Adeane as private secretary came not from the traditional Foreign Office or Armed Forces pool, but from a high-powered job in the City. The Prince had been very specific about the sort of person he was looking for: someone of high calibre, with business and administrative skills, who could sort out the chaos that was his office, who would fit in with the old guard but not be like them and, most important of all, be sympathetic to his views.

Sir John Riddell could not have been better suited. He was a successful investment banker in his early fifties with a young family and a delightful attitude to life. Ace administrator he was not, and the office continued to be as chaotic as ever, but he was universally liked and he guided the Prince through some difficult times with unfailing good humour. As one of his staff said of him, 'I cannot count the number of times I have been into John's office with a disastrous problem to solve, to come out again with the problem still unsolved but feeling that the world was a much nicer place.'

John was in many ways a most unlikely candidate for courtier. The Prince chose him from three men who were presented by a head hunter because he was determined to have someone who would be sympathetic to his ideas. This prerequisite was the cause of considerable apprehension at St James's Palace, and there was much relief when Riddell arrived wearing a pinstriped suit rather than a beard and sandals.

His humour did wonders for the office, which by this time was not always the happiest of places. As thirteenth Baronet from an old Northumberland family, educated at Eton and Oxford, he was not used to dancing attendance on anyone. Nor, despite his City career, was he used to working round the clock. He gave the Prince his wholehearted support and enthusiasm, and admired what he was trying to do, but when his day was finished he wanted to go home to his wife and children. As a complete newcomer to the royal circle, Riddell was much less hidebound than his predecessor, yet sensitive to the niceties of court, and was generally acknowledged to have been another of the Prince's best appointments.

In some ways he gave the Prince a new lease of life. He was much less anxious about the Prince's interests than Adeane had been, particularly with regard to the inner cities and his involvement with BitC. Over the next five years the Prince's public life began to flourish. Having been tortured and uncertain of where he was going or what his role in life should be, he began to see a way forward.

In the same year, Richard Aylard arrived in the office as equerry to the Princess of Wales, replacing Michael Colborne, and three years later joined the Prince's staff as an assistant private secretary. He also played an important part in the Prince's new direction. Aged thirty-three, he had been a naval commander, and latterly worked in naval public relations.

It was the first time Diana had needed an equerry. She had been approached by over 150 charities when she became Princess of Wales and had agreed in her first year to affiliate herself to just five. Now she felt ready to expand her activities, but in her own way and on her own terms, which was sometimes hard for the Lord-Lieutenants who had become used to the punishing schedules prepared for other senior female royals. If she was doing a day in Yorkshire, for example, they would expect Diana to travel overnight on the royal train so that she could start early and fit in six engagements during the day – as the Queen, Princess Margaret or the Princess Royal would do, probably before going home for a reception or a dinner in the evening. In the early days, this was the kind of model that everyone was working to. It didn't cross the minds of any of the people advising Diana on how to handle the public side of her life that a royal schedule could be planned any other way.

However, by this time the Princess had discovered what she enjoyed and felt able to handle and what she hated, and everyone around her knew how best she liked her days to be organised. A day in Yorkshire would begin later in the morning because she was not prepared to spend the night away from home. Ideally she would want to take William and later Harry to school before she set off on her engagements, although that was not always possible if they were far afield. During the course of the day she would do maybe three engagements rather than six, so that she was home again in time for the children's bath and bedtime. Often she would stop at a supermarket on the way home and buy some of their favourite biscuits for tea. She wanted her engagements to be short and she wanted to meet real people. If she visited a hospital, she insisted, as indeed the Prince always did, on sitting on every bed in the ward and speaking to every patient, which meant tours invariably overran. She wanted the simplest possible briefing notes, which left out anything technical and emphasised the human element of any visit. And she conducted conversations on her own terms, never afraid to ask questions, however ignorant they made her look. The more confident she became, the more coquettish she grew, and the result was very powerful. Strong men melted under her gaze and became her devotees.

Anne Beckwith-Smith and Richard Aylard ran her life between them and because they were both new recruits to royal life, neither had any preconceptions about what other members of the Family did or how they behaved on days out. Under their management the Princess felt happy. They knew she did not like formal line-ups and that she hated eating in public. If she had to, she would never want to sit next to anyone who was very clever, or who was old. So they would organise small groups or one-to-one meetings, and instead of lunch they would arrange for her to have a plate of sandwiches in a back room somewhere, so she could unwind and laugh and joke and tell stories with her entourage, before being back on parade.

As time passed, Diana's eating habits became noticeably odd, and they could no longer be put down to post-childbirth dieting, nerves, or any of the excuses her staff had found to explain her behaviour to themselves. One day she would eat her own and everyone else's tea on the way home from a day out. The next, she would eat nothing; then suddenly wolf down four Kit-Kat bars and disappear into the lavatory. No one knew quite what to do about it, and so they said nothing. It was simply accepted as part of a manic day out with the Princess.

The press was fascinated by her weight loss, and her state of health was a national preoccupation. Anorexia had been suggested at various times, and she always said how much it made her laugh. Had these people not seen her appetite, she would say? It was not until about 1986 that her household fully appreciated the problem. By then it was no longer anorexia, but bulimia.

Diana was demanding to work for but she could be very good fun, and she would always make a point, for instance, of asking about people's family – Richard Aylard had a wife and child at home – and of saying thank you at the end of a day out. On a Friday, she would often want to be finished by lunchtime so she could go home to the children, and would say she was sure the others would want to get home early too. She would very rarely telephone staff at the weekend. The Prince, on the other hand, often rang his staff at weekends, and would frequently forget the niceties of thanking the people who made his life work.

Diana, however, was quick to criticise if she felt something hadn't been done properly, or if she thought one of her charities was taking advantage of her or asking too much. She would swing from a situation where there wasn't enough she could do for a charity to cutting it completely dead and refusing to do anything. Organisers were left wondering what on earth had gone wrong. Sometimes it was justified; at other times not. She would never let a charity down if she had already agreed an engagement – she was always one hundred per cent professional in honouring her commitments – but at the next programme meeting their proposals would be ignored. There were only two occasions in fifteen years when the Princess failed to show for an engagement, and they were both when her children took precedence. The first occasion was in May 1988 when Prince Harry was rushed into Great Ormond Street Children's Hospital for an emergency hernia operation. The other was after Prince William had been hit on the head by a school friend with a golf club in June 1991 and he too was taken into Great Ormond Street.

The Princess would also swing in her treatment of friends. She blew hot and cold with them, and caused a great deal of distress. One minute a friend would be her closest possible confidant: she would telephone them ten times a day – and several of those calls might be an hour long – she would lunch with them several times a week, tell them the most intimate details of her life, and shower them with gifts. The next minute, for no apparent reason, she would cut them out of her life entirely, refusing to take their calls. Those who had known her since childhood, in particular, were left hurt and wondering what they could possibly have done to offend. If pressed, she would say they were taking advantage of her. In reality, she panicked because she thought she had told them too much and allowed them to get too close to her.

She was the same with her staff, as Oliver Everett, her private secretary, had discovered. One minute she could not do enough to help them: she would send their mothers flowers on their birthdays, give them presents, be pally and informal and open her heart to them. The next she would cut them dead and might not speak to them for a month, for no reason that they could possibly fathom.

As one of them said, 'I would have given up all the flowers, all the niceness if only we could have avoided the sheer bloody-minded sarcasm, the silences, and sending to Coventry that went with it.'

When either Richard Aylard or Anne Beckwith-Smith had offended her – maybe by allowing photographers to get too close at an engagement, or giving her advice that she didn't like – she would freeze them out for days. If the one she wasn't talking to sent her a memo, she would reply to the other.

She was never entirely comfortable with the press *en masse*, but she had one or two favourites – of which James Whitaker was one for many years; also Arthur Edwards of the *Sun*. In the last four years of her life she developed an entirely different relationship with Richard Kay of the *Daily Mail*, spending hours on the telephone to him and baring her soul in a way she had never done with a journalist before. She was always scrupulously polite to all journalists, calling them by their names, saying 'Good morning', teasing them, flirting with them, and it worked wonders, as she knew it would. She read what they wrote about her avidly and loved to see nice photographs of herself. She learnt very quickly what they wanted and in later years she used the press effectively when she was waging war on her husband. Yet it entirely depended upon what mood she was in. If she felt amenable she would give them the picture they wanted, she would dangle a child on her knee or give them a dazzling smile. If she felt they had taken advantage of her, or crowded in too closely, or been taking photographs for too long, she would simply raise her shoulder to obscure her face or ruin the shot and put an end to it. In the early days she was worried about being accused of upstaging the Queen or the Prince. By the end, when the gloves were off, she delighted in it.

NINE

Marriage and the Media: After Morton

'She thinks he is a bad father ...'
James Gilbey in Andrew Morton's Diana – Her True Story

It was clear to their staff that the Prince was a victim of the Princess's mood swings just as much as everyone else. The shouting that they heard behind closed doors was commonplace, and he would be on the receiving end of sarcastic remarks, no less than the cook or the chambermaid. On greeting one of his staff in full uniform one morning before going off to a formal engagement, the Prince said, 'You only have one medal. We'll have to do something about that.' Whereupon the Princess, following her husband down the stairs said, 'Yes, but at least he earned his.'

Though such remarks were awkward for everyone, no one really knew how serious the situation was. At times they would appear to be very happy together, and in public they were always very civil to one another, but it was growing obvious at programme meetings that the Princess didn't want to do engagements with the Prince, and in private she was gradually cutting herself off from him, not wanting to go to Balmoral with him, refusing to see his friends, cutting short her weekends at Highgrove and, when she was there, spending her time indoors talking to friends on the telephone, never going into the garden – which she had at one time enjoyed – and never going to see the farm.

Many of her friends, like Tally, Duchess of Westminster, née Phillips, were from her teens, and there were those she had shared her flat with before her marriage, like Carolyn Bartholomew, née Pride,

Sophie Kimball and Laura Greig. Sarah Ferguson, who married Prince Andrew, introduced her to several people too, including Kate Menzies, Julia Dodd Noble and the Marchioness of Douro, with whom Diana played tennis at the fashionable Vanderbilt Racquet Club in London's Shepherd's Bush. Julia Samuel, Angela Serota and Catherine Soames, former wife of the Prince's friend Nicholas, were also close for a time. Male friends included James Gilbey, George Plumtre, Rory Scott, two Fergie introductions, Philip Dunne and David Waterhouse, via whom she met James Hewitt.

In later years friends included the Lucia Flecha de Lima, Rosa Monckton, and Mara and Lorenzo Berni, the proprietors of San Lorenzo, her favourite London restaurant.

As well as the moods and the rows, there were rumours that she was being unfaithful to her husband. By 1985 Diana's staff were aware that there was something going on between her and Sergeant Barry Mannakee, her personal protection officer. He was displaying signs of intimacy, which she clearly encouraged; but there was very little gossip because everyone was frightened of the Princess getting to hear what was being said, and they feared for their jobs.

In July 1986, shortly before the Yorks' marriage, the Prince was told that Barry Mannakee had to go. He was given no reason, and told he didn't need to know why. Curiously, he asked no questions but accepted the advice, and Mannakee was moved to the diplomatic protection group and thus out of Diana's orbit. Those near him at the time assumed the Prince must have guessed the reason, but he hadn't. Like most observers, he found the idea incredible, and it was not until some years later that he learned the truth. But Mannakee was not the only affair he knew nothing about until much later.

The Prince never played the jealous husband, and apparently never wanted to know what his wife did when she was out of his sight. If he had thought she might be being disloyal, he never challenged her and never shared his suspicions with anyone. Even during the darkest periods of their marriage, when life, as a friend puts it, 'was one long whinge, it was not always directed at Diana and even at the worst times he did show understanding and sympathy for her position'.

In July 1987 Mannakee was killed in a motorcycle accident. He was riding pillion on a bike which collided with a car in the East End of London. The news reached the Prince at Kensington Palace moments before he and Diana were due to leave for the Cannes Film Festival. He decided it would be better to tell her immediately rather than risk a question shouted from a journalist in the crowd, so he broke the news to her in the car *en route* to RAF Northolt. The Princess was distraught, and spent the journey and much of the trip in floods of tears, with the Prince and Anne Beckwith-Smith both desperately trying to console her. In her despair, she slashed herself, and the dress she wore in Cannes had to be adjusted to hide the damage.

By this time Diana had formed an attachment to Major David Waterhouse, whom she had met along with banker Philip Dunne when the Waleses and the Yorks went skiing together in Klosters in February.

The arrival of Fergie into the royal circle was a mixed blessing for the Princess. On the one hand she was someone closer to her own age and an ally. But she was also a rival. In the early days, Fergie was popular. She was like the girl next door, undaunted by protocol, relaxed, irreverent and determined to have fun: people talked about her being a breath of fresh air. Diana, who had never been confident at the best of times, felt doubly insecure. As she later admitted, 'I got terribly jealous.'

Soon after the Yorks' wedding the Princess unexpectedly announced that she wanted to do some more engagements and gave Richard Aylard and Anne Beckwith-Smith three dates when she specifically wanted them to find something for her to do. It was an odd request and quite out of character. Nevertheless, they fixed things for her to do, and it was only when they had organised it all that the policeman pointed out that they were the precise dates when the Duchess of York had her first three public engagements. Diana upstaged her new rival to perfection.

Diana tried for a while to be like Fergie. She went to pop concerts and out to the cinema and dinner parties and restaurants with friends, including David Waterhouse and Philip Dunne; and at Royal Ascot she poked her husband's equerry in the backside with her rolled up umbrella. She took off in her car without telling anyone or taking a detective. On one occasion, driving herself across London late at night, she was followed by photographers, but it could so easily have been terrorists.

The gossip columnists began to comment, and the press began to speculate, that the marriage was in trouble. One night, as the Princess was emerging with friends from Kate Menzie's mews house in the early hours of the morning, a waiting photographer took some pictures of Diana with David Waterhouse indulging in some horse-play. Diana was distraught when she realised she had been caught on film and she and her detective pleaded with the photographer to hand over his film and say nothing of what he had seen. The photographer duly obliged with the film but went straight back to his newspaper with the story. The next morning it was headline news.

In March 1987 the Prince left for a walk in the Kalahari Desert with Sir Laurens van der Post, and was no sooner back from that than he was off for a week's painting holiday in Italy. By the end of the summer, when he had done his usual stint at Balmoral while Diana had stayed firmly put in London, the press calculated that they had spent one day together in six weeks.

Yet during this period in the mid- and late-1980s, when their private life was so troubled, the Prince and Princess were in many ways a formidable double act.

The Prince had set himself up as a controversial figure, and although some people were clearly bemused by some of his interests and concerns, many of his speeches had struck a chord, as the hundreds of letters that arrived in his office made clear. The Prince's Trust was beginning to have an impact, he was busily importing ideas from America to help solve inner-city problems, and was making waves on the environmental front.

The Princess, meanwhile, although looking ever more glamorous, was making it clear that she had more to offer than her looks. She had taken on unglamorous causes like drug abuse, marriage guidance and Aids, and was proving to be quite unparalleled in her ability to charm, communicate and empathise with ordinary people.

Abroad, they were a sensation and on every trip – to Australia, America, the Gulf States, Italy, Japan – the reception was rapturous. At home the combination was never more successful than as joint patrons of the Wishing Well Appeal. Great Ormond Street Children's Hospital needed £30 million to rebuild, and in well under the two-year target, had raised a total of £54 million with a further £30 million promised by the government.

While everyone who worked for the Prince and Princess knew there were problems, heard the rows and felt the brunt of the changes of mood that affected them both on a daily basis, no one appreciated that there was ever a danger of the marriage breaking down irreparably. While fending off questions from the media about the state of the relationship, those running the press office at Buckingham Palace were far more concerned about how best to manage the run-away success of the royal couple. In terms of providing the perfect foundation for the future of the monarchy, this was a marriage made in heaven. The problem was how to pace the success: not to allow too much exposure, not to allow them to give too many interviews, not to let too much light in on the mystery of monarchy. The popularity needed to be kept going for another twenty or thirty years; because unlike politics or show business or any other career in which fame and popularity are a measure of success, the monarchy is a long-term game. There is no stepping out of public life when the going gets tough, no retreating into anonymity or even retiring at sixty. The work goes on remorselessly and the exposure with it, and as every celebrity knows, the greater the adulation, the faster it can disappear. The danger at that time was too much too quickly.

There was also the danger that if anyone talked too openly about the state of the marriage it might precipitate disaster, when disaster was far from certain. Most of those closest to the couple were aware that there were other people in both their lives. The men who had basked in the Princess's affections were comparatively well known. After David Waterhouse, James Gilbey, who had known Diana since the age of seventeen, had featured briefly. James Hewitt was the one with whom she said she had been very much in love, but there were several men over a period who all seemed to have a claim on her affections, and who came and went from Kensington Palace at all hours of the day and night. She appeared to enjoy the power she had over them, telephoning and having them arrive at her bidding, and dismissing them when she wanted them gone.

Most of the Prince's staff knew he was seeing Camilla Parker Bowles, although he was always painstakingly discreet about it, but none of them assumed that this meant that the marriage was in danger of breaking up. Extra-marital affairs were a traditional part of aristocratic marriages and had been for centuries. Who was to say that this would be any different? Indeed, both Lord Mountbatten and the Duke of Edinburgh had told the Prince of Wales that if his marriage didn't work out, the solution was to find a married woman with whom he could quietly conduct an affair.

Divorce was seldom the solution for couples who had tired of one another in this stratum of society, and many couples lived with great civility, and even affection, under one roof, displaying a united front in public, while pursuing love affairs elsewhere. It meant stability for the children and security for the future of the family estate. Both the Prince and Princess had grown up witnesses to this sort of marital behaviour, and although each was as idealistic as the other and determined at the outset to make their marriage different, they recognised that it was the way people coped. But there was a difference. In previous generations, although their social peers knew who was bedding whom, no one ever broke rank and the gossip seldom went further than their own circle of friends. If ever a whisper reached the newspapers, the proprietors, all themselves members of the establishment, made sure the story never surfaced.

But times, society and newspaper proprietors had changed, and by the late 1980s and early 1990s there was protection for no one, and high prices were paid for information.

The Prince and Princess had already suffered from members of their domestic staff selling the odd story, but no one, not even in their wildest dreams, could have foreseen that the person who would tell the world about the most intimate details of their married life and the Prince's love for Camilla Parker Bowles would be Diana herself. When Andrew Morton's book, *Diana – Her True Story*, was serialised in *The Sunday Times* in June 1992, the Prince and his staff were taken completely by surprise. And for the Prince, the embarrassment, hurt and humiliation was total.

'Diana driven to five suicide bids by "uncaring" Charles', ran the front-page headline on the first day of serialisation. It went on to talk about Diana's bulimia, her husband's indifference towards her, his obsession with his mistress, his shortcomings as a father, and the loneliness and isolation she had felt for so many years, trapped in a loveless marriage within a hostile court and cold and disapproving Royal Family. The book had a compelling authority, and many of the Princess's closest friends were openly quoted. For example, 'James Gilbey explains: "She thinks he is a bad father, a selfish father, the children have to tie in with what he's doing. He will never delay, cancel or change anything which he has sorted out for their benefit.'

At first, Diana denied any involvement with the book and Sir Robert Fellowes believed her. The result of Fellowes's appeal to Lord McGregor, chairman of the Press Complaints Commission, was the issue of a statement condemning the serialisation as an 'odious exhibition of journalists dabbling their fingers in the stuff of other people's souls in a manner which adds nothing to the legitimate public interest in the situation of the heir to the throne'. Having given her word to Fellowes that she had not contributed to the book, the Princess then put on a deliberate and public show of affection for Carolyn Bartholomew, her former flatmate, and one of the most quoted sources in the book. She telephoned in advance to make sure that the press photographers were in place outside Carolyn's London house when she went to visit and the friends greeted one another warmly on the doorstep. The message that Diana approved of what her friend had said on her behalf could not have been clearer. Robert Fellowes realised at once that he had been taken in by the Princess, and that it had caused everyone, including Lord McGregor and the Prince of Wales, acute embarrassment. He promptly handed in his resignation – which the Queen rejected.

It was not until after her death five years later, however, that the full extent of Diana's co-operation with Andrew Morton was known. It transpired that she had spoken into a tape recorder at Kensington Palace during the summer and autumn of 1991, and the tapes were then delivered to Morton via an intermediary, Dr James Colthurst, a friend of Diana who also happened to be a squash-playing partner of Morton. What had puzzled the Prince and those close to him was that much of the book was accurate in some respects, and there were stories told that only Diana or at most only a handful of people could possibly have known about, or memos leaked that nobody else could have seen. But most of the stories had a spin on them, which made them not quite as anyone else who had been present remembered.

There was a memo, for example, which, according to Morton, Richard Aylard had written to the Prince of Wales to encourage him to see more of his children. He had recently been badly censured by the press for his apparently cavalier attitude to William after he had been hit on the head by a golf club. 'At the conclusion of his missive,' said Morton, 'he [Aylard] heavily underlined in red ink and printed in bold capitals a single word: "TRY".'

In actual fact the Prince had sent Aylard a memo saying that William and Harry had said they wanted to do a few things with their father and could Aylard please look in the diary and pick out a few engagements that would be suitable for the boys to go along to. Aylard wrote back with three or four suggestions, including a trip to a naval ship, and said that the next step was to speak to the Princess to make sure she was happy about the plan. It would be best, wrote Aylard, if the Prince could speak to her about it himself. Failing that, he would speak to Patrick Jephson, the Princess's private secretary. The Prince sent the memo back, annotated in his red pen – and he was the only person in the office allowed to use red ink. Against the suggestion that he should speak to his wife, he wrote, 'I will TRY!'

In the immediate aftermath of the serialisation, the office at St James's Palace was a very unsettled and unhappy place. No one knew who was responsible for the leaked information. There were one or two suspects, but they were trusted members of the team and it was deeply uncomfortable not knowing who had betrayed them and therefore might betray them again.

Even before she gave Carolyn Bartholomew such public endorsement, several people suspected the Princess. A number of stories which were clearly very well sourced had been appearing in *The Sunday Times* and other newspapers for some time. One such story was the dismissal of Sir Christopher Airy as private secretary to the Prince of Wales.

In his late fifties, Sir Christopher Airy had taken over from Sir John Riddell in 1990, and from the outset it was apparent that he was not going to fit. As a former Major-General commanding the Royal Household Division, he was not the man to take over a highly disorganised, under-staffed, over-worked office working for an impatient and demanding man with the most disparate collection of interests. One of Airy's first edicts was that everyone should wear their jackets in the office. He never fully understood the difference between the Prince's various organisations, never quite grasped where the Prince's Trust ended and Business in the Community began, or what the Prince's Youth Business Trust had to do with either of them, or where the Prince's interest in organic farming or wildlife fitted into the picture. And when, after a year, he was still very much at sea, the Prince was persuaded that, delightful man though he was, the time had come to part company.

The crunch had come at the end of a tour of Brazil in April 1991, when the Prince hosted a top-level international seminar on development and the environment on board the royal yacht half-way up the Amazon. As private secretary, Airy had insisted on being there although he had no real role to play because three assistant private secretaries, Peter Westmacott, Guy Salter and Richard Aylard, had every aspect of the two-day event covered – Westmacott, the Foreign Office angle, Salter, business, and Aylard, the environment. Nothing irritates the Prince more than supernumeraries on a tour and to see his private secretary left with nothing better to do than hand round the coffee was the final straw. On the night flight back to London, the Prince told Richard Aylard that he wanted him to change jobs with Sir Christopher, having first told the Princess about his plans.

Aylard had been equerry to the Princess for three years from 1985 to 1988. He had then become an assistant private secretary with responsibility for the environment brief, and comptroller to the Prince and Princess.

The Prince's idea was that Airy should run the household and Aylard the office, but was persuaded that this would be unpalatable to all concerned. Better to say the time had come for both Prince and Princess to have their own private secretaries, which up to that time they had shared, and to have a senior figure, namely Airy, to run the household. This was the formula which the Prince put to Airy on their return to London, but the older man saw it as a plot to oust him and refused the offer.

At this point they became aware that *The Sunday Times* was planning to run a story that Sir Christopher Airy had been sacked by the Prince of Wales. It would have to be confirmed or denied, which forced the Prince's hand. He offered Aylard the job of private secretary and determined to sack Airy on the Friday after a meeting of the Prince of Wales Co-ordinating Committee at Highgrove. The Prince is deeply loyal by nature and telling people he likes that they have to go is something he hates doing and is very bad at. He liked Airy and he recognised that the fault had been his own in asking the man to do the job in the first place. When he tackled him, Airy once again refused to accept what he was hearing, so the Prince brought in reinforcements. He asked Allen Sheppard, chief executive of Grand Metropolitan and a member of the Co-ordinating Committee, to take Airy into the garden and tell him that the time had come to hand in his letter of resignation. It was a difficult and highly emotional end to the afternoon, brought to a rather comical conclusion by the Princess arriving at the house, apparently unaware of what was going on, and starting to pour gin and tonics for everyone. In fact, Airy was left so confused by everything that Peter Westmacott found it necessary to explain the situation to him later that afternoon.

The story subsequently appeared in *The Sunday Times*, written by Andrew Morton, with detail of the afternoon at Highgrove that could only have come from one of two people in the room at the time – either the Princess or Sir Christopher Airy. Other stories had had Diana's fingerprints on them too, but no one knew how the stories were reaching Morton. It could quite easily have been that one of her friends, possibly without her knowledge, was passing on gossip that she had told them over lunch or in one of her endless telephone conversations.

There were several people at the time who thought Richard Aylard might have been responsible for the original leak about Sir Christopher Airy's downfall, ambitious as he was for the post and wanting to force the indecisive Prince's hand. Much as he wanted the job of private secretary, Aylard did not want Airy to go yet. He wanted Sir Christopher to handle the household, to be the figurehead and take care of the pomp and ceremony which he was so good at. Aylard himself wanted to be left to get on with writing speeches and pulling together all the different strands of the Prince's interests, and turning his ideas into reality.

There was another possible contender for the job of private secretary in 1991: Peter Westmacott. Of the two candidates he was the more heavyweight. Slightly older than Aylard, he was a senior Foreign Office secondee, who also wrote well and, like Aylard, was responsible for some of the Prince's best speeches, particularly on education. He was a very important influence during his time at

St James's Palace. Like Aylard, he was devoted to the Prince. They got on very well together and it would have been a good team. Unhappily for Westmacott, however, he and the Princess also got on very well together. They became very close; so close that many, possibly even including the Prince, thought they were having an affair.

They were not. But Diana did flirt outrageously, as she did with many men, and did spend many hours confiding her innermost thoughts and fears to him. He had joined the team in March 1990 and first met the Princess when they all went off on a tour of Hungary together. She was on very good form, relaxed and happy, flirtatious as ever and obviously pleased to have a new and good looking face around. Having come from the Foreign Office he was not highly attuned to the finer details of the marriage. At one stage in the tour Diana was being driven around in a horse and cart, and needing to stop quite frequently to go to the loo. The press started saying she must be pregnant, and Westmacott asked Sir John Riddell whether perhaps he should let the Princess know what they were writing.

'Dangerous stuff, Peter,' said Riddell. 'It would take a braver man than you or me to raise that subject.'

At lunch that day, which was a barbecue in the woods, the Princess told Westmacott to sit next to her. They chatted for a while, then he decided she ought to know what was being said. She didn't bat an eye-lid.

'Me pregnant?' she said. 'Chance would be a fine thing!'

Probably like every court that ever was, St James's Palace is a place of camps, a hotbed of internal politics and jealousies, where everyone is jockeying for positions of favour with the Prince and, given the slightest opportunity, will gleefully drop poison into his ear about friends or colleagues. Peter Westmacott was aware that people were talking, and the Princess did indeed seem to regard him as a friend, but he felt that since he was working for both the Prince and Princess he had to speak to them both. If he could help inject a little balance into the way in which the Princess perceived what was going on around her, and be in a position to tell her when something was nonsense – stop her running away with crazy ideas – it might be helpful for everyone. But he was only on loan from the Foreign Office, and was not, therefore, a good long-term bet for the Prince. It was hardly surprising that, in the event, Richard Aylard was given the top job and Westmacott was given the newly created title of deputy private secretary.

Many men found themselves in Diana's thrall, and it was always the Princess who was in control of the situation. She picked them up and put them down at whim, and if she chose to telephone late at night and speak for more than an hour at a time, or plead for someone to drop everything and come and visit, there was no easy way of refusing her. Even Sir Christopher had been entranced by her in his time. On one occasion he was waiting at Highgrove for the Prince, who was late as usual in returning from an engagement. He had just heard that the helicopter was in range, and would therefore be arriving shortly, when the Princess invited him for a drive in her brand new Mercedes soft-top. When the Prince arrived his first question was 'Where's Christopher?' and he was incensed to be told he had gone for a drive with the Princess.

Richard Aylard never found himself caught in the middle, as so many others had been, because after 1988, when he started working principally for the Prince, the Princess looked upon him as an enemy. She accused him of 'defecting to the other side' when his three-year secondment as her equerry came to an end. She began to talk about there being two camps, and wanted to have her own staff and be independent from her husband.

Soon after he had become comptroller and was therefore working for both camps, Aylard was in Switzerland trying to sort out the press in advance of the annual skiing trip. The Princess telephoned from London and acidly asked what her comptroller was doing on the ski slopes. 'Why aren't you back here running the office?'

Aylard explained that he was in Switzerland because the Prince had asked him to go across to organise the press. 'Well that's not good enough,' she said. 'You're needed here,' and slammed the phone down. Having been fond of Diana while working for her he was hurt that she should have turned on him. They had been through a lot together in three years and he was disappointed that she took his departure so personally.

Anne Beckwith-Smith also came to be regarded with suspicion and was eased out as private secretary in 1990. Anne had never allowed herself to get too close to Diana; she wished to keep the relationship professional. Diana was her boss, and Anne kept herself out of Diana's personal life as much as possible. She was unhappy with the way things were going and had a number of fallings out with the Princess. In the past Diana had been receptive to advice, but latterly the advice Anne had to give was not to her liking. Diana had changed and Anne was no longer able to read her or judge how to play things. She tried to persuade her to keep the marriage going, and to make the marriage work, but realised that the Princess was determined to go her own way, and viewed Anne as a stick in the mud. They agreed to a parting of the ways, but Anne remained an extra lady-in-waiting and saw her thereafter about once a month.

Most conversations with anyone who has been involved with the Prince and Princess, either as friends or employees, are categorised as Before or After Morton. There is no doubt that his book spelt the beginning of the end, although at the time, the Prince's immediate reaction was not that he wanted a separation. Despite what the book had said about him, much of which was so devastatingly untrue and unjust, the Prince clung to the hope that Diana had not been involved. He was still desperately keen to keep the marriage going, just as he had always been. He knew separation would cause so much hurt – to the Queen, the monarchy, the country and, most of all, William and Harry – and he thought it was unnecessary. He and Diana both had their own groups of friends, their own interests, their own private lives, and could put on a good public show together for the sake of the country. He did not understand why that shouldn't continue. Before he discovered the truth about the Morton book, he had even cherished the hope that one day he and Diana could be friends.

Curiously, Charles never replied to the accusations against him in Morton's book and gave very firm instructions to his staff and his friends not to reply or offer any kind of defence on his behalf. He didn't want to do anything that would hurt Diana, and he didn't want the degeneration of his marriage to become a tit for tat exercise. He couldn't bear to see the intimate details of their troubled marriage played out on the front covers of the tabloid press for a moment longer. He thought it damaging for his children and damaging for the monarchy. Understandably, the man in the street was left with little alternative but to believe Diana's shocking account of his callous behaviour.

There was another reason why he was loath to retaliate. He had grown bitterly disillusioned about the media during the course of his marriage. He felt, not without some justification, that it had short-changed him. In the early days he had been ignored in favour of his wife. Since their problems first started being talked about in 1987, the newspapers had chipped away remorselessly. They had printed story after story which condemned or ridiculed him; they had analysed his body language, counted the days spent away from his wife, speculated on the identity of mystery blondes seen boarding aeroplanes or spied through long lenses at Balmoral.

During the course of that time he had introduced initiatives to inner city schools which were proving highly successful, he had raised thousands of pounds for the Prince's Trust, he had developed a Volunteer Scheme to give young people a reason for getting out of bed in the morning, he had ensured the future of Shakespeare in our language, he had put architecture into the hands of the people for whom buildings were built, he had raised £5 million for charity on the polo field. The list was endless. Yet all of this, and more, had been largely ignored by the press.

There are a number of theories about why Diana spoke to Morton. It was known in certain circles that some of her telephone conversations had been recorded and were being touted around Fleet Street. There would have been a persuasive argument that she should get her story out and gain public sympathy before a newspaper published any intimate late-night chat she may have had with a man who was not her husband. She had always thought that people were talking behind her back and watching her, and became obsessed with the idea that the Buckingham Palace switchboard was spying on her and listening in to her telephone calls. She was reassured by a member of the Queen's household that this was impossible, but because Diana was insistent, she was given a mobile phone to use instead. Ironically, it was the mobile phone, not the landline, that was tapped.

Diana had been living a charmed existence as far as the newspapers were concerned. Given the number of men who came to visit her by day and night at Kensington Palace, the number of letters she wrote to James Hewitt when he was fighting in the Gulf War in January 1991– any one of which could have been opened or seen by someone else – the number of phone calls she made, the restaurants she openly ate in with male friends, her late-night hospital visits to see a doctor on the pretext of visiting patients, there was surprisingly little gossip about her in the press. She was firmly advised it was highly dangerous to write to James Hewitt in the Gulf, but took no notice. During the course of their relationship she sent over a hundred affectionate, loving hand-written letters to him, which he still cherishes. Sixty-two of her letters were taken from him by a girlfriend who tried to sell them to the *Daily Mirror* after Diana's death. Piers Morgan, the editor, honourably handed them over to the Spencer family without publishing any, although what should become of them is hotly disputed. Diana also wrote to David Waterhouse, who was also serving in the Gulf. She was frightened that both men might be killed.

The fact that she was never seriously exposed by the press was very largely the result of a concentrated charm-offensive on a number of key figures, not least the late Sir David English, who ran the *Mail* titles, whose daily and Sunday papers accounted for the biggest middle-market circulation in Britain. Sir David was charmed and entranced by Diana, as all men who met the Princess face to face invariably were. But he was also a tough and experienced newspaper man, who could see that in a black and white world, taking Diana's side against the Prince in two newspapers with a high proportion of female readers was sound business. Many suspect there was an understanding between the two that in return for stories, and photo opportunities, unflattering aspects of Diana's personal life would remain out of the newspapers. The *Mail* did have a remarkably constant flow of positive stories about the Princess and demonstrated no very great support or affection for the Prince. But Diana targeted other editors too, plus one or two influential journalists, and rang them with stories, invited them to lunch and flattered their male egos.

Despite the show she put on to the outside world, in the early 1990s, the Princess was at a very low ebb. Years of anorexia and bulimia had played havoc with her system and she not only saw a constant stream of conventional doctors but also dabbled in some extreme and strange alternative treatments. One of the problems was a bad back – ironically, a problem shared by both the Prince of Wales and Camilla Parker Bowles. She saw therapists of every sort: she had aromatherapy, reflexology, colonic irrigation, acupuncture, massage, chiropractic treatment, and consulted an astrologer and a medium, and a doctor who runs magnetic pulses through the body. She was also working out at the gym at the Harbour Club in Chelsea on a regular basis. She was spending an alarming amount of money on all of this – and with clothes and holidays thrown in, it was working out at about £3,000 per week.

Whether she believed deep down that as a result of all this therapy she had grown into a strong woman is questionable. She certainly had the vocabulary. She also had the anger. She felt that despite the best efforts of her husband and his family to destroy her, she had managed to pull herself back from the brink of disaster, and she wanted to prove that she had done it by herself. She had cried for help and her cries had been ignored. She had coped with the difficulties, coped with the stress, survived the despair of post-natal depression and bulimia, she had learnt to rely on her own resources, and she had come out the other side, high in the opinion polls, a star in the royal firmament and doing the job better than any other member of the Royal Family – giving the public what they wanted.

Now it was payback time. Whether psyched up by counselling and therapy, or simply angry on her own account, she was determined to have her revenge, and *Diana – Her True Story* was it. The puzzling aspect of the exercise was the effect she must have known it would have on the children she adored. She did subsequently regret what she had done, and told her friends it had been a terrible mistake, but not for some time.

In the immediate aftermath, Diana was elated, and in her triumph she became more and more difficult. The children would not be where they were supposed to be, or she would change her mind at the last minute about arrangements, making life very awkward for the Prince, whose days are tightly scheduled. She became even more reluctant to carry out joint engagements, which made it hard to send positive messages about the health of the marriage to the outside world. Even before Morton there had been an embarrassing trip to India, when the Princess had posed forlornly in front of the Taj Mahal, taking practically every press photographer in India with her, while her husband delivered two speeches and launched a new charity with scarcely one. The potent symbolism of the Princess sitting alone in front of the world's greatest monument to love was enough to wipe anything the Prince did off the map. It was only a couple of days later, when Diana reluctantly agreed to present the trophies at a polo match, that Charles got a mention. And only then because when the Prince came to give her a very public kiss on the cheek as he collected his prize, she turned her head away so as to leave him awkwardly kissing the air. The stories in the newspapers were all about the state of the marriage and that was some four months before Morton's book appeared.

On 25 August 1992 any elation Diana had felt from the publication of the Morton book completely disappeared. Transcripts of a tape-recorded amorous late-night telephone conversation allegedly between her and James Gilbey were published in the *Sun* newspaper. He called her 'Darling' fifty-three times, and 'Squidgy' or 'Squidge' fourteen times, which led to the scandal being dubbed 'Squidgygate'. Once upon a time Diana had used the same sort of vocabulary about Charles. She had said things like, 'My gorgeous sqwunchy man, I love you, I love you, I love you.' And he had gone weak at the knees.

Aside from romantic endearments, Diana also talked about how her husband made her life 'real, real torture', and described a lunch at which the Queen Mother had given her a strange look. 'It's not hatred, it's sort of interest and pity ... I was very bad at lunch and I nearly started blubbing. I just felt really sad and empty and thought "Bloody hell, after all I've done for this fucking family" ... It is just so desperate. Always being innuendo, the fact that I'm going to do something dramatic because I can't stand the confines of this marriage.'

The recording had been made illegally on New Year's Eve in 1989 when Diana was at Sandringham and Gilbey in a car parked in Oxfordshire. Her distress at its publication was excruciating.

Another foreign tour was coming up, to Korea, which had like everything been planned far in advance. Late in the day, the Princess announced that she was not prepared to go. After much persuasion, including intervention by the Queen, she finally agreed to stick to her original plan, but the trip was a disaster. The only angle the press was interested in was the marriage, and for the first time, the Princess made no attempt to disguise her feelings. Normally the master of self-control and a performer of the first order, she looked sad and miserable and frequently on the verge of tears. The Prince looked no happier, and although he worked hard to cover up for her by doing all the talking and smiling, nothing could salvage the situation.

In private there was nothing left between them, not even the enforced civility they had become accustomed to faking for the sake of their staff. To be in the same room with them both, trying to talk to one or other of them, was quite frightful. Meanwhile, journalistic coverage of the Korean tour was confined to obituaries of the marriage and ignored in its entirety the trade deals and governmental ties which had been secured. Peter Westmacott, the deputy private secretary with the unenviable task of accompanying the Prince and Princess, took aside James Whitaker, royal correspondent of the *Daily Mirror*, to complain about the coverage. Whitaker was sympathetic, but commented, 'Peter, you really can't say this is a marriage made in heaven.'

'I am not saying it is,' said Westmacott. 'What I am saying is that you guys are getting it so grossly wrong, you're mis-reporting what's going on and ignoring the substance of the visit.'

Two hours later Sky News was interrupting broadcasts to say 'Palace official confirms marriage is on the rocks.' Whitaker's defence was that he had had a duty to relay what he had been told to the rest of the journalists who were covering the tour, because Westmacott had 'sought him out for conversation'. By the next day the tabloid press was full of the story: 'Palace official in gaffe.' 'Palace official confirms marriage over.'

At the end of the tour the Prince and Princess flew on to Hong Kong. He was staying there; she was to fly back to London. By the time they arrived in Hong Kong, just three hours later, the storm had broken. Shortly after their arrival Westmacott went into the Prince's bedroom with the newspapers to break the bad news. The Prince had been quite unaware of what had happened the night before, but listened to Westmacott's tale and apology with a wan smile. The Prince is always unfailingly gracious if people take problems to him rather than leaving him to hear bad news through back channels. In this case, he was understanding when Westmacott explained what had happened. The Prince had always felt 'it was a waste of time trying to talk sense to these people'.

During the flight to Hong Kong Westmacott had tried hard to talk the Princess out of separation. He tried to persuade her that it would be best for everyone if they could find a *modus vivendi*. She had her own friends, her own life, the children had the stability of two parents and she was good at her job. Why did she want to destroy it all?

It was to no avail. By the time the Prince was looking at the morning papers, the Princess was on a plane bound for London, determined that she was going to end the sham of their marriage.

TEN

The Beginning of the End

'I hope you find it in your hearts to understand ...'
Diana's 'resignation' speech, 1993

On the afternoon of 9 December 1992, John Major, the then Prime Minister, stood up at the dispatch box in the House of Commons before a packed but silent House and read aloud the following statement:

> 'It is announced from Buckingham Palace that, with regret, the Prince and Princess of Wales have decided to separate. Their Royal Highnesses have no plans to divorce and their constitutional positions are unaffected. This decision has been reached amicably and they will both continue to participate fully in the upbringing of their children.
>
> 'Their Royal Highnesses will continue to carry out full and separate programmes of public engagements and will, from time to time, attend family occasions and national events together.'

The Prince was on a Business in the Community visit to Holyhead on the day the separation was announced, followed by a Prince's Trust board meeting in the afternoon. The news had started to leak, and there were shouts from the press 'Give us a statement, Charlie.' Julia Cleverdon, chief executive of BitC, was with him and, much to her amusement, photographed as 'an unknown woman in green' as they boarded the aircraft together. She had been blissfully ignorant about the announcement, and it was only on the flight home that she realised what was going on. They had been working together closely for nearly ten years and shared a lot of the same ideas, frustrations and enthusiasms. That afternoon he told her about the separation and, in all the years she had known the Prince, she had never seen him so deeply miserable.

The crunch had come during a weekend at Sandringham, soon after the disastrous Korean trip. Every year the Prince and Princess had hosted a shooting party at Sandringham for sixteen friends who came to stay for three days with their children, and the Prince had organised it around the Princes' exeat from Ludgrove, their preparatory school, so they could be there and see their friends. Less than a week beforehand, the Prince discovered that Diana had decided to take the children to stay with the Queen at Windsor instead. He explained the situation to the Queen who then spoke to Diana, but the Princess announced that if she couldn't go to Windsor she would take the boys to Highgrove. Charles asked whether she might not at least let the boys come, even if she was determined to stay away herself, but she refused. The Prince's patience finally snapped.

He had put up with years of tantrums and abuse, he had given up his friends to try and please her, he had given up his dog, he had given up shooting for a while, he had sacked perfectly innocuous members of staff because she took against them, he had had no comfort, no companionship in recent years, he had been embarrassed and humiliated by the Andrew Morton book, upstaged by her in the press on more occasions than he cared to think of, she had flaunted boyfriends quite openly, and she had caused acute difficulty in Korea by appearing to be there under sufferance, hardly able to be in his presence. Now she was embarrassing him in front of his friends and making life difficult for their sons. Painful though it would be for everyone, there was no alternative but to call a halt to the marriage.

After the announcement, the Prince's staff had quickly to divide the household in two. He wanted to have the smallest most loyal staff he could reasonably get away with, so that the danger of people selling stories or gossiping would be minimised. He decided to keep Bernie Flannery, the number-three butler, for himself, and let Diana have the two senior butlers, Paul Burrell, from Highgrove, and Harold Brown, who was already at Kensington Palace.

The office at St James's Palace remained intact, and although there was much talk about warring factions, the two teams were remarkably united. They continued to share the same rooms, the same coffee-making facilities, the same secretaries and fax machine, and they continued to talk to one another as they always had done. But there is no doubt there were difficulties, which were never truly resolved until the divorce four years later.

The principal problem remained that the Princess would frequently go off and do things without telling anyone, or change the arrangements for the children at the last minute. It was at the eleventh hour, for example, that Charles's staff discovered she was planning to take Prince William to Wales on St David's Day. This was quite against the spirit of their agreement about the children doing public engagements, which was essentially that they would not do any. However, if there was to be an exception, they would discuss it in advance. The Prince's private secretary heard about this particular outing by chance, and with luck was able to alter Charles's arrangements so that he could be there with them. Diana had not been intending to tell him. Conversely, on the day when the Prince had been planning to take Harry to visit the aircraft carrier HMS *Invincible*, the Princess announced that he had a dental appointment and would not be available. Rather than risk a high-profile row with his estranged wife, the Prince let it go, and Harry missed the excitement of seeing Harrier jump jets take off and land.

On the whole, however, Charles and Diana were scrupulously fair with the children and in total agreement about how they should be treated and educated. They never argued about them, and they never argued in front of them. Both wanted the very best for the young Princes. They had chosen Ludgrove as a prep school for them together, and were both delighted by the choice of Eton as a public school, where William started at the age of thirteen, Harry following in September 1998. Diana's brother had been at Eton, and Dr Eric Anderson, Head Master up until the year William arrived, had been the Prince's English and drama teacher at Gordonstoun. Tom Parker Bowles, the Prince's godson, had also recently left the school and there were plenty of sons of friends either there already or due to go who would make the Princes welcome.

Before making their final decision, Charles and Diana had spoken at length to people connected with the school, such as Douglas Hurd, the then Foreign Secretary, who is an Old Etonian, a fellow of the school and a friend of the Head Master. They both asked the same kind of questions about the teachers (known at Eton as 'beaks'), the people there, and most particularly the privacy.

'I was struck,' Hurd says, 'that they were both, separately, singing from the same hymn sheet.'

There are no dormitories at Eton. Boys all sleep in their own study bedrooms from the day they arrive, in one of twenty-five individual houses of about fifty boys each. The town in which the school is situated is dominated by the school, and it is well used to coping with high-profile boys. William entered historian Dr Andrew Gailey's house, where Harry joined him, and Gailey was instrumental in helping William through some of the most difficult times, when his parents were waging a very public war against each other. He was also there to help William after his mother's death and spent a lot of time talking to him. William and Harry's protection officers have also been a great help to both boys. They were carefully chosen for the job and are very much a cross between friend and uncle.

The Princess was acutely conscious of living in a gilded cage, and saw it as part of her duty as a royal parent to expose her children to real life and give them an understanding of how ordinary people lived. The Prince was in full agreement. He felt that the Palace system had made a mess of him and he was determined that it was not going to wreck his sons too – the very thing that Earl Spencer so unkindly suggested would happen if Diana's blood relatives were not there to save them. Consequently, Charles approved of most of what the boys did with Diana, though he was uneasy that she chose to take them to visit hostels for the homeless, and didn't quite understand why she was doing it. He felt it would have been better to let them be carefree children while they still could. They would have the rest of their lives to carry out public engagements. Why burden them with the plight of the disadvantaged when they were still so young? But he never tried to stop her. She was their parent, he reasoned, just as much as he was, and her point of view about how William and Harry should be brought up was every bit as legitimate as his own.

Charles and Diana unquestionably had very different styles. With their father, William and Harry were typical sons of the landed gentry. They loved hunting, albeit as followers, shooting and fishing, and spent hours on the Highgrove farm with the animals, or on bikes or tractors. More recently, they have both taken up polo, and are mad about skiing, which Diana also loved. When they were with her, they became urban kids. They dressed in jeans and baseball caps and ate in McDonald's hamburger restaurants, went to the movies and hurtled down the scariest runs at all the major theme parks. These were private trips, but Diana always made certain that the newspapers knew about them, which helped to reinforce the perception that she was a loving mother who did fun things with her children, in stark contrast to their father, who looked cold and stiff, with hands clasped firmly behind his back, a picture of distant old-fashioned formality.

If they are at home, Charles's philosophy is they can do exactly as they please and have fun; but when they are doing anything remotely public as royal princes, he expects something a little different. The sight of Prince Harry, aged thirteen, dressed in a suit at the World Cup football match in France in July 1998, when England played Argentina, was typical. Prince Charles was criticised for making him dress up in a suit, when it was so obvious what his mother would have dressed him in. What the commentators failed to recognise was that Prince Charles and Prince Harry both met the President of France while they were at the match. They were not there as anonymous punters, and it would have been discourteous to President Chirac to dress in any other way. Whether he likes it or not, Harry is not a normal teenager, and never can be. He is third in line to the throne of England and, as he discovered long ago, this sets him apart from his peers.

In reality, Diana wasn't the only one who handed out the laughter and the hugs. The Princess was very often warmer and more demonstrative in public than in private. Away from the cameras, the boys saw the extremes of her moods as clearly as everyone else, and were often quite frightened and bewildered by what they saw. She had taken no effort to spare them her emotions. When a friend once suggested it was unwise to have hysterics in front of Prince William, who was at that time in a cot, Diana said he was too young to notice, and anyway he would have to learn the truth sooner or later.

The Prince's private persona is also completely different from his public one. He fools around with the boys, they tease each other, laugh, joke, rough and tumble, and even hug and kiss. On the last night of their skiing holiday in Klosters in 1997, there was a big farewell dinner party in their hotel restaurant. In the middle of dinner Harry got to his feet and, in front of a table full of people, made a little speech to thank 'Papa', as both boys call him (to rhyme with 'supper'), for giving him such a wonderful holiday. He then walked smartly up to his father and smothered his face in kisses until, in mock embarrassment, the Prince begged for mercy. It was a touching scene.

When William and Harry were small, one of the biggest problems Charles's valets had was keeping his suits clean. Whenever Charles arrived home at Highgrove by helicopter, it would land in the front field, where sheep graze. As soon as William and Harry heard it overhead, they would come running out to meet him. Once it had landed safely, they would race across the field and jump up into his arms for a hug, smearing one suit after another with the sheep droppings they had trodden in on the way. He built them a massive tree house in a holly tree, affectionately known as Holyroodhouse, after Holyroodhouse Palace, the Queen's official residence in

Edinburgh. They share the same silly sense of humour, as Diana did too, and they are great practical jokers – another of their mother's legacies. They are also both very funny mimics, like the Prince, and take him off better than anyone. These days, William is taller than his father so any physical horse-play invariably ends in cries of 'Get off, you great big enormous lout.'

After the separation Charles recognised he was going to need some practical help looking after the boys when they were with him. They were too old for a nanny but needed someone who could be around to do things with them, drive them to their friends', take them shopping or shooting and, being a hopeless disciplinarian himself, exert some discipline over them. Alexandra Legge-Bourke, known as Tiggy, was the twenty-eight-year-old daughter of a family friend, and perfectly qualified. She was a delightful, dizzy nursery school teacher, who had a brilliant rapport with children of all shapes and sizes, who were known as her Tiggywigs.

William and Harry took to her instantly. She was like an over-grown child, very good fun to be with. She treated them as a big sister might, rather than as a nanny or a parent would. She loved doing all the outdoor things they enjoyed, like shooting and following the hunt, she told jokes, liked the same kind of music, watched the same videos, yet at the same time she managed to get them to do what they were told, without ever being officiously strict. If their father tells them to go to bed, they ignore him or wheedle him round. If Tiggy tells them to, they call her a 'Bossy Old Bat' but go.

The Princess looked on the blossoming relationship between her sons and Tiggy Legge-Bourke with horror; and this was the one area in which Camilla Parker Bowles was entirely sympathetic. As a mother herself, she could understand how painful it must have been for the Princess to see her children fooling around and enjoying themselves with another woman, who was allowing them to do things she might not have done, and to whom they were inevitably growing closer emotionally. She was angry and jealous, and the Prince was not overly sensitive to her feelings.

These years of separation were not happy ones for the Princess.

She developed a passion for Oliver Hoare, an art dealer friend of the Prince of Wales, whom she had met through her husband. He was often seen arriving at Kensington Palace and there was much gossip. Hoare was married, with no intention of leaving his wife and, when he realised that the situation was getting out of control, he tried to cool the relationship. The Princess was not happy about it. She liked to be in control. As a result she started telephoning Hoare's wife, Dianne, at the family home. When Dianne picked up the receiver there would be a long silence, or the caller would hang up. Eventually she reported the matter to the police and a trace was put on the calls, which all seemed to have emanated from Kensington Palace. When the story appeared in the press, Diana was livid, and to their complete fury, accused one of the Prince's staff and her husband of leaking it. She was convinced that her husband's office was running a campaign to discredit her, and was certain that this was yet one more example of their treachery. The leak had actually come from a boy who was at school with one of the Hoare children.

There was no campaign to discredit Diana. In fact, in August 1993, when Charles declared independence from Buckingham Palace and, with the Queen's agreement, set up his own press office at St James's Palace, he had given specific instructions to his staff to say and do nothing to reflect badly upon Diana. Constitutionally the Monarch and Prince of Wales do very different jobs, and for some time it had seemed common sense that they each should have a dedicated team to handle the media. What is more, there had been a great deal of bad feeling between the press and Buckingham Palace in the latter part of the marriage. The more it became apparent that there were serious difficulties, the less the Palace press office would say. At best, the information they gave was misleading, with the result that most of the papers had stopped talking to the press office at all. The Princess, meanwhile, was talking privately to journalists and editors, and the whole situation was a mess. Much as he despised the press, the Prince was well aware that it was important to him.

He recruited two highly experienced press officers, both from solid civil service jobs: Allan Percival, from the Northern Ireland Office, and Sandy Henney, as his number two, who was with the Crown Prosecution Service. The Prince said he wanted no games and no spinning; and he wanted nothing going out of his office that might be even mildly damaging to the Princess. He left them in no doubt about his views. No matter what she did or said, she would always be the mother of his children, and anything that hurt the Princess would hurt them.

Nonetheless, Diana saw conspiracies everywhere. She left disturbing messages on a number of people's pagers and answering machines. They were all unsigned but there was no doubting where they came from. Patrick Jephson, her private secretary, was a regular recipient, with messages like, 'We know where you are and so does your wife. I know you're being disloyal to me.' Richard Aylard was another target, and there were others in the office. But some of the most poisonous messages were reserved for Tiggy. In the late-1980s Camilla also had a number of threatening and unnerving telephone calls in the middle of the night. Diana would never say who she was, but would say things like, 'I've sent someone to kill you. They're outside in the garden. Look out of the window; can you see them?' For a woman alone at night in a large house in the country and no protection, it was frightening.

No one dared confront the Princess about the messages, for fear of provoking a scene and, in the case of staff, being sacked. Diana's sackings had cost the Prince a lot of money over the years. With modern employment law it was not possible to dismiss people without warnings and good reason, and most of the people she took against had done nothing wrong. Diana had decided, sometimes quite arbitrarily, that she no longer wanted them around. On each occasion the office had to work out what that person would have been awarded by an industrial tribunal and add twenty per cent. Awards for unfair dismissal in those days were a maximum of about £11,000, depending upon length of service. As the succession of cooks, housemaids, dressers, secretaries and butlers left, each one cost between £12,000 and £14,000.

One person dismissed for no good reason was Steve Davies, a thirty-two-year-old chauffeur who had been having an affair with Helen Walsh, one of the Princess's pretty young dressers, who lived in a grace and favour cottage at the back of Kensington Palace. The Princess didn't like the relationship, and thought that they were taking advantage of their position and having fun when they shouldn't be. As a result the chauffeur was paid off, and the dresser told that her boyfriend wasn't to come on the premises again. Furious that the Princess should be interfering in her personal life, the dresser consulted the Personnel Department, who told her that she was perfectly entitled to have any guest she wanted in her home, provided the police on the gate knew they were coming. When the Princess heard this she got someone to check the rules and discovered that, technically, visitors had to be off the premises by midnight. At ten past midnight she banged on the girl's front door, like a woman possessed, shaking with rage and shouting, 'I know he's in there, I want him out now!'

Another victim of Diana's erratic behaviour towards friends and staff was Victoria Mendham. She was the Princess's secretary for seven years, and was totally devoted to her. The relationship was exceptionally close – she even began dressing like her employer – and was treated by Diana as a friend and a confidante. It was a measure of their friendship that Diana asked Victoria to go on holiday with her four years running. For the first two, one to America and the other to the Caribbean, Diana paid the full cost. When they went to the Caribbean again at Easter in 1996, Victoria assumed she was there as a guest once again. It was a great treat and all was going well until half way through the holiday when the Princess suddenly said, 'Oh, Victoria, I've written a note to Tony Burrows to make sure you get your share of the bill. I think it's about £5,000.'

'But, Ma'am,' spluttered Victoria, 'you asked me to come.'

'Yes,' said the Princess, 'but you always knew you would have to pay your way.'

Victoria telephoned the office in London in floods of tears, saying she didn't have £5,000 in the world and not knowing what on earth to do. The Prince paid.

Nine months later it happened again. This time Victoria said she could pay the airfare to the Caribbean, which had been economy class, but they had stayed at the K Club where beach-side villas cost £1,700 a night, and paying that kind of money was out of the question. When the Princess learnt that her husband had footed the previous bill she 'went through the roof' and Victoria was frozen out as others had been before her. On her anti-landmines campaign to Angola, Diana took Paul Burrell with her instead of Victoria, who was very upset. On Diana's return, they had a confrontation, which resulted in Victoria tending her resignation. She was told to clear her desk and leave at once without serving her four weeks' notice.

The Prince picked up a lot of Diana's casualties. He also picked up Diana herself. She drove him to distraction in many ways. He was angered by some things she did – not least her decision to retire from public life, which she did dramatically on a public platform, despite pleas from him, the Queen and the Duke of Edinburgh to withdraw if she liked, but to do it quietly so that she could change her mind at a later date if ever she wanted to. She ignored them all. At a charity luncheon on 3 December 1993, she said, 'Over the next few months I will be seeking a more suitable way of combining a meaningful public role with, hopefully, a more private life. I hope you can find it in your hearts to understand and give me the time and space that has been lacking in recent years ... Your kindness and affection have carried me through some of the most difficult periods, and always your love and care have eased the journey.'

Charles was in Kentish Town in north London the day before the announcement and in a filthy mood, which his private secretary thought must have been because of something he had done. Colin Trimming, Charles's policeman, reassured him. 'It's nothing you've done,' he said. 'Wait until you get back to the office and all will be revealed.'

The Prince was furious with Diana. He saw it as her job to support all the institutions and charities she had taken on, and the faxes that arrived in the office in the aftermath of her speech indicated just how much they would miss her. The one from the Welsh National Opera was typical. 'Your Royal Highness, it is just so helpful to be able to use your name. We only ask you to do one engagement a year, which is a reception followed by an opera, but twenty per cent or so of all our fundraising is achieved that night. What are we going to do now?'

The Prince found conversations with Diana very difficult and upsetting, but he never felt she was entirely responsible for what she did. He regarded her as an injured soul, a poor damaged creature who needed help. He had come to learn that he wasn't the person to give that help. Everything he had tried had failed, and he seemed to do nothing more than provide a focus for her anger, but he did care very much that she should be looked after. He worried about her, and was always there at the end of a telephone, right up until the time of her death, when things went wrong with a love affair or the children or even the press. She would ring him up in tears, and he would do whatever needed to be done to sort out the problem.

ELEVEN

Camillagate

'There were three of us in this marriage.'
Diana on 'Panorama'

For a man obsessed about his privacy, the publication in January 1993 of a highly intimate late-night telephone conversation with Camilla Parker Bowles was the ultimate humiliation. Known as the Camillagate tapes, they were recordings said to have been made four years before, which left no one in any doubt that these were two people who were very much in love, and who enjoyed a close physical relationship. Everything that the Princess of Wales had told Andrew Morton appeared to be confirmed.

A full transcript of the eleven-minute tape was first published in an Australian magazine, but swiftly reproduced in the British press, where millions of people digested it with their breakfasts. What they read was allegedly the heir to the throne's wish that he could be with the woman he adored, and musing on the possibility of turning into a tampon in order to be closer to her. It was a conversation which should never have been overheard – the sort many lovers might have in bed, after a bottle of wine, when they are tired, relaxed and entirely alone – and of toe-curling embarrassment for the two participants.

The puritanical outburst that followed was hysterical and out of all proportion. The widespread feeling was of a nation in crisis. There were lurid headlines and cartoons, wide condemnation of the Prince, questions about his fitness to be king and, in the mounting fever, demands from Cabinet ministers that the Prince give up Mrs Parker Bowles.

Charles: ...He thought he might have gone a bit far.

Camilla: Ah, well.

Charles: Anyway, you know, that's the sort of thing one has to beware of. And sort of feel one's way along with, if you know what I mean.

Camilla: Mmmmm. You're awfully good at feeling your way along.

Charles: Oh, stop! I want to feel my way along you, all over you and up and down you and in and out.

Camilla: Oh!

Charles: ...particularly in and out.

Camilla: Oh, that's just what I need at the moment.

Charles: Is it?

Camilla: I know it would revive me. I can't bear a Sunday night without you.

Charles: Oh, God.

Camilla: It's like that programme 'Start the Week'. I can't start the week without you.

Charles: I fill up your tank!

Camilla: Yes, you do!

Charles: Then you can cope.

Camilla: Then I'm all right.

Charles: What about me? The trouble is I need you several times a week.

Camilla: Mmmmm. So do I. I need you all the week, all the time.

Charles: Oh, God, I'll just live inside your trousers or something. It would be much easier!

Camilla: (Laughs) What are you going to turn into? A pair of knickers? (Both laugh) Oh you're going to come back as a pair of knickers.

Charles: Or, God forbid, a Tampax, just my luck! (Laughs)

Camilla: You're a complete idiot! (Laughs) Oh, what a wonderful idea!

Charles: My luck to be chucked down the lavatory and go on and on for ever swirling round on the top, never going down!

Camilla: (Laughing) Oh, darling!

How the conversation, which went on in a similarly ridiculous vein, demonstrated in any way that Charles was unfit to be king was a mystery. What it revealed, in the silliness and crudity of the jokes as well as the rest of their sleepy ramblings, was that the Prince had found in Camilla what he had so much hoped to find in Diana. It was clearly a loving, friendly, familiar relationship, with no suspicion or tension or jealousy. They took pleasure in hearing each other's voice, they had fun in their friendship, and they made each other laugh. And as his staff will say, no matter what sort of a day he has had, a conversation with Camilla last thing at night – which he will try and have wherever he is in the world – will always cheer him up.

The Prince likes people who are fun to be with, and one of the greatest disappointments in his marriage was that the sense of fun which had so attracted him to Diana when he first met her, quickly vanished. But it was more than her sense of humour that attracted him to Camilla; and some of the other elements that made her so important to him were evident in that tape. Camilla was interested in the Prince: she boosted his ego, she wanted to hear about his work, she was straightforward, she made no demands on him, she was happy to see him but understanding when he had to be elsewhere. She was sexy and giggly and pulled his leg when he was angry or pompous, but didn't criticise or put him down. She asked to read his speeches, wanted to hear about his plans and schemes, and on the rare occasions that she met someone from one of his organisations, said she had heard so much about them and wanted to know more. She was friend as well as lover; and shared many of his enthusiasms.

How the conversation was taped that night is unknown, and the Prince would still dearly love to get to the bottom of. It mystifies them both to this day. The tape was not one single conversation, but a compilation of many, which they worked out they had had over several months around Christmas 1989. The original notion that it was some radio buff accidentally tuning into the Prince's mobile phone signal was quickly dismissed, and an official government inquiry into MI5 and other intelligence agencies dismissed their involvement too. The Princess was one of very few people who knew the Prince's mobile telephone number, and it was known that she had been worried about bugging on her own account and had installed some sophisticated equipment at Kensington Palace.

The real agony of the tape is that it will haunt Charles for ever. He knows that it will be recalled at his coronation and all the serious moments in his life, and his humiliation and that of his parents and two sons, also of Camilla and her family and children, will go on indefinitely.

He was in Liverpool the morning the tape was published, and had seriously to steel his courage to climb out of the car and face the crowds, not knowing what kind of reception awaited him. He behaved as though nothing had happened, and the crowd, in turn, behaved similarly. There were no sniggers, no shouts, no catcalls, and no absence of people. Throughout all the difficulties and revelations, no one who accompanied the Prince on any engage-ments ever saw so much as a single placard or heard the faintest jeer. Despite the brave exterior that day, it was nonetheless one of the very worst days of his life: he was excruciatingly embarrassed on a personal level, extremely annoyed with the media for having published the tape, terrified for his children, and miserable that yet again he had managed to drag the monarchy through the mire. The Queen had called 1992 an 'annus horribilis' and 1993 was obviously going to be no improvement.

Charles was also devastated for Camilla. The Morton book had turned the spotlight on Mrs Parker Bowles for the first time in all the years of their friendship. The press took up residence outside her house in Wiltshire, making her a prisoner in her own home, and she was on the receiving end of some unpleasant mail, which accused her of breaking up the royal marriage. But the Camillagate tapes were infinitely worse, and effectively brought an end to her marriage to Andrew Parker Bowles by making his position untenable. Having the explicit nature of her relationship with the Prince of Wales all over every newspaper made life extremely unpleasant for her children and elderly parents too. She was the butt of jokes up and down the country. She was never pelted with bread rolls by a bunch of abusive women shoppers in a car park in Chippenham, although the story has been told time and again; but she did get dozens of abusive letters and telephone calls, which she found enormously upsetting, and even quite scary. She scarcely went out, and when she did it was always with the protection of friends. Friends shopped for her and delivered supplies to her home, and were her lifeline.

Her children were innocent victims, and it was deeply unfair that her husband should have had to run the gauntlet of media scrutiny as a result of someone illegally bugging the phone line to his home. But Andrew Parker Bowles was by no means the poor cuckold, stepping aside dutifully for the heir to the throne to exercise his *droit de seigneur*. The very qualities which had attracted Camilla to him in the early 1970s, and made him such an exciting catch, had not diminished. Good looking, charming, slim and fit, he was still the womaniser he had always been. Camilla liked Andrew; they were good friends despite the infidelity, and have remained so. Having been brought up by her mother to have a strong sense of family and to put the children of a marriage before the wants of their parents, Camilla had settled for the life she had, put up with Andrew's behaviour which she couldn't stop, and happily devoted herself to her house and garden, her children and her horses. When the Prince of Wales reappeared in her life, he brought excitement, which had been missing for a long time. She, likewise, brought light into his life, which had been steadily closing in on him in dark despair.

The Prince loved Camilla. She had rescued him from the depths and brought laughter and sunshine into his life, but it didn't mean he wanted to marry her or escape from his marriage to the Princess. The separation from Diana in December had been a desperate and difficult time. What distressed him as much as anything was the feeling that he had let so many people down. It had taken a severe toll and left him at a very low ebb. He knew he had tried as hard as was humanly possible to keep his marriage together, but whatever the excuses, whatever the reasons, the fact was that he had failed. It was no comfort to know that his marriage was no different from a high percentage of the population's. He had known from the outset that his marriage was different and must be for life, which is why he had been at such pains to find the right bride. As the man who would be king as well as Defender of the Faith, he couldn't easily walk away from the vows he had made before God 'to love and to cherish, for better or worse, in sickness and in health'.

He felt, in admitting defeat, that he had disappointed many people, the Queen, the Queen Mother, his children, not to mention all the millions of strangers who had watched his marriage to Diana, heard the spine-tingling notes of the Trumpet Voluntary and Dame Kiri te Kanawa, seen the pomp and ceremony, the glass coach, the kiss on the balcony, and had believed in the fairytale.

The Queen and the Duke of Edinburgh had been shocked and appalled by the Andrew Morton book. They were shocked still further by the publication of the Squidgygate tapes, and were deeply disappointed by the separation.

Yet despite their disappointment, the Queen and Prince Philip were not unsympathetic. They had seen the difficulties at first hand, particularly over the recent Sandringham weekend when Diana had been so awkward about the children attending, and although over the years they had tried hard to resist taking sides, now that the crunch had come, they recognised he had had no alternative. The Duke, normally sparing in the extreme with any kind of praise or support for his eldest son, wrote him a long and sympathetic letter saying that in his opinion, Charles had displayed the fortitude of a saint.

In the summer of 1992, before the Andrew Morton book, the Squidgy tapes, and Camillagate, the writer and broadcaster Jonathan Dimbleby began working on a double project: a television documentary about Charles and an authorised biography. Both were timed to coincide loosely with the twenty-fifth anniversary of his Investiture as Prince of Wales in July 1994. What began as an innocent and well-intentioned exercise had unimaginable consequences, and was ultimately responsible for Camilla's divorce from Andrew Parker Bowles, terrible ructions within the Royal Family,

Diana's devastating 'Panorama' interview, Richard Aylard's downfall, and the fiercest controversy yet about the Prince's fitness to be king.

The moving force behind the exercise was Richard Aylard, who chose Dimbleby for the task and convinced the Prince that he should give maximum co-operation. Dimbleby was experienced, distinguished, and sufficiently heavyweight to appeal to the Prince and be trusted by his friends. Having never previously written about the Royal Family he was also suitably neutral. He was a passionate country-lover, with a small organic farm near Bath, married to the writer Bel Mooney with whom he had two children. In all sorts of ways there was a useful synergy between the two men and they got on well.

The producer for the film was Christopher Martin, who had made the Prince's two previous films, 'A Vision of Britain', about architecture, and 'The Earth in Balance', on the environment. It was a winning combination of people whom the Prince liked and trusted, and the crew became part of his life over the next year and a half, as they filmed at Highgrove and St James's Palace, at Windsor, Balmoral and Sandringham, abroad, at work and play. The result was a sensitive and illuminating film called 'Charles: The Private Man, the Public Role', which ran for two and a half hours and attracted an audience of fourteen million viewers, many of whom understood for the first time what the Prince of Wales actually did when he was not playing polo.

What most people remembered of the film, however, ran to no more than three minutes.

Dimbleby asked the Prince about his infidelity. 'Were you,' he said, 'did you try to be faithful and honourable to your wife when you took on the vow of marriage?'

'Yes,' said the Prince, and after a brief and rather anguished pause said, 'until it became irretrievably broken down, us both having tried.'

When asked about Camilla in the film, he said she was 'a great friend of mine ... she has been a friend for a very long time.'

At a press conference the next day Aylard confirmed that the adultery to which the Prince had confessed was indeed with Mrs Parker Bowles.

The question had had to be asked. By the time the programme was shown in June 1994, the Prince and Princess had separated, Morton and both sets of tapes had been published, as had a series of prominent articles in a variety of publications, which talked quite openly about the Prince having been unfaithful to his wife. There was serious discussion between Aylard and Dimbleby about whether in the light of all of this the project should be abandoned, but they decided that would give quite the wrong signals to the outside world, and it was important to go ahead. However, given what had happened, it would have been impossible for Dimbleby to have ignored the one topic that was fascinating people up and down the country. It would have entirely destroyed his credibility as a serious journalist. So although no one doubted that the question had to be asked, what the Prince's friends, colleagues and advisers still disagree violently about was whether the Prince should have answered it. At the time, many thought his answer might cost him the throne.

As the author of it all, Aylard was convinced that the Prince did the right thing, and was deeply cynical about the moralistic and hypocritical tabloid outcry. As one tabloid journalist said to Jonathan afterwards, 'You shot our fox.' They didn't want this coming out in the programme because there was a million pounds worth of exclusive in this story for someone, which they weren't going to get.

Aylard was also convinced that if the Prince had said 'No' and denied he had been unfaithful, it would only have been a matter of time before someone intercepted another telephone call or came up with photographs, or the evidence of a disaffected housemaid, which would have proved he had lied. He knew the *News of the World*, in particular, was spending a vast amount of money in having both the Prince and Camilla Parker Bowles followed, day and night.

The other option would have been to bat the question away, to say that he was not prepared to answer personal questions, but that would have done nothing to kill the speculation, nor indeed the determination to find evidence of an affair. And since most people who either watched television and read the tabloids were already pretty sure he had been unfaithful to Diana, he would simply have looked as though he was not prepared to be honest with the people who would one day be his subjects.

'It wasn't being honest to Jonathan that was the problem,' Aylard said when accused of allowing the Prince of Wales to make what many people regard as one of the most serious mistakes of his life. 'If you want to start placing blame, the fault was getting into the relationship in the first place.'

But it was the book that followed that, in the view of most of the Prince's friends, did the real damage. Not the book itself, which few people will have read from cover to cover, but its serialisation in *The Sunday Times*. It was a formidable tome, running to 620 pages, meticulously annotated and painstakingly detailed, which the Prince had been over with a fine-tooth comb checking facts, and which is now widely used as a handbook amongst 'the rat pack', as the tabloid royal reporters are known. For the first time in his life, Charles had made every source available to a writer. Dimbleby had a free run of everything, including his personal letters, diaries and journals, and his archives at St James's Palace and Windsor Castle. Furthermore, the Prince had positively encouraged friends and relatives to talk about him, many having never previously done so. Each one spent many taped hours talking about the man they knew, in the belief that this definitive, comprehensive and authoritative book would do him good and put right the injustices they felt he had endured for so long. When they saw what happened, they recoiled in horror and felt that the blood was partly on their hands. They had helped destroy the man they had all so wanted to help.

The deal Aylard struck with Dimbleby was quite extraordinary and left the Prince dangerously exposed. While Dimbleby under-took 'to take into account any comments made by HRH with respect to factual inaccuracies', he had the final say and 'sole discretion about the contents' of what he produced. In other words, Dimbleby could write whatever he liked and, provided it was accurate, the Palace was powerless to remove it from the book, no matter how much embarrassment or damage it might cause. In fact, Dimbleby took quite a lot out that would have been awkward for the Prince, but there were other details which he thought important to retain.

The Prince's relationship with his parents and other members of the Royal Family was one damaging element, which was deeply illuminating about the personality, but not enormously helpful in terms of the continuing relationships. Also, Aylard had no control over serialisation. *The Sunday Times* inevitably sensationalised the book, and the lasting impression, once the headline writers had finished, was of a whinging Prince, whose parents had never shown him any affection, who had loved Camilla for most of his adult life, and never loved the wife that his father had bullied him into marrying. All the juiciest bits were picked up by the tabloids and by columnists, and the Prince was given another very sound kicking.

Initially, the Prince had been rather pleased with the whole exercise. He had been over the book and watched the film, and was comfortable that he had made the right decision in answering Dimbleby's question about adultery. And then his telephone started ringing and one friend after another said, 'Oh, sir, what a ghastly programme. Wasn't that awful? You were led up the garden path, weren't you? What was Richard Aylard thinking of? Why on earth did you let him persuade you to do it?' And all the resolve and the certainty began to evaporate.

The decision had been his own, albeit with a strong recommendation from Aylard, who had been convinced by Dimbleby that he should tell the truth. They had discussed the pros and cons, and he had been given the advice. But the Prince is the boss, he was the one facing the camera, and he could have simply said 'No.' One of his constant complaints is that he is always made to do things he doesn't want to do by the people he pays to advise him. A stronger character would stand up for what he believes himself and let his advisers advise, and not dictate.

Aylard had not consulted with anyone else over the Dimbleby deal. He played the whole project very close to his chest, as he did most things, and his critics say that was his big mistake. When it all began to unravel, he had no supporters. No one was prepared to fight his corner because they had not been involved in the process, and many were angry that it had been sprung on them. There were plenty of people he could have gone to for advice, even within the office at St James's Palace. Belinda Harley, for example, an assistant private secretary, had been a PR in the publishing world but she had not even been asked to have a look at the contract. She felt the Prince could have had a much better deal and been properly safeguarded. Tom Shebbeare, chief executive of the Prince's Trust, and Julia Cleverdon of BitC, both of whom featured heavily in the film as key players in the Prince's two major activities, knew nothing about the venture until it was underway.

'We all tried to say it was a frightfully good idea to the outside world once we heard about it,' says Shebbeare, 'but it was all happening before anyone could have any influence on it. The first thing I knew about it was when television cameras started wandering into everything we did.'

The film could not have come at a worse time for Camilla, and she blames herself for not having taken a greater interest in what the Prince was telling Dimbleby. In the wake of his admission that they had had an affair, an assortment of friends and relatives appeared in print to condemn the Prince on her behalf.

'Frankly,' said one, 'he has behaved like an absolute pig and landed Camilla right in it. She has done absolutely nothing to deserve this after all the support she has given him over the years through difficult times.'

They said she had begged him not to talk to Dimbleby, but that he had ignored her pleas and selfishly exposed her to public vilification. This was not true. She never begged him not to talk to Jonathan. She was too busy with her own problems to worry about what Prince Charles might or might not say to Jonathan Dimbleby. Her life was a mess. Her marriage had virtually fallen apart thanks to the

Morton book and the Camillagate tapes. Her children were being teased and tormented. She couldn't go out of her house; and there were photographers camped on her doorstep. On top of everything, her mother was dying. Her lively, lovely, sparky mother, the Hon. Rosalind Shand, the much-adored bedrock of her tightly knit family, was slowly and painfully dying of osteoporosis. She had had the disease for some years, and as her spine gradually collapsed in on itself, she lost a foot in height. To have to stand by, feeling so helpless, and watch her mother suffer was more distressing to Camilla than anything the media could throw at her. She died on 14 July 1994 in hospital in Brighton, with Camilla and the rest of the family by her side, and was buried in the Sussex village of Plumpton, where she had lived throughout her married life. To add to the family's distress, the number of photographers that day almost outnumbered the mourners.

Though still married, Camilla and Andrew had been leading separate lives for years. However, the horrors of Morton and the tapes had made his position impossible. After Dimbleby, there was absolutely no way they could carry on as man and wife, and by January the following year the Parker Bowleses were divorced and a line finally drawn under their twenty-one-year-old marriage. Although it was precipitated by the Prince's confession, the truth was that Andrew had been wanting a divorce from Camilla for some time. He was keen to marry his own long-standing love, one of Camilla's friends, Rosie Pitman, who lived nearby in Wiltshire. The grounds for the divorce were that the couple had been living apart for more than three years, and it went through uncontested.

Knowing that the divorce would cause a sensation in the tabloid press, and could rake up the tapes and everything else all over again, Alan Kilkenny, the PR consultant who had masterminded the publicity for the immensely successful Great Ormond Street Wishing Well Appeal, was brought in by the Prince to help manage the publicity. Since Great Ormond Street, Kilkenny had helped with a number of projects, which included organising the Symphony for the Spire, a spectacular open-air event in the precinct of Salisbury

Cathedral, to raise money for the crumbling edifice. He had also been involved in the Prince of Wales's Charities Trust, and given advice on the Institute of Architecture. After the Parker Bowles's divorce he assisted Camilla in handling the press on an informal basis for almost three years, but that role came to an end shortly before Diana's death, when the Prince's office at St James's Palace took Mrs Parker Bowles under its protective wing.

The plan was that on the day the divorce was heard, Camilla's lawyer, Hilary Browne-Wilkinson, would make an announcement to the Press Association, and all enquiries would be directed to Simon Elliot, Camilla's brother-in-law. The day before the announcement, Andrew Parker Bowles went to see the woman who lived in a tied cottage at the end of their driveway in Wiltshire to tell her what was happening. Margaret Giles worked as a housekeeper and looked after the property when the Parker Bowleses were away. Andrew wanted to warn her that she might be pestered by the press. The plan backfired dramatically. Mrs Giles immediately contacted the South West News Agency – where the editor of the *Sun*, Stuart Higgins, once worked – and within minutes he was on the phone to Simon Elliot to say he had heard the Parker Bowleses were about to divorce. Unable to deny the story, it was all over the next day's newspaper, followed by some personal photographs. Some had come from the Parker Bowles's private family photograph album which was subsequently found at the *Sun*'s offices in Wapping. Others, such as a photograph of the four-poster bed in which Camilla slept, had been taken by someone with access to the house. Mrs Giles had a key to the Parker Bowles's house and subsequently admitted having agreed to sell the photographs for £25,000. The money was never paid. The Parker Bowleses sued the *Sun* and the newspaper settled out of court for the same sum it had offered Mrs Giles. The money went to charity.

When the interest in Camilla's divorce was past, the fuss over Dimbleby long gone, and life was pleasantly uneventful, the Princess of Wales released another Exocet which took everyone back to square one. It shattered the Prince, shattered Camilla, and dealt yet another serious body blow to the monarchy.

Diana gave a theatrical performance on the BBC's flagship current-affairs programme 'Panorama'. Sitting forlornly in a chair at Kensington Palace, occasionally pausing to recover her composure or wipe a tear that threatened, she told journalist Martin Bashir about her life. The scene could not have been more dramatic. With black kohl lining her eyes, Diana looked vulnerable and wretched, but talked about being a strong woman, and other phrases straight from the counsellor's couch. Much that was said echoed what she had told Andrew Morton. She talked about her bulimia, her cries for help, the Prince's friends who waged a war in the media against her, his obsession with Camilla, 'the enemy' within the Palace. She confessed that she had been unfaithful to her husband, with James Hewitt, whom she had adored, but who had also let her down. She talked about her desire to be 'a Queen in people's hearts ... someone's got to go out there and love people and show it.'

The most memorable moment of the whole broadcast was her simple description of what had destroyed her marriage. 'There were three of us in this marriage,' she said, 'so it was a bit crowded.'

The most damaging remark, however, was her doubt that the Prince of Wales should ever be king.

The programme had been filmed and prepared in total secrecy, and announced at the last minute. The BBC governors had not even been told about it, for fear that the establishment mafia would interfere and have it stopped. Until the opening credits rolled at 9.30 p.m. on Monday 20 November 1995, no one at either St James's or Buckingham Palace had any idea of what was about to follow.

A group of courtiers gathered in the Buckingham Palace press office to watch it together. They included Charles Anson and Philip Mackie, from the Queen's press office, Richard Aylard, Allan Percival and Sandy Henney from the Prince's press office, and Geoff Crawford, who was Diana's press officer and as much in the dark as anyone else present. He resigned as a direct result, as did Patrick Jephson, her private secretary. Both had been taken entirely by surprise and felt they couldn't carry on.

Philip Mackie, a genial Scot, who was always telling people he had the inside track on a story, and that he had his sources, said reassuringly, 'I've been doing a bit of ringing around, and there's nothing to worry about. It'll be a damp squib – I bet you a bottle of Champagne.'

About fifteen minutes into the film, Aylard said, 'Philip, we're up to a whole case by now!'

On the notoriously tough discussion programme, 'Newsnight', immediately after 'Panorama', Nicholas Soames – clearly one of the 'enemies' the Princess had been referring to, and not the most sensitive of men – explained that Diana had endured 'a period of unhappiness [that] led to instability and mental illness'. Her theories about her telephone being tapped, which she had talked about in the interview, exhibited 'the advanced stages of paranoia'. While some people might have agreed with him, it was not the most helpful remark under the circumstances. He had gone into the studio quite unprepared. The script that the BBC had promised to send him hadn't arrived. The programme had asked for Charlie Palmer-Tomkinson but, being a politician – the Armed Forces Minister – Soames, who was used to being put on the spot, seemed a safer bet.

'What shall I do?' he asked of one of the Prince's staff, who was as much in the dark.

'Just be careful!' were the memorable parting words.

The Prince was at Highgrove that evening and chose not to watch the 'Panorama' programme himself, but was soon told about it; also about the remarks his friend had made on 'Newsnight'. Despite speculation in the newspapers the next day that it might end their friendship, that was not the case. Rather, the Prince was worried that Soames might have damaged his own career by going out on a limb on his behalf.

Camilla watched the programme at home with her family and laughed at the sheer theatricality of it, as did many people who knew Diana.

Martin Bashir, 'Panorama' and the BBC were all being expertly manipulated in just the same way as Andrew Morton had been. The

Princess was using them to inflict maximum hurt on the Prince, and she could not have been given a better platform from which to do it. But it was still essentially a very private battle, and in her determination to make the Prince pay for having failed to make her happy, she hurt her sons and also the monarchy, which was not just about the Queen and the Prince of Wales. It was the throne that William would one day inherit.

The Queen had had enough. She was concerned about William and Harry, and thought the tit for tat nonsense that had been going on through the media was undignified and damaging. The time had come to bring the marriage that had caused such grief and heartache to an end. After consulting with the Prime Minister and the Archbishop of Canterbury, she wrote formally and privately to her son and daughter-in-law asking them to divorce as early as could practicably be done. Negotiations began, but while they were still in the very early stages, to everyone's surprise, on what Diana called 'the saddest day of my life', she put out a statement to the press.

'The Princess of Wales,' it said, 'has agreed to Prince Charles's request for a divorce. The Princess will continue to be involved in all decisions relating to the children and will remain at Kensington Palace with offices in St James's Palace. The Princess of Wales will retain the title and be known as Diana, Princess of Wales.'

The Queen was furious and issued an immediate response. 'The Queen was most interested to hear that the Princess of Wales had agreed to the divorce. We can confirm that the Prince and Princess of Wales had a private meeting this afternoon at St James's Palace. At this meeting details of the divorce settlement and the Princess's future role were not discussed. All the details on these matters, including titles, remain to be discussed and settled. This will take time. What the Princess has mentioned are requests rather than decisions at this stage.'

Richard Aylard handled the divorce for the Prince, and on top of the other demands on his time, including a marriage of his own that was falling apart, he was closeted with lawyers for several hours almost every day for many months. The Princess had engaged

Anthony Julius, a high-profile divorce lawyer from the well-established firm Mishcon de Reya, and the Prince was represented by Fiona Shackleton, from the royal solicitors, Farrer and Co. Negotiations could not have been more difficult or acrimonious, but by July they had agreed a settlement, widely perceived as generous towards the Princess in terms of money, which was the Prince's express intention and instruction from the outset.

It was a financial package thought to be worth more than £17 million, although both parties signed a confidentiality agreement about it and the precise deal was never known. They retained equal access to their sons, and equal responsibility in the children's upbringing. Diana was still to be regarded by the Queen and the Prince of Wales as being a member of the Royal Family and would receive invitations to some state and national public occasions. She would carry on living in Kensington Palace, but her office would be there rather than at St James's Palace, as she had wanted. There was one detail in the settlement that was widely perceived as petty, and which rankled. She was stripped of the title Her Royal Highness. It was not a detail that the Prince had wanted, it was a decision for the Queen. In public relations terms, it turned out to be a blunder, as her brother made so painfully obvious in his funeral address at Westminster Abbey.

TWELVE

Difficulties at Work

'It's not you I'm cross with, it's the situation.'
Charles

'Matthew, you work in public relations,' said the Prince, taking him by surprise, 'what do you think I should be doing differently?' They had been looking at ways of streamlining the Prince's Trust. 'How can I do it better?'

Matthew Butler had joined the Prince of Wales's office on secondment from Allied Dunbar as an assistant private secretary in July 1993, to look after the UK side of things in terms of the Prince's relationships with the business world. On appointment, like all secondees, his salary was frozen.

'Remember,' said Sir James Mellon, former ambassador to Denmark, who knew the Prince, 'the worst thing that can possibly happen to you is you get sent back to your £40,000 a year job in PR.'

With this advice in mind, plus a little reckless courage, Butler began to tell the Prince what he thought. He was not employed to do PR for the Prince but that was his field. Few people dare say what they really think to the Prince of Wales, even when asked, and the new recruit rapidly realised why. After he had proffered some advice to the Prince on the subject of his public image, Charles quite suddenly flew into a towering rage. 'I'm sorry, it's not you I'm cross with,' he said, mid rant, 'it's the situation.'

Butler retreated, shaken, and immediately telephoned Sir James. 'I've just had a rather interesting conversation,' he said, and told him what his advice had been. He believed that the Prince needed to be more focused in his activities, with a far greater distinction between what was public and what was private – not in the marital or extra-marital sense, but in terms of his private interests. It was not easy to explain to the outside world what relevance organic farming had to unemployed young people on peripheral housing estates in Glasgow, and it would be better if he kept the farming, likewise the architecture, as private interests.

Sir James reassured Butler that he had given exactly the right advice. 'The only thing I would have done differently is make the point about why his sister gets a better press than he does.'

'I'm afraid I did,' said Butler. 'That was when he really got agitated!'

The Princess Royal has been hugely successful. She may not have achieved as much as the Prince has in his scatter-gun way, but no one has ever suggested that she is neither hard working nor professional and everyone knows what she does. An image of the Princess in a sensible head scarf visiting African children as president of Save the Children is indelibly etched on the national psyche – not cuddling them, as the Princess of Wales did, but observing, making sure no one forgot their plight. And she is ever present on formal occasions: never glamorous, seldom smiling but a dependable pillar of respectability. Her private life has been no more saintly than his. She has been through a divorce, and there were rumours of affairs during her first marriage, but she has managed to keep her private life entirely private and earn the respect of the public and, more importantly, the media. It is a remarkable recovery since the 1970s, when she was one of the most unpopular members of the Royal Family, with a reputation for telling photographers to 'Naff off.' She is still surly and bad mannered on occasion, and quite capable of snapping people's heads off if they annoy her, but she has always been much more straightforward than her eldest brother, and has managed her public image with great skill.

Ask people what the Prince of Wales does and, even today, not many have a clear idea. It has not been helped by the fact that since 1981 the scandals, rumours and revelations about his private life were infinitely more fascinating to the public than anything he ever did in the line of work. Furthermore, to his intense frustration, the opportunity to have a photograph of Diana on any given occasion was instantly guaranteed to drive him off the pages of almost every newspaper – as she was well aware. In the five years after the separation, Diana was engaged in a PR war with Charles and the Royal Family, and in the black and white world of the media, she held all the cards.

It is only since Diana's death that the press has begun to take an interest in Charles again. When he visited Canada in 1996 only one press photographer went on the trip. When he went to the Gulf States before her death in 1997, there were two photographers and one journalist. An ITN crew happened to go because they were making a film about the royal yacht, not because they were interested in the Prince. Yet when he visited South Africa with Harry in early 1998, all forty seats on the aircraft were taken and many more photographers made their own way. It was the same in Sri Lanka when he was on his own, and again in Nepal and Bhutan.

Having hardly changed one iota in style or substance in the last ten years, the Prince was less than enthused to hear that the press were saying, 'This guy's great. Why haven't we seen him like this before?' The answer was that for the last sixteen years no one had really looked.

His involvement with the Prince's Trust is well known, although not many people understand what the Trust does, apart from hold pop concerts. Most people associate him with architecture. Some know about the organic farming and Duchy biscuits; and much of the business world is aware of his activity in the inner cities. But the overall impression is of a butterfly, moving from one random issue to another, most of them slightly off-beam.

John Major, when he was Prime Minister, used to worry about the Prince's lack of focus, and the two men frequently talked about trying to find some kind of role which would establish him firmly in the public consciousness. 'Although The Prince's Trust ought to fit the bill,' he says, 'it does it by stealth, and does not have sufficient public impact; it is, by its very nature, a series of small packets. There is nothing immediate about the work it does, nothing photogenic that generates the publicity to fix in the public mind: Prince's Trust, Prince of Wales, Good Thing. He deserves more public recognition of the work he does.'

The ideas, though not always good, have been the easy bit. Raising the money and making the ideas work is the tricky part. The only reason the Prince's Trust has succeeded is because the Prince has worked tirelessly on its behalf, hosting lunches, nobbling likely donors, bringing groups together to find solutions to problems, lobbying government to cut the red tape, and taking an interest in the young people it helps. Without him, several thousand people might never have had a chance to make something of their lives.

Business in the Community was not the Prince's idea, although he has contributed plenty of ideas to it since he joined forces with Stephen O'Brien in 1984. It has grown immeasurably since then, and succeeded in altering the face of many of Britain's inner cities. Once again, much of this is due to the Prince of Wales, with his determination and energy to keep pushing and pushing until he gets what he wants. But it hasn't been without the odd complaint.

'Oh, Julia,' he will say in a pained voice, when he has been up working on his official paperwork until two o'clock in the morning. 'So much paper, Julia, I can't cope. I spent two and a half hours on it yesterday.'

The ideas often arrive on what Julia Cleverdon calls Black Spider Memos. When the Prince is on form, she gets about one a week, as does Tom Shebbeare. They are impassioned notes about some campaign he wants to run, some person one of them ought to do something about, or organise some event with, or some opportunity that he thinks they should not miss.

'I remember getting one saying could we please help resettle the Army. The Army was being flung out of various regiments all over the place. Could we take the project on of resettling them? And some reasonably mad character inside BitC said, "Oh, frightfully good

188

idea," and I said, "Absolutely not. We are not resettling the Army; it's the Army's problem. Of course, we'd be interested to talk to them about ways in which young soldiers could be helped to set up their own businesses – send them off to Tom at the Prince's Trust." You have to be reasonably firm about knowing what is the mission and what isn't the mission.'

More frequently, the Prince will telephone. 'Do you know, I sat next to a Swiss gnome at dinner last night who appears to run that confectionery company and he knew nothing at all about anything we did. I've got his phone number here, will you ring him up?'

The ideas and thoughts come at any hour of the day or night, and the Prince will track down who ever of his staff is appropriate for the particular thought.

'Last night, on the train going home,' says Tom Shebbeare, 'something to seven, the Prince just back from Canada, rings me up: "I've just met the Poet Laureate, Ted Hughes. He has some ideas about how he might help young people with their writing and I would love to involve him. Would you mind terribly meeting Ted Hughes?"'

His work has been a lifeline throughout the years of personal anguish, and it has been a real boost to see some obvious benefit, but nothing thrills him more than when either of his parents notice what he has achieved. Recently the Queen was due to visit Hull and Buckingham Palace rang Julia Cleverdon to see if there was anything the Prince had been involved in nearby, which the Queen might be able to visit. There was, said Cleverdon, a staggeringly good Compact running in Hull, the idea for which the Prince had brought back from America.

A Compact is a bargain between companies and school children in the community in which they operate. If the children keep their literacy skills up, the company rewards them with, perhaps, tickets to the local football match. The idea is for business to talk to the schools to make sure that they are teaching the kind of skills the companies need from their workforce, so that the children are working towards the goal of potential jobs at the end of their education. Business provides the incentives for the children to go to school and succeed, and the schools provide a supply of skilled employees for the local businesses. Everyone benefits.

The Queen was given a presentation by a group of children who told her what they had achieved and came away impressed and enthusiastic about what she had seen and heard. But did she pick up the phone and tell her son? The news that she had been impressed filtered its way down on paper to Julia, who passed it on to the Prince of Wales. He telephoned straight away. 'I gather it went terribly well,' he said.

'Yes, sir, the children were stunning.'

The Prince used to agonise over the problem of having no role, of seeing no positive benefits from his toils at the end of a long working day. It was one of the reasons why he became so passionate about his garden. He enjoyed the physical exertion of digging because he could see the results of his labour and felt gratifyingly tired when he had finished. It was also one of the reasons why he hunted and played polo so obsessively. Pushing himself to the limit physically made him feel alive. It is also, he says, 'one of the best cures for jet-lag'. To be told he had raised thousands of pounds by shaking a lot of hands was thoroughly unsatisfactory, and the curse of people born to his position, where fame and esteem come from an accident of birth rather than hard work or achievement.

Nowadays, the Prince knows he is making a real contribution to society. The frustration is people not making his ideas happen fast enough, or people telling him something can't be done. What he enjoys so much about Business in the Community, almost more than any of the other organisations he is involved with, is that when he has a good idea, not only is it put into practice, the results are immediate and there for everyone to see.

Typical is the Seeing is Believing programme which he dreamt up in 1990. His idea was that if, instead of telling chief executives about the problems of poor housing, drugs, crime and racism, you could let them actually see for themselves what was going on in run-down parts of the country, and meet some of the people who lived there, they would have a far better understanding of the problem and might be more inclined to help. His instinct was absolutely right. In the last seven years more than 700 business leaders have been taken to the inner cities, to community projects, prisons, housing estates – about three tours a year led by the Prince himself. At the end of it the businesspeople are asked to write reports for him on what they've seen and, over lunch at either Highgrove or St James's Palace, discuss what they might be able to contribute. Most of them have found the experience shocking, the more so because they were so unaware of the deprivation that was often on their own doorsteps. They have given not just money, but equipment, property, secondees and volunteers, and many have created work experience, training and job opportunities for the unemployed.

The Prince reads the reports and follows them up. 'He's got a memory like a bloody elephant,' says Cleverdon. 'He cares very much whether any grass came off the mowing machine, and he's an absolute stickler for "What happened as a result of that? Did that hostel for thirty-four homeless people get built after we'd been given 40,000 square feet in Liverpool by Ladbroke Hotels?"'

The answer was, 'Yes.' Forte equipped it with beds from one of its hotels and the hostel was built and ready for business within five months of the Seeing is Believing visit. Another astounding success was Great Yarmouth. After a visit, which the Prince attended, the local business support group produced £1 million to run a re-generation programme called SeaChange. And in Manchester, Charles Allen, the chief executive of Granada Television, was so impressed by what he had seen that he announced he wanted to go one step further and produce a Seeing is Doing programme. He twinned five companies with five housing estates where there was heavy unemployment amongst young people, got each company to give five middle managers for five hours a week, and filmed what happened over a five month period. It was hugely successful. The companies and their suppliers gave the project £7.5 million, which built five community centres on the five housing estates, several of which the Prince opened.

Realising that his intervention and ideas could make a difference, particularly to the young, was one of the things that really gave Charles the confidence to keep going through the darkest patches, and still gives him an enormous sense of fulfilment. He also gets pleasure from the people he meets in the course of his travels. Occasionally he hears remarks that make him roar with laughter, and sees a side of life that others miss.

One day Charles was visiting an Indian family at a housing association in Smethick, near Birmingham. Once the press had gone, he said how nice it was to meet the whole family. The man of the house said, 'Yes, we are all here apart from my father who is out at work.'

'What?' said the Prince. 'You must be fifty, and your father is still working?'

'Yes, he's seventy-four, but he still goes out to work every day.'

'How's that?' asked the Prince.

The man looked very worried and said, 'You are my future king, I cannot tell a lie. In India there is no provision for old age and so my father and his friends, when he came over to Britain in the 1950s, he was forty-six, but on his form he said he was aged thirty-six, so he can go on working for ten more years and earn a lot more pension.'

Once he was back in the car, the Prince picked up the mobile phone and with a mischievous grin asked if he should call the Home Secretary.

The Prince has tramped around more inner-city streets and spoken to many more tenants in high-rise blocks than any politician, and what he understood early on is that to be effective, change must come from the bottom and work its way upwards. Government initiatives alone won't work. You have to help the community entrepreneurs in the housing estates, so that they can fight the crime, vandalism and drugs. But as well as pouring money into projects, they need to learn how to tackle the problems. So in collusion with Anne Power, an expert in housing at the London School of Economics, who is a great advocate of two-storey back-to-back housing, he had the idea of setting up a National Tenants Resource Centre, to teach local committees how to manage their estates. They found a building in Cheshire, which Grand Metropolitan gave to the Prince for the project; Richard Rogers – the modern architect who had once been the Prince's most vociferous critic – ran an appeal. Money came in from business leaders, Laings did the work for free, Sir John Riddell became chairman and, despite a certain amount of scepticism, the centre has been busy ever since. It is just one example of many.

'At heart, he's a campaigner and a world-changer,' says Cleverdon, 'and driven with passion. "It's the primary schools, Julia, that we have to focus on. Do you take in that, it's the primary schools?" "Yes, sir, oddly enough I do." "Yes, but what can we *do*?" "Why not have a reception for the primary head teachers who have been a beacon of achievement?" "Oh, that's a good idea, we'll have a reception. But that's not enough. What else can we do?" So we have a drive on literacy and get all the Seeing is Believing teams to go and visit primary schools and report back on what they've seen.'

And all the while he is power-brokering behind the scenes. Hundreds of computers, for example, will go into the community because of the pressure he brought to bear on the Treasury about charging VAT on gifts in kind.

Matthew Butler believes that the Prince has a problem in reaching Mr and Mrs Average Briton, living in their three-bedroomed, detached Barratt home in Didcot, catching the train to London every day, both out working because they need the money for the mortgage. 'What does monarchy mean for them?' he asks. 'At the top end of the social scale and the bottom end the Prince is very much in touch. It's the middle where there's a problem. If ever it came to a referendum on the monarchy, it would be the husbands and wives in the Barratt homes in Didcot that settled the matter. It's not going to be the kids on the inner city estates, sadly.'

He feels there are flaws in the way the Prince's diary is planned. 'There are a number of formal events, which will increase as time goes on. The remainder of his time is up for grabs, which encourages all his patronages and interests to compete for it, instead of driving the process proactively. He very seldom carries out engagements over weekends, which is the obvious time to attract crowds. If he turns up at Cardiff, for example, on a wet Wednesday morning, it is hardly surprising if there are only a handful of old-age pensioners to greet him. Everyone else is at work. Go at the weekend, as he did to Llandudno on the Sunday night of his twenty-fifth anniversary trip – organised deliberately over a weekend – and the promenade was jammed as far as the eye could see. It's not rocket science,' he says. But being the son of a Bradford and Bingley branch manager from Yorkshire, he knows more about how ordinary people live than many a private secretary before him.

The magic touch has not worked as smoothly as Charles might have hoped in the architectural world. The Prince of Wales's Institute of Architecture was opened to students in 1992, following on the success of a couple of pilot summer schools held in Oxford, Rome and a glorious villa lent to the Prince by the Italian government near Viterbo. The Institute had brave new ideas, and was going to provide an alternative architectural education. Launching it, the Prince said, 'We are told that our contemporary built environment must reflect the "spirit of the age". But what concerns me most of all is that we are succeeding in creating an "age without spirit" ... What I would like to be taught and explored and studied in my Institute, is the fact that the architecture which nourishes the spirit is not so much a traditional architecture, which resembles or apes the past, but rather a particular kind of architecture whose forms, plans, materials, are based on human feeling.

'At the end of their course, I would like the students to leave my Institute with a feeling that they have experienced something rather special in their lives; that a new dimension of life has been revealed to them which has struck a chord in their hearts that will never stop resonating. I hope this will enable them to have the true vision to see that although styles may vary, proportion is in itself a reflection of the order inherent in the Universe. They will need to discover these great truths, I believe, in order themselves to provide the beacons of civilised values in a world increasingly in need of real meaning and of that most precious of commodities – hope.'

Alas, hope was not enough. The students who left the Institute may indeed have experienced something rather special in their lives, but they did not leave with a qualification that would ensure them a job – in as much as any qualification ever can. Good as the idea that drove it and the architects and academics connected with it were, the venture was nonetheless little short of a fiasco. Jules Lubbock, the art historian who had helped write the Prince's famous Hampton Court speech, ran the first summer school, organised the second, and was to have run the Institute as director. But he resigned and went back to his job in Essex because he could not agree the terms of his contract. He had identified the flaw that has dogged the Institute ever since. He thought it imperative that one person should be responsible for running the Institute; but the governing council wanted a division of power – a director to oversee the academic side of life and an administrator to oversee the director. The man who picked up the reins was Dr Brian Hanson, an architectural historian, who, like Jules Lubbock, had formed part of the Prince's advisory group on architecture, and had been shaping his views and speeches since 1987. He became Director of Studies, and Keith Critchlow, who was not by nature a team player, became Director of Research. In the late-1980s, these people had direct access to the Prince and could push his ideas forward, but once Richard Aylard became private secretary in 1991 he took a much tighter grip on things and the direct line they had enjoyed was considerably weakened. By the time the Institute finally opened, the Prince seemed to have lost his appetite for a fight and was wanting to pull in his horns.

Without strong support, a venture of this sort, which challenged conventional wisdom, had no chance of survival; and those in-volved felt badly let down. The Prince didn't stand up for the principles he believed in. He allowed his teaching staff to be overruled and undermined by the council, and failed miserably to back the people he had put in place. The Institute had four directors in six years, which was hardly an encouraging start. The first two were Brian Hanson, who lasted until March 1994, and went on to run the Prince's Urban Design Task Force programme, and a young and fanatical classicist, Richard John, who was another architectural historian. Richard John lasted a year before he was removed and replaced by Richard Hodges, an archaeologist with no particular view on architecture at all; and finally, Adrian Gale stepped into the musical chair as Head of School. Gale was one of the team of architects at Ludwig Mies van der Rohe, the company which designed the 'glass stump' proposed for No. 1 Poultry in the City of London, which the Prince had lambasted so famously in 1984. It was the final irony, and yet another example, some felt, of the Prince being manoeuvred into betraying his ideals.

The foundation course students were unaffected by the less than solid administrative base and went on to places like the Mackintosh School, in Glasgow, widely recognised as the best in the country, where they were welcomed as quality students. However, the changes in directors meant that most of the graduate course students were seriously disrupted in their studies. The Institute failed to get the Royal Institute of British Architects to agree that the graduate course could qualify as a Part II exemption for architects. The RIBA had been receptive in early discussions and it was assumed there would be no problems, but the Institute did not keep up the rapport, and when the RIBA saw such instability at the helm, it refused the qualification. Changes and political in-fighting at the RIBA did not help.

The Institute swallowed up vast sums of money, much of it from the Sultan of Brunei, and Arab sheikhs, and constantly lived in a state of under funding. To avoid any accusations of élitism, it opened its doors to anyone it felt right for the course, so there was an extensive system of student bursaries, which led to the accusation that the Institute paid students to attend. Students came from all corners of the globe, and they were careful not to turn anyone down simply because they couldn't afford the fees. The fees were too low to start with, set at a level to match other foundation courses in the arts, but other schools offering courses had a high level of public funding. The Institute had none.

At the end of 1996, in an attempt to put an end to the internal intrigue and bickering, the Prince sacked the entire governing council and appointed a group of lawyers in their place, chaired by Lady Browne-Wilkinson, Camilla Parker Bowles's divorce lawyer, who openly admitted having neither knowledge nor interest in architecture. Many people in the know have been predicting doom for the Institute for some time, and are not impressed by the latest reorganisation. In August 1998, the Prince announced that he was launching a new Foundation for Architecture and the Urban Environment. It was to be an umbrella for a number of schemes that have been spawned around the urban design theme in recent years, and would include the Institute – renamed the Prince of Wales's School of Architecture and the Building Arts – the Urban Villages Forum, Regeneration through Heritage and the Phoenix Trust; and the whole lot would be housed at a cost of £4.6 million in a former fur warehouse in the East End of London.

'So, once again, in a triumph of hope over experience,' wrote Giles Worsley in the *Daily Telegraph*, 'Prince Charles rides forward in his architectural quest. Perhaps this time it will work. But if the new Foundation turns out merely to be a presentational device to paper over the failure of the institute, if it has been cobbled together to give the appearance of action because nobody dares tell the Prince that it is time to close down, then the old flaws are doomed to re-emerge.

'One longs to be proved wrong, for the Foundation to work. But the suspicion lurks that this is just the Institute mark two. Same trustees, same confusion of purpose, just a new building, a new name and a few new victims to be sucked into the maelstrom.'

Giles Worsley was himself a victim, having been made redundant as editor of architecture magazine *Perspectives* on its demise in January 1998. The magazine had been set up to widen the architectural debate, and attract lay readers. It struggled on for four troubled years, accumulating debts of almost £1.8 million – money it borrowed from the Institute. Apart from the debts, there were irregularities over advertising. Space had been sold on wildly exaggerated sales figures, which had been falling dramatically since its launch. The first issue, with articles by the Prince, Clive James and Lucinda Lambton, sold around 20,000 copies, but that figure steadily declined. In April 1997 it was as low as 2,109 copies. What infuriated many of Charles's friends in the architectural world was that, although the magazine was set up by the Prince to promote his ideas, his own favourite projects – like Poundbury in Dorset and Paternoster Square in London – were scathingly knocked, while modern schemes, by far Charles's least favourite architectural projects, were lavishly praised.

Arguably, it was an area into which the Prince of Wales should never have ventured. He expects too much of his staff, depending on them to have expertise in areas where they have none. Publishing is a specialist industry, and difficult at the best of times. When he first said he wanted a magazine, someone should have had the courage to say 'no'.

The Prince's ideas on architecture have not changed since he made his first speech on the subject in 1985, but he has allowed himself to be pushed around yet again, and he has failed to support the people whose ideals he shares. He would doubtless say it wasn't his fault, it was the fault of those who advised him. Some of his once staunchest supporters are very critical. Mira Bar-Hillel, planning corre-spondent of the London *Evening Standard*, says, 'The Prince could have made a real difference to the way architecture is viewed and practised in this country, giving a voice to millions. But he has allowed himself to be compromised, marginalised and ultimately silenced altogether. His direct influence is now negligible.

'What is both ironic and tragic is that the Prince's own views have never changed. He loathes the Millennium Dome every bit as pas-sionately as he hates other buildings by Lord Rogers, Sir Norman Foster, Sir Michael Hopkins and others who have flourished regardless of his views of them.

'But we can no longer expect him to add his weight to any future anti-modernist campaigns. His success in defeating "a monstrous carbuncle on the face of a much-loved friend" and the "glass stump more suitable to Manhattan" will, tragically, not be repeated.

'This is all very sad, but we must now accept that, while his views have not changed at all, we can no longer expect the Prince to voice them in defence of his architectural realm.'

THIRTEEN

Organic Highgrove

'We live in an age of rights – it seems to me that it is
time our Creator had some rights too.'
Charles

If Camilla has been Charles's emotional lifeline throughout the
darker moments, and work a mental escape, Highgrove has always
been his spiritual refuge. All the while his marriage was disin-
tegrating, he was creating, ever more furiously, a garden which,
whether by accident or design, is an uncanny reflection of the man
who made it. It became a sanctuary where he could clear his mind,
feel close to the natural world, pause briefly from the demands of the
job, and escape from the torment of the media and the failure of his
marriage. Today, it is simply home.

'The garden at Highgrove really does spring from my heart,' he
wrote in the introduction to a book about the estate published in
1993, 'and, strange as it may seem to some, creating it has been
rather like a form of worship.'

It is still his passion, and he spends many happy hours there, no
matter what the weather. He has five full-time and four part-time
gardeners, but he knows every square metre of the ground
intimately, and planted most of the trees and plants himself. He
notices every spurt of growth, every weed, and is constantly
changing and improving and dreaming up new ideas, adapting
schemes he has seen in other gardens and in other parts of the world,
and experimenting with different materials. The latest addition is a
stumpery, a faintly surreal, almost sculptured area of vast and aged
tree stumps that he has collected from different parts of the country

and arranged to extraordinary effect. He likes nothing more than the opportunity to show it all off, and watch the surprise on people's faces as they move from one part of the garden to another, like rooms in a house, each one quite different from the last.

There is sculpture in the gardens too, and a fountain, and giant Ali Baba pots. Poignantly, outside the walled vegetable garden, there is a figure of Diana the Huntress. He is genuinely pleased when people take an interest, and time and again, he has had letters from quite hard headed people saying that they felt something almost spiritual there.

'In some strange way, when I took on Highgrove,' he wrote, 'I knew what I wanted to do even though I had absolutely no experience of gardening or farming and the only trees I had planted had been official ones in very official holes! I experienced no sudden conversion to a new way of thinking, but merely developed an almost unconscious train of thought that seemed, now I reflect upon it, like some powerful echo that arose, inexplicably, from within.

'I knew I wanted to take care of the place in a very personal way and to leave it, one day, in a far better condition than I had found it.'

After Diana's death the Prince was thrilled to have back an album of photographs she had taken of the garden during its transformation in the early years of their marriage. It had gone missing from Highgrove some years before. She had captioned each photograph – 'Charles digging the Rose Garden', for instance – and it was a record that he treasured as an indelible memory of happier times. The Prince had realised it was missing when he wanted to include some of the photos in the book about the estate, written after the separation, and finally learnt the album was at Kensington Palace, and that was where it was staying.

Though he loves the garden, he feels no less passionately about the land. The Prince regularly takes the dogs up to Broadfield, and roams the fields and woods of the Home Farm with a little pruning saw in his pocket, which he uses to tidy up the lower branches of saplings. While Tigger, the remaining Jack Russell, whose daughter Pooh was lost down a rabbit hole, and William's black Labrador bitch, Wigeon, snuffle around after rabbits, he makes notes about things he has spotted, like a dead tree which needs to be removed, an untidy bit of hedgerow, a damaged stone wall, or some other detail, and fires off memos either to David Wilson, the farm manager, or to Nick Mould, the deputy land steward for the Eastern Region of the Duchy of Cornwall.

Sometimes the Prince and Wilson will walk round together and exchange stories, the Prince talking about ideas he has had, things that he has heard during the course of his travels, or things that have excited or troubled him. Recently a butcher they deal with in Essex told David a horror story, which he passed on to the Prince of Wales. A friend of his has steers which graze on the Essex marshes that had started to grow udders, from drinking the water. Oestrogen-mimicking chemicals had evidently seeped into the marshes. Stories like this serve to convince them that what they are doing at Highgrove is the only responsible way of farming for the future. There have been wild quail nesting on a particular block of land for the last two summers and that has been a thrill for everyone. It is important to the Prince that the land is managed in a way that encourages wildlife, and the arrival of quail, not normally seen so far north, is a compliment.

The farm is now fully organic, and Charles is adamant that it must be an example of best practice, and on the principle that Seeing is Believing, has regular tours for visiting groups of interested people, like farmers, researchers and agricultural students. The result is an estate which looks beautiful. Where he has had to replace buildings, he has never gone for the practical and economic option. He has brought in architects. He has a cowshed that commanded more work and expense than many a modern house. He has planted copses and mixed hedges to enhance the landscape, and to encourage birds – skylarks sing above; there are wild poppies growing through the fields of wheat, gates that hang properly on their hinges, and smart wooden fencing that sits well with the landscape. For many years there was not even a strand of barbed wire on the estate.

This pastoral idyll is not just personal vanity; it is at the root of the man. 'In farming, as in gardening,' he wrote, 'I happen to believe that if you treat the land with love and respect (in particular, respect for the idea that it has an almost living soul, bound up in the mysterious, everlasting cycles of nature) then it will repay you in kind. But if you fail to respect the complex, universal laws to which every living creature is ultimately subject, and if you discard that essential humility which recognises the subtle balance that has to be struck between Man's ambition and the finite nature of the physical world, in the end the consequences could be painful and deeply destructive.'

In David Wilson, the Prince found a kindred spirit, in total agreement with him about the environment and future sustainability of the planet. However, the men in suits who were running the Duchy of Cornwall at the time when the Prince decided he wanted to farm organically were another matter. They thought he was about to make a fool of himself by getting involved with some wild and wacky loss-making enterprise that was better left to oddballs.

Highgrove is owned by the Duchy of Cornwall, which, since its creation for the Black Prince in 1385, has been providing an income for successive Princes of Wales, and it has a duty, enshrined by an Act of Parliament, to continue doing so. The Prince's council of eight men, chaired by the Prince himself, has a statutory obligation, therefore, to make enough money for the Prince of Wales to live on, without diminishing the capital assets. No major projects can be undertaken at Highgrove without consulting the council and, although the Prince finds it intensely frustrating at times, it has a tempering effect on some of his more impulsive schemes. But on this matter the Prince was adamant: 'If the Duchy of Cornwall can't afford to try organic farming, then who the hell can?' he argued.

The conversion was gradual, and not entirely free from anxious moments. They experimented first with an eighty-acre block in 1986 and, three years later, after much consultation and visits to other organic pioneers, decided to go with their convictions and convert all 1,080 acres. But in the early 1990s, when the conversion was about half way, they had a succession of very poor harvests, like everyone in the Cotswolds, and the books began to look decidedly wobbly. The Prince's preference for post and rail fencing everywhere instead of barbed wire, and wooden tree guards instead of the plastic sleeves most farmers use, and even stone and wood state of the art cowsheds, did not help. They have not been cheap, but where once the cost would have had to be written off over five years, there is now no need. The final block of land was converted in 1996, the farm is fully organic, and to everyone's delight, it has now been in profit for five years running. Even the council has come round to thinking that organic farming is rather a good wheeze.

One of the farms the Prince took comfort and inspiration from when so many people seemed to be telling him he was mad, was Kite's Nest near the Cotswold town of Broadway. It is farmed by a remarkable family: Mrs Mary Young, who is a disarmingly forthright woman, and her son and daughter, Richard and Rosamund. Mary Young's husband, Harry, was alive at the time of the Prince's visit, but died in 1993.

'Are you a graduate of English literature?' she said, greeting Charles Clover, who was writing the Highgrove book, on his arrival at the house. 'They're the only people I have time for.' And when the Prince's staff were going over plans for his visit in 1989, and said they wanted him to drive round in his own Range Rover, Mary Young said, 'If he's not prepared to drive round in our Range Rover then you can tell him not to bother coming!' And so it was that the Prince was driven around in a battered old blue Range Rover – albeit newly serviced and freshly polished in his honour – and had a highly entertaining day.

This unusual turn of events was not dictated by pride, it was simply Mary Young's concern for her cattle, which happily roam the pastures in family groups, each one, in a herd of 200, individually named with something suitably literary. She thought they would be frightened if they saw a vehicle they didn't recognise. She cares about her animals' welfare in a most commendable way – right through to the end. When the time comes for any of the animals to be slaughtered, Richard and Rosamund take them to the abattoir and comfort the creatures until the bolt strikes. This is not simply sentimentality: there is strong evidence that the meat tastes better from animals which have been slaughtered without the stress and fear normally associated with abattoirs. The Youngs are practically self-sufficient: they grow their own vegetables, mill their own flour, make their own bread and sell their meat in their own shop.

The Prince didn't go quite as far as the Young family, but he came away with plenty of ideas. He has a herd of Aberdeen Angus beef cattle, which live in family groups; also a dairy herd – Ayrshires because he likes their brown and white colouring – and sheep. There are also three glossy brown Gloucester heifers, and a few other rare breeds dotted around the farm, which the Prince, as patron of the Rare Breeds Trust, keeps to provide a gene base. In 1998 they tried outdoor pigs for the first time, in a share-farming arrangement, where a local pig farmer runs his business on Highgrove land – also vegetables, as an experiment. The Prince already has five rather special pigs, which are extremely friendly and pleased to see people. The boys love them. Three are Large Blacks, a breed in danger of extinction, which were a birthday present to the Prince from some friends last year, and two rare Gloucestershire Old Spots, which were also presents, one for a birthday, the other for Christmas. They are supposed to live in the woods in an area specially fenced off, but are forever escaping and coming back to the farmyard in search of company.

The Gloucestershire Old Spots will have to go to the abattoir shortly. They have failed to breed, and in the practical world of farming that means they are no longer of any use alive. There is no boar at Highgrove, so they were sent off to be mated with the Princess Royal's Old Spot boar at Gatcombe. Sadly, they both appear to be barren.

The Prince lives about six miles from his sister, but seldom sees her; although her children, Peter and Zara, have become close to William and Harry recently. The Queen Mother came once to

Highgrove to look at the Prince's herd of Aberdeen Angus. She has a herd of her own at the Castle of Mey and sold Charles a few heifers in 1988. The Queen has also visited Highgrove, but she is very unaware of what her eldest son does. A visitor invited to afternoon tea at Sandringham not long ago complimented the Queen on the Prince's delicious Duchy Original biscuits. The Queen appeared not to know of their existence, and yet the Prince has been marketing his own biscuits made with organic oats grown on the Home Farm for more than six years.

Although they have not done much riding for a few years, the boys have recently become keen on polo. When they were younger, they both rode on ponies loaned by a local horsewoman, Marjorie Cox, who used to teach them – indeed James Hewitt also taught them. The ponies went when the marriage was in trouble, because the children were spending so much time in London, but they are great enthusiasts for the hunt. They love to follow it in a four-wheel drive vehicle, or on the back of one of the terrier men's quad bikes. They also spend hours on the estate shooting and roaring around the fields on trial bikes. They are fascinated by the animals; at lambing time, they spend hours in the lambing pens with Fred Hartles, the shepherd.

The Prince is delighted that William and Harry get so much pleasure from the countryside, which he loves so much, and is keen to let them enjoy themselves in any way they like.

Hunting is still one of the Prince's greatest passions, and he views the move to ban it with great sadness. He sees it as a natural part of the management of nature and an extension of man's involvement in the countryside. It is also a great leveller. As a fellow member of the Beaufort says, 'There's very little protocol on the hunting field, particularly when you're covered in mud and being hauled out of a ditch!' The killing of the fox is almost incidental. What Charles enjoys is the danger, the adrenalin and the challenge and the fact that in the process of trying to stay alive, it's very difficult to worry about anything else. As Trotsky once said, 'Hunting works on the mind like a poltice on a sore.' The danger, however, is very real. Many people, even the most skilled horsemen and horsewomen, have been killed, maimed or confined to a wheelchair as a result of an accident on the hunting field.

Charles didn't start hunting until 1974, when he was twenty-five, because he was never brought up to it. The Queen was a supporter, but never participated. Her father, King George VI, had hunted with great enthusiasm, and was fully supported by Queen Elizabeth, although she never hunted herself. Before George became king they rented a house in the Pytchley country, a hunt in Northumberland, where he hunted regularly. Princess Anne made her name as a three-day eventer, but at one time she hunted frequently, especially when she was married to Mark Phillips. But Charles had only ever played polo, and had therefore never done any jumping. It was one of Mark's horses that the Prince of Wales rode when he hunted for the first time. The late Duke of Beaufort laid on a special meet with some friends, specially for his benefit and, on that one day out, Charles was hooked.

It was not easy starting so late in life, and in the early days he fell off a lot, but he was remarkably brave and always went for the biggest and most difficult jumps. To the Queen's concern, he still rides fast and fearlessly, and she has said that she wished he wouldn't be quite so daring on the hunting field. He tests himself against every obstacle, and pushes himself and the horse to the absolute limit. Like all who wish to stay out to the end of the day, which he does whenever possible, he has a second horse in reserve. Most people who ride at Charles's pace get rid of a horse after a few seasons, but he gets desperately fond of his horses and puts great pressure on his head groom, Tom Normington, to keep his favourites going.

Camilla has a very different style. She takes the day at a much gentler pace and jumps when necessary, but does not leap blindly over every hedge, ditch and five-bar gate that presents itself. She was brought up hunting – her father, Bruce Shand, a wildly popular man, who won two Military Crosses during the Second World War, was joint Master of the Southdown Foxhounds. The social side of hunting is important. There is enormous camaraderie amongst the hunting fraternity, like any group who regularly face danger together, and they have a lot of fun. It is predominantly a sport for the rich, who have the time and money to do it, although there can be a surprising mix. For the Prince, it's an ideal opportunity to meet locals, particularly farmers. He always stops and chats to farmers whose land the hunt crosses, and every year holds a lunch at Highgrove for them by way of thanks.

The Prince is not a regular at the annual Hunt Ball, but he did enjoy a couple of very blue evenings laid on in recent years by the hunt at Badminton, home of the Duke of Beaufort.

'Matthew,' said the Prince after the first of these, 'I was at this marvellous hunt dinner last night and they had a wonderful comedian, a man called Jethro.'

'What?' said Matthew Butler in disbelief. 'I thought Jethro was for people who found Bernard Manning too subtle!'

Jethro is a Cornish comedian, whose act is extraordinarily crude: 'My pal Denzel got a Hoover stuck up his bum and I took him to hospital. When I phoned the hospital next day to see how he was getting on, they said, "He's picking up nicely."

'Denzel's dog swallowed a condom. The vet agreed to come over. Ten minutes later, Denzel rang back saying, "Don't bother. We found another one."'

Jethro had the hunt audience falling off their chairs with laughter. At the end of what was a very drunken evening the Prince swore everyone present to secrecy, then proceeded to tell a very filthy joke himself.

In the summer of 1998 there was a second Jethro evening, which members of the Beaufort were fighting to get tickets for. It was every bit as funny, and every bit as rude and, once again, at the end the Prince told a joke that was not out of keeping. He was telling it, he said, as a reward because everyone had been so good in keeping his last one out of the press. Most had actually been too drunk to remember it, but members of the Beaufort Hunt are entirely discreet.

The young of the Gloucestershire set are now doing much the same for Will, as he is known locally. He regularly goes to parties,

The Prince of Wales in his element, with his faithful dog, Harvey. Charles cut his friends out of his life at Diana's insistence, and even gave away the dog he loved in an effort to make Diana happy.

The fateful trip to Korea in November 1992, when the marriage was all but over and the pretence gone.

The PR war was on, and photographers were telephoned and told where they should go if they wanted a good picture. The laughter and enthusiasm Diana put on for the cameras were not always in evidence at home.

Diana's father, Johnnie Spencer, died in March 1992 while she, the Prince and the boys were skiing in Austria. She was determined to go home alone, but the Prince insisted on accompanying her. When Jane, Sarah, Charles and Diana took the ashes to the family crypt, interestingly, it was Diana who carried them.

In 1993 Diana announced her retirement from public life. Charles saw it as a dereliction of duty, and was furious.

Diana became obsessed about Camilla, who after 1986 was a regular visitor to Highgrove and occasionally with others to Balmoral. Anonymously, Diana would make threatening telephone calls to her in the middle of the night.

Charles with his arm in a sling after falling from his horse during a polo match in 1990. Pushing his horses to the limit was an outlet for his frustration.

A hug for Carolyn Bartholomew, who had talked to Andrew Morton, told the world that Diana approved of his book.

Diana's dramatic
performance on 'Panorama'
in November 1993 prompted
the Queen to insist she and
Charles seek a divorce.

Diana wearing a
deliberately sensational
dress on the night the
Dimbleby documentary was
shown in June 1994. She
knew which picture would
make the front page.

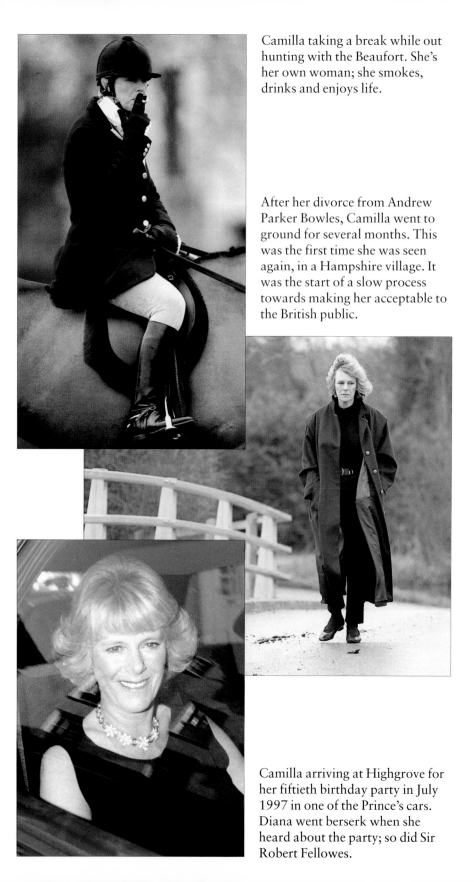

Camilla taking a break while out hunting with the Beaufort. She's her own woman; she smokes, drinks and enjoys life.

After her divorce from Andrew Parker Bowles, Camilla went to ground for several months. This was the first time she was seen again, in a Hampshire village. It was the start of a slow process towards making her acceptable to the British public.

Camilla arriving at Highgrove for her fiftieth birthday party in July 1997 in one of the Prince's cars. Diana went berserk when she heard about the party; so did Sir Robert Fellowes.

July 1997. Diana, William and Harry with
Mohamed al Fayed and his daughter
Jasmin on the St Tropez holiday which
turned into a media circus. Diana was
heavily criticised for exposing her sons to it
all, and Charles feared she was being
sucked into the al Fayed publicity machine.

Prince Charles in Manchester in September 1997. It was his first public engagement since Diana's death and he was terrified. He was touched and relieved by the warmth of the crowds.

There is a spring in his step as Charles begins to enjoy life once again. In March 1998 he took William and Harry to Canada.

Camilla with her daughter, Laura. All she wants is to be a legitimate part of the Prince's life. William and Harry approve – they can see how happy he is when she's around.

often with his friend Mark Tomlinson, who is the son of polo playing neighbours, and he has already made such an impression on the local youth that even sixteen-year-olds close ranks and shield him with a protective wall of silence – sometimes against their own mothers' curiosity.

The Prince's impatience, and his desire to see his ideas implemented before the ink has dried on the page, makes him highly vulnerable. He doesn't want to hear good reasons why it might be ill advised to leap into a new venture without first thinking through all the possible consequences. He wants immediate action. So when people come along promising they can deliver, he takes them into his embrace as the answer to all his problems. But in every area that an idea takes him, there are groups and individuals waiting to hi-jack his name and exploit his enthusiasms for their own ends.

In 1989 he delivered a strong message of support to the organic movement. He also charged David Landale, secretary of the Duchy of Cornwall, with finding ways of giving added value to farm produce. David met a man called Michael Silverman, a management consultant who had contacts with Tesco, the giant super-marketing chain. They approached Tesco with the idea of selling Duchy produce and, spotting a marketing opportunity, Tesco was interested. The Prince was delighted. He had toyed with the idea of selling produce from Highgrove for years. He had thought it might be fun to sell apples and put them in carrier bags with the Prince of Wales's feathers on the side, but everyone wrote it off as another of his impractical ideas. Tesco promised to deliver.

Thus, in the summer of 1990, bread made from Highgrove's very first organic wheat crop went on sale in a selected number of stores in the south-east of England. It was called the Highgrove loaf, but couldn't be labelled organic because it didn't meet the Soil Association's strict guidelines: the palm oil used 'to give good loaf volume' was not organic. The loaf sold well initially, but in the recession of the early 1990s demand fell off and the loaf was discontinued.

In the meantime, still capitalising on the Prince's organic credentials, Silverman was hatching a plan to sell lamb reared by Duchy tenants to Tesco. But there was a problem. Wheat from the Home Farm for the bread had been organic; Duchy lamb was not. So Silverman set about writing a new set of guidelines for lamb production which lamb from Duchy farms would be able to meet sooner than the normal three-year period needed to qualify under the Soil Association guidelines.

Richard Young, from Kite's Nest farm, was then deputy director of British Organic Farmers, and number two at the Soil Association. He was asked to come to London to give them some advice, but told not to talk to anyone about it. Silverman wanted Richard to give the organic movement's seal of approval to a non-organic farming regime, and had drawn up detailed standards which allowed the use of chemicals. Richard flicked through a weighty volume Silverman put on the table in front of him and told him there was no chance of this being accepted. It completely missed the point of organic farming. Silverman then showed him a Code of Practice for free-range lamb production.

The draft, drawn up by Silverman, was a masterpiece of writing, with reassuring phrases about sustainability and the environment, but nothing of any real substance. Young asked whether he might consult Patrick Holden, director of the Soil Association, or Lawrence Woodward of the Elm Farm Research Centre, and was told he couldn't consult anyone: the project had to be confidential. It was only when Young protested that he was told he could discuss the broad principles with Patrick and Lawrence, but he was not to show them the Code of Practice. His instinct was to write, 'This is crap – an appalling dilution of organic standards'; but having the clear impression that the Prince wanted this code to be approved, Richard sat down and wrote a seven-page diplomatic critique of the draft. His major criticism was that it allowed the use of nitrogen fertiliser. It banned pesticides, which sounded good, but the sort they were banning, namely insecticides, were rarely used on grassland in that area anyway, while herbicides, which were used, were to be allowed. He then wrote a second letter putting his reservations more forcefully: the code was not acceptable to the organic movement, it would create big problems for the movement, and it would not achieve what the Prince wanted in terms of sustainable production.

'I think I had been identified,' said Richard, 'as someone who was a bit naïve and sufficiently involved with the organic movement to carry some weight, but not so involved that I was battle-hardened like Patrick, who would have seen through it straightaway.'

David Landale was on the telephone to Young at 7.30 a.m. to say that things now had to be done in a great hurry, and that he was sending Silverman to visit him at Kite's Nest. Silverman arrived in a Rolls Royce on 17 December 1990. Thinking he had been sent by the Prince, the Young family entertained him politely. Silverman wanted approval for the Duchy lamb initiative, and would not take no for an answer. In the end, Richard agreed to sign a hand-written statement, drafted in front of him, which said he would give limited backing to the scheme – his 'broad sympathy' – subject to a number of conditions being satisfied.

The Young family did not take to Silverman. They put up with him because they believed the Prince had sent him. During the course of his visit, Silverman twice said that he was worried the Queen would abdicate, which would be hopeless because once the Prince of Wales became King, he would no longer be able to use him in this way. He said this in a very direct manner, with a lot of impatience and nervous energy. Richard had the impression he was dealing with someone who was single-mindedly intent on exploiting the Prince of Wales's concern about the environment and animal welfare in an unpleasant and mercenary way.

He also felt within minutes of Silverman leaving that he had made a terrible mistake in signing the statement of support. Silverman, he felt, had used every trick to win his confidence and allay his concerns. He rang Silverman as soon as he arrived back in London that evening and told him he had had a change of heart. Silverman was not at all pleased and said he had already spoken to the Prince of Wales and everything was going ahead.

It was only at this point that Young broke his vow of silence and sent a fax to Richard Aylard, who unfortunately was in the Gulf at the time and didn't see the note for some days. Aylard was appalled when he read what had been going on, as was the Prince. Charles was furious that his name was being used in this way, and telephoned Richard Young to say how uneasy he was about the scheme, and that he shared all his reservations. He assured Richard that it would be dropped.

A few weeks later, Richard Young happened to be having lunch at Highgrove with the Prince and a group of people, including Patrick Holden. The Prince sought them both out. 'I can't get out of it,' he said with pent-up frustration. 'It's gone too far down the road.' The argument from Silverman that he had been presented with – which had not pleased him one jot – was that because of his initial support for the idea, the Duchy tenants had invested such time and energy, as well as money in starting to modify production, that it would cause major problems if the Prince pulled out. This was not entirely true: many Duchy tenants were extremely unhappy. They bitterly resented being presented with a set of guidelines telling them how to farm by 'a blue-suited bugger from London', as one referred to Silverman.

'Prince sells 3,000 stress-free lambs, humanely reared on a vegetarian diet from his own Good Life farm' was the story in the *Today* newspaper as the first lamb hit Tesco's shelves in March 1991, shortly after the Prince had made another big speech about organic farming; 'Baa Royal Appointment', the headline. Although the labels did not make any false claims, the link between the Prince of Wales and organic production was already established in the public's mind.

The farming press was quick to react. 'The Prince of Wales's Duchy of Cornwall Estate is trying to pull the wool over consumers' eyes with marketing gimmicks that could lead people to believe Duchy lamb is produced organically,' said *Farming News*, under the headline 'Royal woolly lamb fools buyers'. Use of his crest was giving the Duchy a fifteen per cent premium for the lamb.

'Real organic farmers are livid. It is unfortunate that Tesco has begun marketing the Duchy lamb so soon after the Prince's speech on organic farming last week,' said British Organic Farmers' chairman Bill Starling. The Prince had delivered a major speech to the Royal Agricultural Society of England in which he called for wholesale reform of farming methods and better labelling of foods.

After some heated debate at Highgrove, the Soil Association managed to convince the Duchy that there was a serious problem in labelling this product 'Duchy Lamb'. It was stopped. The meat thereafter was known as Cornwall Quality Lamb, and later still, West Country Lamb.

The Prince was still convinced that the basic idea had been good. It was a question of finding the right way of making it happen. It was John Lister who runs Shipton Mill, a couple of miles down the road from Highgrove, who came up with the answer. He suddenly said to David Wilson one day, 'I think I could make a biscuit with your oats.' David Wilson presented the idea at a management committee, and the Prince snapped it up.

The Duchy was not so enthusiastic, but after a certain amount of argument, Guy Salter, the Prince's then assistant private secretary with the business brief, was given the go-ahead to develop a product. Salter was a maverick who didn't obey the rules, and was dangerously cavalier in using the Prince's name, but much liked by the Prince. He had useful connections in the media and was good company. He also had extraordinary energy and a capacity to make things happen. It was he who set up the Prince of Wales's Business Leaders Forum, through which Business in the Community ideals were extended into a global context. He organised a highly successful conference, which involved getting the Prince of Wales, plus 200 business leaders, their wives and luggage, to Charleston, South Carolina, just eight weeks after a fearsome hurricane had all but flattened the town. He was one of a rare breed of 'can do' men who have passed through the Prince's office, who brooked no opposition. When told there were no longer any tiles on the roofs in Charlston, he said, 'Well get some,' and when told that the Prince could no longer stay in the very large beautiful house that Salter had found for him, because the garden had disappeared, he said, 'Well just deliver 4,000 tons of top-soil plus some cactuses by Tuesday and I don't want to hear any more nonsense about this.' After that, developing a biscuit was child's play.

Knowing that the key to success was not what you know but who, he immediately brought in some experts to develop the idea of Duchy Originals. What the Prince liked about the idea was three-fold: use of his name would give added value to Duchy produce and help his tenant farmers, it would encourage his tenants to go properly organic by providing an outlet for their produce, for which the market would pay a premium, and by running the company as a charitable trust, it would make money for his charities. Unlike Richard Aylard, who had a tendency to go for the less high profile characters, Salter went straight to the top. He recruited the head of the country's leading advertising agency and the head of the country's leading market research company to form the Duchy Marketing Advisory Group, chaired by Keith Holloway of Grand Metropolitan. The group then recruited Chris Nadin, a secondment from Grand Met, to run the business. Things couldn't have been going better. The first product was an oaten biscuit, made with organic oats, mostly from the farm, milled at Shipton. It went on sale in 300 independent retail outlets in 1993, and a year later, that number had doubled. The result was stupendous. Most people who tasted it agreed it was a delicious biscuit. Then followed a ginger biscuit, equally good, apart from a few minor setbacks with shelf-life, and Duchy organic bread. The future looked promising.

Then Nadin left, his secondment over, and was replaced by Mike Cornish, marketing manager of VW-Audi, who was of a much more conventional mould. He knew nothing about organics but a great deal about marketing. If the business was going to make real money, he said, it needed volume, and since there wasn't enough organic produce available to create volume with the biscuits and the bread, he struck a deal, first mooted by his predecessor, with Coca-Cola Schweppes bottling to produce a range of fizzy drinks. Before anyone had really caught up with what was happening, Coca-Cola Schweppes was churning out more fizzy drinks than anyone could possibly handle or sell. They were a disaster. There was nothing organic about the drinks, and most people thought they tasted like cough mixture. Furthermore, so that they could have some tenuous claim to the Duchy label, estate workers had to pick elder flowers from the farm, which amounted to no more than two per cent of the drinks' ingredients, and could have been bought dried, for a fraction of the cost, from the Eastern Bloc with a much stronger aroma than they were able to produce by improvising a drying system in the grain store.

For a while the drinks traded on the integrity of the biscuits, but it didn't last. By 1996 the business was in a parlous state. It had accumulated huge overheads, and spent a lot of money developing products, which it never recouped. In six years of trading it had lost £373,180 and reached the point where it either had to stop trading entirely, or expand at speed so that it made money quickly.

In 1996 the Prince thought he had found the person who could rescue Duchy Originals from the mess it had got itself into – the latest in a long line of people who he hoped might provide the answer to the problems that none of his advisers seemed able to do. Sue Townsend was a marketing wizard, who had had great success with Crabtree & Evelyn, the up-market toiletries and jam firm, which she co-founded. He had met her through Robert Kime, the interior designer who had redecorated Highgrove after the separation. She was an engaging blonde, with lots of energy, a husky voice and plenty of charm, which the Prince immediately fell for. He announced that he wanted her to take over Duchy Originals and, although her references were not encouraging for this particular job, the Prince didn't care and was deaf to advice; he was adamant she should be appointed.

Like her predecessor, Townsend knew nothing about organics, although she went to the Home Farm often to glad-hand and talk to visitors. She appeared to be more interested in the garden at Highgrove and in the domestic arrangements than in the produce she was marketing. She worked slavishly for the bottom line, and had a good eye for an appealing image, introducing smart designs to all the packaging, but she set about it in a way that irritated almost everyone with whom she had dealings. The direct access she enjoyed to the Prince caused jealousies, and she created extra work throughout the Duchy, the gardens and the house. She failed to appreciate that the Prince of Wales was not like any other commodity or brand name that could be prettily packaged and sold in bulk for maximum profit. The departure into fizzy drinks had started the compromise, but Sue Townsend went further and introduced a whole range of products which had no pretence to be organic in any way. They included soap, bath oil, perfume, chocolates, tea – twenty-three products in all, and most of them made by well-known conventional companies, like Crabtree & Evelyn, Fortnum & Mason and Floris. Even the pork sausages and jams were no different from any other you could buy in an upmarket food shop. All that was different was the label and the price.

The labels did not make any claim to be organic, so there was no suggestion of any deception. Nevertheless, for the last ten years the Prince of Wales had been widely viewed as a champion of the organic movement, and consumers seeing a Duchy Original product could have been forgiven for assuming that it would be organic. Even the biscuits, which once *were* organic, were no longer. Yet they were still being sold in what was basically the same packaging. All that had changed was the wording, which consumers who had been buying the biscuits from the beginning would have been unlikely to notice.

The situation was causing great nervousness all round, not least at the Soil Association, but Sue Townsend's position seemed unassailable, until a meeting at Highgrove in the summer of 1997. The Prince was confronted by all the big names in the organic movement who all told him that Duchy Originals was heading for catastrophe, and would take the Prince with it, if it was allowed to continue on its present course. Sue Townsend stoutly defended herself, but in so doing made it clear that her commitment to marketing and developing the image of Duchy Originals took precedence over the product pedigree and organic integrity of the production system. 'There was blood on the carpet that day,' said one of the participants, 'but it wasn't arterial.'

At the next meeting a couple of months later, it was. Sue Townsend had a set-to with Helen Browning, chairman of the Soil Association, which was said to have been 'like putting a couple of cats into a cardboard box'. In the heat of the moment, Townsend accused organic farmers of being 'a bunch of hillbillies' – not the most sensible remark to make in front of the Prince of Hillbillies himself. 'It was a watershed meeting,' is the deliberate under-statement of one of those present. The Prince recognised that the situation could not continue, and Sue Townsend departed as swiftly as she had arrived. She was replaced by her deputy, Fiona Gately, and in January 1998 Guy McCracken, a senior if unexciting director of Marks & Spencer, was hired as non-executive chairman, charged with the task of trying to restore the company's integrity.

Patrick Holden, who has watched in dismay the rise and fall of Duchy Originals, has every sympathy. 'It was a brilliant aspiration, and he was exactly right to create the company in the first place,' he says. 'What went wrong was the people running the company were tempted by the commercial element, because they were wanting to create profit for the Prince's Trust and run a viable business. And they were right: all their training, their mindsets, said volume equals profit. You can't make profit instantly on tiny volumes of expensive, high integrity product. Where they were wrong was compromising the story, which is the essence of what it's all about. In the long run it would be an own goal, because ultimately you lose the trust of the consumer and the mechanism for that is exposed by journalists.'

It was what they all feared could happen at any time, but it wasn't until January 1998, ironically the very month that Guy McCracken arrived to put things right, that Sheila Dillon, producer of Radio 4's 'Food Programme', who had been such an admirer of the project when it first began, could stand her disillusion no longer.

Food writer Henrietta Green, amongst others, was interviewed.

'When Duchy Originals was founded in 1990,' she said, 'I, and I think lots of other people, got very excited about it because what it was setting out to do was very, very different. It was unique. It was all about sustainable farming and linking the farmer right the way through to the product. And also, I think one of the intentions, although perhaps they didn't express it, was to use themselves as a model, so that other farmers could see how it could be done, how they too could get into a niche market. And I think it's fair to say that over the years they have, well, perhaps, drifted a little from their intention to ... what they have ended up with now is, in essence, no more than a range of gift foods.

'Prettily packaged, taste good, fine. But they've just been brought in from other manufacturers, other producers. Nothing particularly interesting about them. I mean, take, say, Ackermans chocolates. Well, Ackermans chocolates do very nicely, thank you ... What is there about these chocolates that could possibly help the British farming community? I mean, the cocoa solids are imported, the orange flavours ... Similarly, what's satsuma marmalade got to do with the British farmer? What have fine teas blended by Taylors of Harrogate?...'

As the presenter, Derek Cooper, commented, 'Even more depressingly, in the last eight years, only two Duchy farmers have gone organic.'

The whole sorry saga of Duchy Originals was typical of so many of the Prince's good ideas. His interest is just as keen as it ever was, his principles are intact and he is just as radical as he ever was, but he allows himself to be led by anyone whose star is currently in the ascendant.

Nonetheless, as Patrick Holden is the first to acknowledge, Charles's influence on the organic movement cannot be overstated. He helped make organic farming respectable, and his involvement has persuaded a lot of influential people to take it more seriously than they would otherwise have done. Organic production in Britain is still smaller than in any other country in Europe – about 1,000 farms account for 0.4 per cent of total production – and consumer demand is far greater and growing all the time. The people who once mocked the organic movement are now queuing up at their local supermarket to pay over the odds for chemical-free food. Conventional farmers, who have been propping up the agro-chemical industry for years, are seeing that organics are good business, and are busy converting. Organic production is likely be up to two per cent by the millennium.

Charles has been most powerful in the work he does behind the scenes, bringing together people who would not normally meet, very often people of opposing views, and exerting gentle pressure on government. It is the way he operates in all his areas of interest. One of his concerns is 'greening' the Common Agricultural Policy. To this end a seminar was organised in Brussels in October 1996 for seventy-five people, including both agricultural and environment commissioners, and five people from each member state, which the Prince attended. He spent a morning listening to the debate, spoke himself, and hosted a dinner. At Sandringham he has hosted three seminars for environmentalists, organic and conventional farmers, to try and move farming in a greener direction.

But there is still work to be done, and anyone who thinks that the Prince of Wales has lost his campaigning edge is mistaken. The latest danger in the environmental world is the encroachment of genetically modified crops, which threaten the very heart of sustainable agriculture. They are plants which have been given genes from bacteria, which make them resistant to a broad-spectrum weed-killer, available from the manufacturer that supplies the GM seed. When the crop is sprayed with this weed-killer, every other plant in the field is killed. The result is an essentially sterile field, providing neither food nor habitat for wildlife. More frightening yet, these crops are capable of interbreeding with their wild relatives, creating new weeds with built-in resistance to weed-killer. They have also been found to have spread more than a mile away from their own field, which poses a threat to other methods of farming, both conventional and organic. GM production is owned by half a dozen giant multi-national companies, and if things continue unchallenged, within ten years everyone's staple food, whether they like it or not, will come from genetically engineered plants.

Since 1995, the Prince has chosen to write newspaper and magazine articles on matters of importance as a safer way of communicating his thoughts and ideas than via speeches, where he was prone to being quoted out of context. Genetic modification had been a concern for some years and it was a question of firding the right moment to launch an attack. The moment was deemed right in June 1998, and the *Daily Telegraph* carried a powerful leader-page piece calling for a moment's pause to consider the consequences of crops that take 'mankind into realms that belong to God, and to God alone. Apart from certain highly beneficial and specific medical applications, do we have the right to experiment with, and commercialise, the building blocks of life? We live in an age of rights – it seems to me that it is time our Creator had some rights too.'

FOURTEEN

The Prince's People

'I wouldn't go on advising him if I didn't think he
was doing very, very important work.'
Adviser to the Prince of Wales

In October 1993 Charles's cousin, Viscount Linley, married. The Prince was entertaining a group of overseas businessmen, called British Invisibles, on board *Britannia*, in an attempt to drum up trade abroad. The appointment had been fixed at a programme meeting before the Linleys even announced their engagement, let alone the date of their wedding. He was going to have to miss the church service, because he couldn't be back in England in time, but would make it to the reception. It would have to be a life or death situation for the Prince to let down someone who had been expecting him. James Whitaker, then writing for the *Mirror*, decided this was nonsense; the real reason he wouldn't be at the wedding was because he couldn't bear to be seen near an altar with the Princess of Wales.

'This is total crap, James,' said Sandy Henney, as she patiently explained the chronology. 'You would be the first to bark if he said, "Sod the country, I'm going to a family wedding."'

The next day the front-page story in the *Mirror* was all about the Prince not wanting to be seen in church with Diana.

In July 1994 the crescendo of his twenty-five years as Prince of Wales celebrations was a return to Caernarvon Castle, where Charles had been invested by the Queen in 1969. There he had won the hearts of millions of Welsh people, not all of whom were pleased to have an English prince foisted on them, by taking the trouble to learn the language and giving the Loyal Address in a mixture of English and Welsh. He had returned in 1981 to present his new bride on their first tour together. The Welsh people once again fell in love, this time with Diana. In July 1994, just a month after the Dimbleby film, in which he had admitted being unfaithful in his marriage, there was no certainty the visit would go so well. In fact, *Daily Mail* readers the following day were given the impression that the Prince was very badly snubbed when the paper published a photograph with a small gathering of people behind a police barricade and the headline, 'Welsh stay away in their droves'. According to the article, between 200 and 300 people had turned up. According to the police, an estimated 5,000 were there – so many people that they had to mobilise their strategic reserve for crowd control.

It was the kind of negative press coverage that drove the Prince to distraction.

More damaging yet were sensational revelations in the *News of the World* by Ken Stronach, the Prince's valet for fifteen years, about the Prince's affair with Camilla Parker Bowles. Stronach was tricked into selling his story, although, in the end, he never received any payment. The newspaper had first contacted his son, also named Ken, who persuaded his father to come with him to meet a reporter from the *News of the World* in a pub. With a bit of encouragement and a few drinks inside him, Stronach began to talk, but the following day he had decided he was not interested in saying anything for the record or for any money. Neither he nor his son had realised that the reporter had a tape recorder hidden during their conversation which had picked up everything.

The *News of the World* was not slow to point out the tricky situation he was in. It was going to publish the material it had whatever Stronach's views on the matter. He was trapped, so when the newspaper asked for photographs too, he obliged.

The story ran under the headline, 'Charles Bedded Camilla As Diana Slept Upstairs', with photographs he had taken himself in the Prince's bedroom. It was as damaging as it could possibly be, particularly given the timing. The newspaper had had the story for some time, but sat on it until the Parker Bowles's divorce was announced in January 1995, when it was guaranteed maximum impact.

In the wake of this, an informal media advisory group was set up chaired by Richard Aylard, with Alan Kilkenny, the PR consultant, Jonathan Dimbleby, Allan Percival and Sandy Henney from the press office, and Stephen Lamport, Aylard's assistant, to discuss ways of improving the situation. Everyone agreed that their strongest asset was the Prince himself. No one who meets him face to face is ever unimpressed. So, in the absence of sympathetic media coverage, why not go on the offensive and invite opinion formers down to Highgrove to meet the Prince and get to know him in a social context? There could be newspaper editors amongst those chosen, MPs, and influential people in all his fields of interest, like medicine, architecture, farming and business. But the real problem he faced, they all acknowledged, was the incompatibility of being both heir to the throne and a public figure in a media age.

Some months later a larger and more formal Media Advisory Group was set up at Matthew Butler's suggestion, to discuss how to put over more effectively what the Prince did. The group included people like Charles Allen, head of the Granada Media Group, a number of eminent journalists, several leading PR consultants, including Alan Kilkenny, Simon Mayo, the Radio One disc jockey, also Tom Shebbeare from the Prince's Trust, Julia Cleverdon from BitC, and Richard Aylard.

The first meeting was hugely invigorating and professional, and produced a number of good ideas and observations – also questions, which Matthew Butler undertook to convey to the Prince for feed-back to the Group. He duly sent the Prince a memo detailing the meeting, which the Prince annotated liberally, clearly enthused by some of the ideas.

The Group never got to see the Prince's notes. Matthew was on the point of circulating them but was stopped by Richard. As a result, with no feedback from the Prince, the second meeting proved to be a complete waste of time, and a significant part of Aylard's downfall. In the months when he was working on the Prince's divorce settlement, plus coping with the normal office load and the collapse of his own marriage, his behaviour became increasingly puzzling. 'It was a terrible existence, poor chap,' says one of his former colleagues, 'and because he couldn't share a lot of the stuff with anyone else – the stuff he was dealing with ten hours a day, when he was locked in with the solicitors – I think he got into a mindset that spilt over into nobody could know anything else either.'

It became clear as a result of that second meeting that Aylard wanted to keep aspects of the Prince to himself. He felt that the private Prince and the Prince who was heir to the throne was his responsibility, and wanted the Group to concern itself with the Prince's charitable activities and nothing else. 'But don't let's forget,' he said, 'that there are two quite separate Princes here. The Prince I am dealing with, and the Prince's Trust Prince.'

The Group pointed out that they couldn't be marketing two separate Princes. As one of them said, 'Richard saw this as a bit of a threat and the issue really was, are we going to have someone who, however talented and devoted to the Prince, is going to do all of this on his own? Or are we going to have someone who's a bit more of a team player with a single message coming out? Richard wasn't very good at working with other people and, when things went wrong, he got in his bunker and managed as best he could on his own. These people, some of whom were quite distinguished, clearly wanted it to be done in a different way.' Their voices joined the chorus that was already telling the Prince it was time for Aylard to go.

Another voice in the chorus was Camilla's divorce lawyer, Hilary Browne-Wilkinson, who had become a good friend. More significantly, she had a suggestion about who might strengthen the team. Over dinner at St James's Palace she judiciously brought the subject up while Aylard was present.

Also at the table were Hilary's husband, Law Lord Nico Browne-Wilkinson, and former Head of the Bar Council, Lord Alexander, and his wife, Marie. The party had reached the coffee without anyone saying anything very alarming, when Lord Browne-Wilkinson cleared his throat and launched into a fearsome attack on the way the Prince's staff had handled the media and the legal profession's collective view that the situation could not be worse, nor more damaging for the monarchy. As the man responsible for the office, Richard Aylard found himself in an uncomfortable position.

Hilary Browne-Wilkinson was also on the board of the Press Complaint's Commission, and therefore probably knew better than most how St James's was regarded by the press.

'Have you come across a man called Mark Bolland?' she asked. 'He works for the Press Complaints Commission,' and proceeded to describe this Canadian-born, comprehensive-school educated, bright, entertaining thirty-year-old from Middlesbrough, who had been director of the PCC for the last five years. 'You should hire him,' she said, 'and see if he can do anything to help.'

The Prince leapt at the suggestion, said he must have him at once, and would arrange a meeting. Here was a new wonder man who would solve all his problems.

Sure enough, a couple of days later Aylard invited Bolland to lunch and offered him a job as Sandy Henney's assistant, on terms which Bolland thought rather peculiar for an assistant press secretary. He had been warned the job he would be offered would be 'crap' but had been told to take it; there would be better things to come. He accepted.

Soon afterwards he was following Richard Aylard up the stairs at St James's Palace on his way to meet the Prince, when they bumped into Allan Percival, who was then press secretary. 'Oh, Allan,' said Aylard, 'this is Mark Bolland. We've just offered him a job in the press office.' Neither Percival nor Henney had been told of Bolland's appointment. Sensing what was coming, Percival opted for a post in Downing Street.

'I've heard lots of rumours about you from people,' said the Prince to Bolland. 'If you could bear to do this ...'

Bolland said that he could certainly bear to do the job; what is more, he intended to have some fun doing it. 'If you don't have fun in a job, there's no point in it,' he said. 'It doesn't all need to be so terrible. Things can get better.'

'If you say so,' said the Prince.

'Well, I do, actually.'

The two men struck an instant rapport and in July 1996 he took up his unlikely and lowly post in the press office, where he spent his first month poring over the file on Dimbleby, reading all the notes and memos, wanting to understand how it had all come about, and taking calls from the Prince, which he enjoyed. Whilst not being the greatest admirer of Aylard, and believing Dimbleby to have been a mistake – easier with the benefit of hindsight – he acknowledges that 'Richard became a lightning rod for quite a lot that was wrong.'

It soon became obvious that Richard Aylard and Mark Bolland could not continue in tandem. While Stephen Lamport, who was then Aylard's deputy, Mark Bolland and Colin Trimming, the Prince's protection officer, were on a recce to Central Asia, a plot was hatched to remove Aylard. The Prince had to be the one to tell Aylard to go, however. This was one conversation he could not duck or pass on to someone else. He did it in a typically clumsy way, at the end of a week's fishing on the Duchess of Westminster's Scottish estate, Lochmore. He was deeply fond of Richard and knew the conversation would be more painful than he could bear, and had postponed it all week. As one observer said philosophically, 'Richard is a classic case of that S-Level cliché: "The victims always get a bad press because the victors write the history books".'

Apart from Sir James Mellon's reminder that if the worst came to the worst he could go back to his well-paid job in PR, the other good piece of advice that Matthew Butler was given on joining the Prince's office in July 1993 came from Robert Fraser, the equerry, who had been in the job a while. Matthew was off for a fortnight to Birkhall, one of the Queen Mother's homes on the Balmoral estate, which was regarded as one of the best parts of the job. The five people in the office did a two-week stint each, staying in a little cottage on the estate.

'The Prince will ask you to go and have dinner with him most nights,' said Fraser. 'He will say, "Oh, you will come for dinner, won't you?" My advice is to plead a previous engagement, because he's only doing it out of old-fashioned courtesy. He's there with his friends and doesn't really want someone from the office there. Do it once, but otherwise stay clear.'

It is a shame for Richard Aylard that he was never given the same advice. Although he would say he never presumed upon a friendship with the Prince of Wales, he became so close over the seven years he worked for him that, to everyone who watched the relationship at first hand, it seemed almost symbiotic. Aylard gave one hundred and ten per cent of himself and his time to the Prince, and in the end it cost him his job, and his marriage.

He worked long hours, and was with the Prince over many weekends as well, sometimes fishing or shooting with him, but there was scarcely a day when the Prince would not do some work at some point. Whatever recreation he is engaged in, whether fishing, painting, gardening, or even reading a book, his mind never stops. As an idea occurs or a worry clouds his day, he wants someone to bounce it off. He is also a great writer of memos. If he has a sudden thought, or notices something he's not happy about, or decides there's someone he ought to see who might be able to help solve a problem or raise some money, he commits it to paper for his private secretary to action. There are even memos from the Prince dated 25 December, written from Sandringham, the one date in the year when perhaps even the Prince thought twice about telephoning.

If ever there were three people in a marriage, it was in Richard Aylard's. Because the Prince never stops working himself, it doesn't occur to him that his staff might need a break, and unless something is pointed out to him, he is curiously blind to what is going on in other people's lives. The Princess was always very acute at picking up vibrations from the people around her, and solicitous for their well-being. Once alerted, the Prince could not be more concerned, but his antennae are poor. For all the time spent together, and the obvious closeness, the Prince was unaware that his private secretary's home life was in serious difficulty. Aylard had two young children at home and a wife who had suffered severe post-natal depression, whom he seldom saw. She lived in Surrey, and he lived in a grace-and-favour apartment at Kensington Palace. On the rare occasions when he was at home, he would be interrupted by the telephone. It was not the formula for a happy marriage.

'I don't know what I would do without Richard,' the Prince said to Belinda Harley, an assistant private secretary, one day. 'He's helping me so much through this difficult situation.'

'Yes, sir,' said Belinda, 'and it's difficult for Richard, as you probably know. His own marriage is in difficulty at the moment as well, so he's getting it at home as well as at work.'

'I had no idea,' said the Prince. 'Why didn't anyone tell me?'

The following morning Aylard came storming into the office. 'Well, thank you very much, Belinda,' he said. 'Thanks to you, the Prince was on the phone from a quarter past ten until midnight last night sympathising with me.' Though he feigned anger, he was clearly quite touched.

Everyone who has worked for the Prince has experienced the pressure. He is demanding and if allowed will take over every waking hour. Whether others were more determined, or simply more successful than Aylard in making sure they kept a life for themselves, it is difficult to know. There is no doubt Aylard saw the Prince through infinitely more difficult times than any other private secretary, and perhaps felt that he needed the extra support. He was with him when Andrew Morton's book came out, he was with him through both the Squidgy and Camillagate tapes, and the 'Panorama' interview, and he was with him through the painful process of separation, and divorce – times when the Prince was desperately low, and his confidence all but gone. There were days when it took a real effort to motivate him, and Richard gave his life over to keeping the Prince going.

He was also with the Prince in Klosters on 10 March 1988, when his friend Major Hugh Lindsay was killed by an avalanche, which must rank as one of the very worst days in the Prince's life. Nothing since the death of Lord Mountbatten had distressed him more. Hugh Lindsay had been his guest, he was newly married and his wife, Sarah, who worked in the press office at Buckingham Palace, was pregnant with their first child. They had been skiing off-piste, down a particularly difficult run known as the Wang, which runs below the Gotschivagrat cable car. They were skiing with Charlie and Patti Palmer-Tomkinson and a local guide called Bruno Sprecher. Fergie had fallen and hurt herself that morning, and Diana had stayed behind with her in the chalet. As the party paused at the top of a steep and narrow gully, there was suddenly a great roar, a noise the Prince has never forgotten, and they looked up to see giant blocks of snow tumbling down the mountain towards them at terrifying speed. The guide shouted 'Jump!' and, trained to move when he is told, the Prince jumped, escaping death by no more than a couple of seconds. Patti had been caught under the falling wall of snow. She had appalling injuries and was initially thought unlikely to live, or at least unlikely to recover fully. It took many months and countless operations but, miraculously, not only did she recover, she was able to ski again. Hugh Lindsay was not so lucky.

The Prince blamed himself for his friend's death, even though he was in no way responsible. Everyone understood the risks they were taking in skiing off-piste. The situation was not helped by the media, which blamed him too. The *Sun*'s headline read, 'ACCUSED. Official: Charles DID cause the killer avalanche'. There were stories that the Prince had led the party down a 'closed' run, despite warning signs to stay away, and had thereby triggered the avalanche. An official enquiry, however, found him in no way culpable: the run was not closed, and there were no warning signs.

Sarah Lindsay, whose baby, Alice, was born two months later, went through some very black times after Hugh's death, but amongst the welter of support and kindness from friends and strangers alike, both the Prince and Princess were memorable. She was desperate for details of what precisely had happened, what precise time he had died, how he must have felt as he looked up and saw the avalanche, and Charles talked to her endlessly. Unlike so many people who tried to avoid mentioning Hugh's name, Charles understood Sarah's need to talk about him. It was important to her to know that wherever he was, he was all right, which he also understood. She tried mediums and automatic writers, who claim to write what they are instructed from the spirit world, and the Prince suggested a number of people who could help her, including Mervyn Stockwood, the former Bishop of Southwark, who put her on to the Institute of Psychic Studies. Diana's support was even more exceptional. For three years after Hugh's death, she telephoned Sarah every Sunday night or Monday morning, which were always difficult times; and on Alice's first birthday, she invited her to Kensington Palace, where they had a birthday cake with the boys.

The Princess told Sarah she would never go back to Klosters, and she kept her word. The Prince, however, has been back many times, and was accused by the media of great insensitivity. But he has never been there since without thinking of Hugh Lindsay. As Patti Palmer-Tomkinson explained, 'We all agreed that we would never go anywhere else ... It would have been like turning our back on him and leaving him there. We can't ski together, the three of us, without remembering Hugh.'

The Klosters disaster happened soon after Richard Aylard had become assistant private secretary, and a bond was formed in the mountains, and an understanding and admiration for the Prince, which never diminished. Although from quite different back-grounds, they shared a lot of common interests. Aylard was sympa-thetic to all the Prince's ideas and ideals, and keen to push forward and find ways of achieving what the Prince wanted. What he lacked was confidence. He was deluged with work, which he refused to delegate, and tried to handle himself. There was pressure coming from every direction. He even had a furious telephone call from Tiggy Legge-Bourke's father blasting him because his daughter was always in the newspapers, but resisted the temptation to say she was in the newspapers because she did such stupid things. The more he did, the more the Prince asked for, and Richard found it difficult to say 'No.' Meanwhile, all semblance of a home life, or any other kind of life, disappeared.

To others watching the relationship develop, watching the hours he put into the job, and knowing about the tensions at home, it was clear that the situation was going to end in disaster. Julia Cleverdon discussed her fears with John Riddell. 'This is awful,' she said; 'you must stop him working like this or he's going to ruin another marriage.'

Riddell looked at Julia in complete astonishment and said, 'Of course he will. Everything he does has to be one hundred and ten per cent dedicated to the Prince, so of course he will. It's quite impossible. That's what will happen.' Sure enough it did. He subsequently went through a very acrimonious divorce.

By 1996 he had been fatally wounded by the Dimbleby exercise, and, although he was the last person to see it, his days as the Prince's right hand man were numbered. The all-powerful friends thought the Prince had been wrong to confess adultery and blamed Aylard. He might have survived the initial furore, but too many things followed that kept reminding them all about the fatal question, and St James's Palace constantly seemed to be caught on the wrong foot. It was a period of intense fire fighting, with the media perpetually having the upper hand. As horror heaped on horror and the Prince's popularity plummeted, his friends all said it would never have happened if it hadn't been for Aylard. Gradually their influence chipped away the Prince's confidence in his trusted private secretary and, exposing his own fundamental weakness, he gave in to them. He knew that it was not fair, and he knew that Aylard had served him loyally and well, and helped him get through the most traumatic years of his life, up to and including sorting out his impenetrable divorce settlement. Yet he bowed to pressure and agreed he had to go. He is now, however, working as an environmental consultant to the Prince and is happily remarried.

Stephen Lamport was asked to take over as private secretary, and Mark Bolland was pulled out from under the cloak as his deputy. Bolland is an immensely charming but dangerous man, another maverick, whom the Prince finds stimulating and fun to have around. Bolland creates as many enemies as friends, and has caused havoc in St James's Palace, and suspicion at Buckingham Palace. He places stories in the press which unnerve his colleagues, but he is a skilled operator and, after five years at the PCC, his contacts in Fleet Street are second to none. He has built on the work done by Alan Kilkenny in making Camilla acceptable to the British public. And it is a measure of their joint success that just nine months after Diana's death a story which appeared in the *Sun* that Camilla was spending nights with the Prince at St James's Palace scarcely raised an eyebrow.

Stephen Lamport had been in the Prince's office since 1993, and as a much more traditional courtier, was a good antidote to Bolland. Educated at Winchester and Cambridge, he arrived at St James's from the Foreign Office, where he had worked for Douglas Hurd when he was Foreign Secretary. He took over foreign tours and the architectural brief from Peter Westmacott. He is highly orthodox, cautious and discreet. Where Bolland is prepared to stick his neck out, Lamport is loath to take decisions, as a colleague says, 'lest the gun-boats come over the hill'. Bolland makes decisions then worries about how he's going to break the news of what he has done to the Boss. Recently, Bolland presented the Prince with a *fait accompli* that he wasn't overjoyed by. The *Sun* newspaper had agreed to sell prints of a watercolour he had painted on a trip to Bhutan in 1998, and in return promised to make a £50,000 donation to a local charity running a home for girls rescued from prostitution, which the Prince had been impressed by during a visit there. Believing the *Sun* to be a rag from the lower reaches of the tabloid sewer, the Prince was deeply reluctant, and the marmalade wasn't the only thing that flew on the morning he was told, but since no other newspaper was prepared to pay the money, his private secretary was insistent. The money was raised, but his friends would say at what price? He shouldn't have had to go begging to a newspaper which had caused him such torment with intrusive and negative coverage of his marriage.

Lamport has a first class brain, but is generally thought a bit rarefied. 'Take him a completely insoluble, knotty problem,' say colleagues, 'and he will think a way through it.' Bolland is very clever, and he's the one you go to if you really want to know what the Prince thinks and what is going on. Lamport is tougher than he looks and is more than happy to play the nice guy while Bolland attracts the flak; and while Bolland may not be the most reverent man on earth, nor the closest timekeeper, nor even the best keeper of appointments or returner of phone calls, he has not yet put a foot wrong as far as the Prince is concerned. He gets on famously with the Prince's women friends; he loves intrigue, lunches regularly at the Caprice, drinks Champagne with enthusiasm, has friends in high places – including Lord Wakeham, chairman of the Press Complaints Commission, and Peter Mandelson, Secretary of State for Trade and Industry – and is, as he promised the Prince he would, having the greatest fun.

There are people who predict Mark Bolland is riding for a fall, and many more who will enjoy watching it happen – a few of them across the road at Buckingham Palace – but the Prince is entranced; he enjoys his company, recognises that he has been good for his public image, and believes that he has finally found the man who can solve his problems. He came in at a time when the Prince needed above all to have his confidence and his courage restored – emotional needs, for which Bolland, with his exuberant manner and reassuring optimism, was well suited.

Whatever the manner of Richard Aylard's departure, it was time for a change, as with hindsight he would be the first to admit. Seven years was too long and he had become so involved that he had lost his sense of perspective. Inevitably he was also tarred with the brush of the most difficult days of the past, when nothing that came out of the press office could be believed. No matter what he did, the situation was not going to change until the man at the helm changed. His departure and the arrival of a new team sent powerful signals to the outside world that, post-divorce, this was a brand new beginning for the Prince of Wales. It also sent signals to the team in St James's Palace, where from the dark days of bunker mentality, three emotions prevailed: a hatred of the media, a hatred of Camilla Parker Bowles, and a hatred of the Princess of Wales, who terrified most people in the office.

Bolland's attitude was that if Mrs Parker Bowles was a non-negotiable fixture in the Prince's life, which she clearly was, then a way had to be found of making her acceptable to the British public. As for the Princess, he rather liked her. Despite her divorce from the Prince, she still took a lively interest in his office, and she had been to inspect the new recruit on his third day and invited him for tea, to try and establish whether or not he might be an ally. She knew one or two people who knew him and they had obviously been talking. After tea she took him to his car, parked on the gravel outside. 'Oh, Mark, you'd better be quick,' she said mischievously, pointing to Richard Aylard's house across the courtyard. 'He'll probably clamp it!'

With his fiftieth birthday approaching, there was an imperative to improve the Prince's image, not just because he preferred to read nice things about himself, but because it has a serious bearing on the future security of the monarchy, which Bolland understands very well. The fundamental purpose of monarchy is to be a symbol of unity, to represent the nation to itself. If it is a source of division, it loses its purpose. Therefore to have a figure accede to the throne who was as controversial as Prince Charles then was – and to a lesser extent still is – would have been highly dangerous. If the Queen lives as long as her mother, it could still be a very long time before the Prince becomes sovereign, but it would clearly be foolish to presuppose such certainty. Unless fifty years of preparation and dogged devotion to duty were to be wasted, it was time to get the scandal off the front page, and present the Prince of Wales as less of a crazed crusader lashing out at farmers and architects and all the other orthodox establishments he had had in his sights, and more as a king in waiting.

The Prince has moaned and complained about the press to his staff and friends for years, and some of them have been too sympathetic for his own good, encouraging his self-pity. He didn't understand why they turned against him, why they ignored the things he tried to do, why they were so dishonest, as he saw it, in their reporting, why they were so intrusive when he had asked them not to be, why they were concerned all the time with the trivia of his personal life. At one time he read nothing but *The Times*. Now he reads no newspaper regularly and listens instead to Radio 4's early morning news programme, 'Today', and relies upon others to tell him anything he needs to know.

Some of the people he works with find his capacity for self-pity quite irritating. As one who has been advising for years says, 'There are times when all I want to do is say "For God's sake, just get a grip, stop going on about it. We know what it's like out there. Yes, the media are ghastly; yes, things have been rough, but you still have an enormous amount to do. You've still got a huge amount to contribute to this stuff, so just stop banging on about how awful it is and settle down to the things you can do, and go on doing them, and go on doing them, and go on doing them." Eventually people will respond to the deeds and not to anything else. That's what you've got to keep coming back to. I wouldn't go on advising him if I didn't think he was doing very, very important work and keeping things moving on a host of progressive agenda issues which I think are crucial, as he does.'

The press has circumscribed his life for a very long time. The Prince would love to be able to hunt with Camilla, for example, but he doesn't. She keeps her horse at Highgrove, and, very often, will go hunting for the morning, then go home. He will then go out in the afternoon, because they still have a horror of being seen and photographed together. It is the one picture every newspaper and magazine in the world wants, and which every photographer knows he would get big money for. Members of the Prince's staff are regularly offered bribes for a tip-off about when they will be together, but so far there have been no takers.

The closest they have come was in August 1995, when the Prince and Camilla were photographed with their friends Nic and Sukie Paravicani at their house in South Wales where they sometimes spend the weekend. Nic was previously married to Mary Ann Parker Bowles, Camilla's former sister-in-law.

It is no longer a secret that Charles and Camilla spend time together, including nights together, but they are damned if the media are going to get a photograph until they are good and ready. And so they forgo simple pleasures like hunting or even just going for walk with each other. A night spent with friends in the North Country, where the Prince had engagements the next morning, was typical. They woke up to the most glorious day, in the most glorious countryside. Camilla suggested a walk. 'We can't,' said the Prince, 'there will be photographers out there.' And he was right. Yet to his frustration, the photographers never appeared to be interested in taking photographs when he was doing anything useful. How could people possibly know what he did if the newspapers didn't tell them?

The Prince is well aware of his problem relationship with the press and desperately worried for his children. How, he wonders, are they ever going to be able to have girlfriends or find wives if they are subjected to the sort of personal intrusion he had been? Their lives will be completely insupportable, and the only sort of girls who will be able to endure the media attention would be quite the wrong sort. He is deeply fearful for them.

FIFTEEN

'Mrs PB'

'Do you really think I will do you any good?'
Camilla to the National Osteoporosis Society

A good relationship between St James's Palace and Buckingham Palace is hugely important. Both incumbents work for the same 'firm', and although they go about their work in very different ways, it is crucial for the people of Britain to recognise that they are two parts of a whole. The institution of monarchy is above individuals and above governments. It is part of the history and heritage of Britain and can be a force for great good; but it has to embrace the people because it is here to serve the people. It is also here by the consent of the people. Yet ever since the Prince set up camp in St James's Palace, across the Mall from Buckingham Palace, the relationship between the two private offices has been strained, and is possibly worse today than it has ever been. While they just recognise Stephen Lamport as one of them, the Queen's courtiers do not share the Prince's enthusiasm for his number two, Mark Bolland, and sense that private discussions are probably safer held in his absence. So blackened is his name, that even leaks from the Prime Minister's office in Downing Street are likely to be attributed to Bolland. The Prince puts such remarks down to jealousy.

It is not hard to see why the two offices clash. It is a matter of age and style. The Queen's private secretary, Sir Robert Fellowes, who took over from Sir William Heseltine in 1990, is the nicest of men and very able, but he comes from a highly privileged background. His father was the Queen's land agent at Sandringham for nearly thirty years, he was educated at Eton, was an officer in the Scots Guards before spending fourteen years in the City, and is much more aware of what the burning issues are around the polished mahogany bars of the gentlemen's clubs in St James's, than what is being said in the pubs and clubs of Bristol, Birmingham or Bolton. At fifty-seven he has already announced his retirement after twenty-one years in service, and will be succeeded by his deputy, Sir Robin Janvrin, in February 1999. Aged fifty-two, Janvrin is another immigrant from the Foreign Office, but has a much more realistic view of the modern world, and an understanding that the monarchy must be seen to adapt to it. Having begun his career at the Palace in the press office, he has a better feel for the media too.

Buckingham Palace has often been blamed when the Prince's plans have been thwarted, and not always quite fairly. It has been easy for his staff to stir up trouble. 'Sir, your idea was so good,' they might say, 'but I couldn't get those people over there to listen.' Charles is predisposed to believe that the Queen's courtiers are out to scupper him, and is easily encouraged to launch into an attack, when the truth is that a private secretary just doesn't dare disagree with the Prince and tell him outright that an idea wouldn't work.

'Those people over there are getting in the way of me doing my job as Prince of Wales,' he will say. 'Why don't they get on with looking after the Queen and let me do my thing?'

'The private secretaries ought to be building bridges all the time,' says one former private secretary. 'It was the right thing for the Prince to have his own office and press office, because what he does is so specialised and so different. You've got two people who are from different generations, doing different jobs with different personal styles. To try and run the whole thing from Monarchy plc in one office isn't the answer. The answer is to have separate offices but have very good communications, and to operate on an absolutely "no surprises" basis. It will never be a relationship of equals because the Queen's team will always be senior. On the other hand, they have to recognise that the Prince's team must have autonomy on a great deal of issues relating to him. When a problem is Monarchy plc, as it was when the Princess died, they should all get together and sort out the best solution. Unless both sides are trying constantly to bring it together, they can drift apart, and what the media wants is, "Buckingham Palace says this, St James's says something else." That is what creates and fuels stories. You have to be constantly bending over backwards to talk to Buckingham Palace, and realise you can have honest disagreements about things without falling out.'

As the Queen slows her pace, and the Prince takes over more and more of the formal tasks which will eventually all fall to him, communication between the two offices becomes even more relevant.

Foreign tours are one of the most obvious tasks that he is taking on; and former Foreign Secretary, Douglas Hurd, who saw him in action on many occasions, has no doubt that he is 'a unique asset to this country in its dealing with foreigners'. One of the most memorable occasions was the half-centenary celebrations in Hamburg, the German city which fifty years before had been virtually destroyed by the British during the Second World War. The reception could have been cool. 'He had mugged up a twenty-minute speech in German – he doesn't speak German but he had learnt it specially. And I said, "You must do a bit in English, because this is a big story at home", and he said, "Oh, do you really think I need to do that?" His whole mind was focused on making a success of the occasion, in the open in the big square in Hamburg, surrounded by thousands and thousands of Germans. He didn't have to do it, and that he should have gone and taken such trouble – they thought it remarkable.'

Stephen Lamport was also there. 'The impact there was electrifying. And it is important because he helps define what German people think of this country, and helps open doors and arouse sympathy and helps others who have to do business there. The same is true in Italy and much of Europe and even to a degree in France. His impact is more emotional and deeper than that of a politician.'

Neither is that difference lost on the British public. The Prince was visiting the scenes of the Paisley floods in Scotland some years ago, accompanied by Tom Farmer, chairman and chief executive of Kwik-Fit, also the Prince's Trust in Scotland. A crabby old woman in the crowd, obviously mistaking Tom Farmer, who was fifty-five if he was a day, for a local councillor, waved at him. 'Hey you, boy,' she shrieked. 'Come here.' Then stabbing the air with her finger in a menacing way, said, 'You're here because you *have* to be here. He's here,' she said pointing at the Prince, 'because he *wants* to be here.'

Vernon Bogdanor, the constitutional historian and Oxford don, believes that most of the conflict between the two Palaces is fundamentally generational. 'The Queen's formative period was during the war and afterwards,' he says, 'with the transformation of the Empire to the Commonwealth. She grew up in a period when social obligations were taken for granted. That broke down under the pressures of affluence in the 1960s, which was when the Prince of Wales grew up, and he is therefore more conscious of rebuilding communities, and the fact that the Commonwealth isn't the Empire; and whatever one's attitude to European integration, the most important relationship for Britain is with the Continent and not the far away Commonwealth. These generational differences are very fundamental and there is a danger that his view of monarchy could be seen to be in conflict with her view of monarchy. But in a way they complement one another, because her role is primarily symbolic, and his can be slightly different. He can go into areas where she cannot tread. But it is not easy for the Queen to keep in touch with the modern world, and very important for her advisers to keep her in touch.'

The simple fact is that the Queen doesn't live in the modern world as most of her subjects know it. When Matthew Butler arrived in 1993 his predecessor told him that if he fancied it, he could get lunch at Buckingham Palace. He decided to give it a try and, expecting a staff canteen, was astonished to find four tiers of eating, and men in tail coats. The Queen and the Duke of Edinburgh ate in one dining room, members of the household in a second – which included private secretaries, keepers of the royal stamp collections and chaplains; and then below stairs – in the basement – were the senior officials' dining room and the junior officials' and lady clerks' dining room. The year he arrived, the Palace was opened to the public for the month of August for the first time, and one of the rooms that could be seen was the household dining room. The result was some very unpopular rearrangement, which offended the natural order of things. The senior officials had to double up with the junior and lady clerks, and the members of the household were sent below stairs, which caused chaos. Half of them had never been into the basement and so many got lost they had to put up signs to direct them.

All the Queen's residences feel as though they belong to another age. They are run by uniformed staff, they have antiquated heating systems and are short on creature comforts – but so are most houses belonging to the British upper classes, particularly in the country. The Royal Family are great lovers of fresh air, and even in the midst of winter the Prince will have a window open. At Sandringham he works in a little room with a primitive three-bar electric heater, which he rarely turns on, and visitors freeze. When the heating is working, the Victorian system that has never been replaced in either Sandringham or Balmoral pumps out so much heat that everyone boils.

Highgrove is different. The Princess was a perfectionist and she liked to be comfortable and although the décor was changed when she moved out, it is still smart and visitors don't feel they are stepping into a 1950s time-warp as they do in most of the Queen's residences.

Camilla's house is very largely given over to her dogs, which sleep on the furniture and cover everything with paw prints and hair. Muddy wellington boots clutter up the doorway, and the furnishings are worn and comfortable. There is a slightly chaotic feel to her house, which is in perfect keeping with the woman. She has no interest in designer clothes, manicures, smart salons, shopping or doing lunch. She is a strong, practical, independent woman who doesn't particularly care what she looks like, and unless she is going somewhere special, doesn't bother with her hair or with make-up. She has dozens of friends, and a few who are very close. Patti Palmer-Tomkinson, Candida Lycett-Green, Frances Shelburne, Amanda Ward, Emilie van Cutsem and Jilly Cooper are amongst them, but her sister Annabel, two years her junior, is probably closer to her than anyone. She is less conventional than Camilla: while Camilla came out as a debutante, Annabel did the hippy trail in her youth and now runs an antique business in Dorset. They have similar features, the same husky voice, laughing eyes and earthy sense of humour; and they have a brother, Mark Shand, two years younger than Annabel, who is less conventional still. He writes about travel and is married to Cleo Goldsmith. Their children are all good friends and it is a close and mutually supportive family.

The children often come to stay, and bring friends, which she enjoys, but Camilla is perfectly happy alone. She has the dogs for company and she gardens and paints. She is not the least bit house proud, and not the greatest cook – but she does know about wine, having had a father in the trade, and has taken the Prince's wine cellar in hand at Highgrove, much to the relief of his friends.

The Prince, like all of his family, is quite ignorant about wine – the Queen drinks martinis, and if she must drink wine it will be mostly sweet, white and German. For preference Charles drinks strong gin martinis and Manhattans, even with a meal.

Dinner is the main meal of his day which he usually has at about nine o'clock, and he will choose the week's menus. He usually skips lunch or at most will have a sandwich – a favourite is egg mayonnaise on wholemeal bread – with fruit juice to drink. Breakfast is also light, usually a bowl of odd looking cereals, nuts and wheat. On the royal train one morning one of the stewards, a Liverpudlian, asked the Prince whether he would like yoghurt on his cereal as usual. 'No,' said the Prince, uncorking a large bottle of black liquid. 'I'd like this rather splendid date oil I was given in the Middle East last week. It's very good.'

The steward, rather more doubtful, replied, 'It looks like sump oil to me, Your Royal Highness.'

When the Prince goes to Sandringham he takes his own staff, who also dress in uniform – as they do at Highgrove and York House, where he stays when in London. There is a minimum of formality, although the way in which he lives in any of his houses still bears no relation to the way in which normal people live their lives. But then nothing about the Royal Family is normal. The Queen thinks and reacts how she is told to by her advisers, as, to a lesser extent, does the Prince of Wales – and friends say he is retreating ever more into a world of his own and leaving his staff to run the detail of his life.

When, in the spring of 1998, the Prince gave a weekend party for a group of friends at Sandringham he took advice about inviting Camilla. Stephen Lamport and Mark Bolland both said, 'Invite her. It will be a two-day wonder in the press and then it will go away. It won't be a problem.' The weekend was important in terms of defining what Camilla's future role in the Prince's life would be, and what was private and what was not. There was another consideration. Camilla was becoming increasingly fed up with being abandoned like a piece of left luggage, and it was important from the point of view of their relationship that they spend some time together. When he knew the story would be in the newspapers, Bolland rang Sir Robin Janvrin and told him there would be an issue in the press of whether the Queen had known about the weekend, and whether she had given her permission for the Prince to invite Camilla.

Robin Janvrin said he would deal with it and, on his advice, the Queen's reaction was that this was a private party, it was up to Charles to invite who he wanted, and she would not have expected to be consulted. They say that if Sir Robert Fellowes had made the call to the Queen, her reaction would have been entirely different. 'There would have been rows, hysteria, battles.'

Robert Fellowes was absolutely furious when he heard that the Prince had plans to give a fiftieth birthday party for Camilla at Highgrove in the July of 1997. He said that if the party went ahead he would have to advise the Queen to tell the Prince that he must give up Camilla for good. In his view, all the difficulties that had befallen the monarchy in the previous ten years had been because of the Prince of Wales and his relationship with Camilla Parker Bowles, and he wanted rid of her. There is a view that Robert Fellowes doesn't much like the Prince, a view shared by his mentor, Lord Carnarvon, the Queen's close friend and racing manager. Robin Janvrin and Mary Francis, his deputy, were appalled by his attitude over the birthday party, and horrified by his lack of simple humanity. They told him in no uncertain terms that if he advised the Queen as he intended, then they would have to offer very different advice. He backed down.

The Queen has not seen Camilla for some years and does not choose to discuss her. A couple of days after Camilla crashed her car on her way to Highgrove shortly before her fiftieth birthday, the Prince was at Sandringham with the Royal Family. Everyone asked whether Camilla was all right, including the Duke of Edinburgh. The Queen said nothing. At one time she was very much a part of the royal scene, and the family were very fond of her, particularly the Queen Mother. She had grown up in that circle. She, her sister and brother all went to all the same parties together as children, and after she married Andrew Parker Bowles, she was ever present. He still is, as Commanding Officer of the Household Cavalry, with the improbable title of Silver Stick in Waiting. It is a title from Tudor times – the incumbent kept close to the Sovereign to protect him or her from danger, and carried a staff of office, topped in silver.

Andrew Parker Bowles was amongst the guests at the birthday party, also Camilla's father Bruce Shand, her children Tom and Laura, and all her closest friends. Camilla was the first to arrive at Highgrove. She came with her sister Annabel and her husband, driven by one of the Prince's drivers. She looked quite radiant, in a black dress with a diamond and pearl necklace, and there were glowing reports and photographs in the press the next day. The evening had been a triumph.

Appearances aside, Robert Fellowes was cross about the party because he knew that the Princess was unhappy about it. Diana had gone completely berserk when she heard about the party and put around all sorts of stories that Camilla was about to start writing newspaper articles and coming out into society in a big way. These stories circulated for three days, and then the Princess telephoned Bolland.

'Mark, I'm very cross,' she said. 'What on earth's going on?' This was the Princess's usual phraseology to indicate that there was trouble. 'I don't know what's going on. People keep telling me all these things, I don't know what to think. I'm really cross.'

Diana had seen the headlines and read the reports. The *Daily Mail*'s write-up of the evening began with the line, 'She was the first to arrive, sweeping into Highgrove last night with all the confidence of a queen.' That particular headline did little for Diana's blood pressure.

Bolland reassured the Princess that nothing untoward was about to happen, and that Camilla was not on the verge of launching herself as a public figure; indeed nothing could have been further from the truth.

In April there had been an announcement that Camilla had become a patron of the National Osteoporosis Society, which was accompanied by the first glamorous portrait of her that had ever been seen, taken specially by Sir Geoffrey Shakerley. There were reports then that this was the start of a PR push to bring Camilla out into the open, raise her profile and make her acceptable to the British public as a companion to the Prince of Wales. Diana had been incensed.

It was true that there was a move to make Camilla acceptable, but only so that she didn't have to skulk around like a criminal. She had no desire to be a public figure in any way. She hates publicity and shies away from any kind of exposure, as Diana was quickly reassured. She had become a patron of the National Osteoporosis Society only after much persuasion, having been approached by the charity in 1994, just as her life seemed to be crashing around her ears. Linda Edwards, the director, had read an article about Camilla, which mentioned that her mother had osteoporosis, and wrote at once enclosing some literature, which she thought might help, and inviting her to get in touch if she wanted any further information. After a while, Camilla wrote back to say that her mother had sadly died since the article was published, but how she wished she had known about the society earlier. Could she please come and see them? In due course she arrived at their new headquarters and research centre near Bath and after seeing round and chatting to Linda Edwards, said that she would like to do something help. She had known nothing about the disease during the years of her mother's illness, and if anything could be done to educate people and prevent others suffering the way her mother and every other member of the family had, she wanted to do it. There was one condition: she didn't want any publicity. That, said Linda, was no problem at all.

What the charity needed most of all was money, and it was not long before donations started arriving as Camilla talked to friends. When the charity was formed in 1986, very few people knew about osteoporosis, and even doctors tended to dismiss it as nothing more than the normal ageing process, a disease suffered by little old ladies. However, it can also strike young women, and is now affecting an increasing number of teenagers because of their obsession with slimming. More women die from osteoporosis than from cancer of the ovaries, cervix and uterus combined, but it is not the sort of disease that has people instantly reaching for their wallets – as child or animal charities do – and raising funds to improve diagnosis, treatment and prevention, as well as support for sufferers, had always been a very uphill struggle.

The first thing Camilla did was donate her half of the £25,000 settlement from the *Sun* for the photos published from the family album at the time of her divorce.

While she looked for a house to live in after her divorce from Andrew, she was staying with friends, the Earl and Countess of Shelburne, at Bowood House, and it was there in September 1995 that she held a private soirée. The setting could not have been bettered, nor the weather more perfect. There was Champagne, music, sculpture and theatre, and in front of 200 guests, including her ex-husband, despite great nerves, Camilla gave a touching speech about her mother's illness, which Tom, her son, recorded on video. In one night, Camilla raised £20,000 and was absolutely thrilled.

Some months later, Linda Edwards wrote to Camilla, inviting her to become a patron of the society. 'Do you really think I will do you any good?' Camilla asked. She was under no illusions about just how unpopular she was; and she recognised that her association with the charity could even be positively harmful. Linda was adamant.

'Look,' she said, 'your mother died of osteoporosis, your grand-mother, you now realise, died of osteoporosis. You have spoken from time to time about the devastating effect it had on your family, so you are very aware of how osteoporosis can destroy someone's quality of life. You've learnt that at first hand. Inevitably, people want to read about you, and if at the same time they are reading about osteoporosis and putting osteoporosis on the map, then you are helping an awful lot of people. We can make it a household word and give it the recognition it needs to get something done about it.'

By the time of Camilla's fiftieth birthday party Diana had actually become quite relaxed about her as a presence in the Prince's life, although she hated the idea of Camilla becoming acceptable as a public figure. She had met Dodi Fayed by this time, and no longer seemed to mind so much. Importantly, she had never seen Camilla as a threat to William and Harry, which undoubtedly would have caused problems, because she knew the Prince had always kept them apart. She had even become slightly more relaxed about Tiggy, about whom she had at one time been vitriolic. At the staff Christmas lunch at the Lanesborough Hotel in Knightsbridge in 1995, which the Prince and Princess continued to attend together even after their divorce, Diana couldn't resist the temptation to wreak her revenge on the woman she thought had not only stolen her children, but was possibly having an affair with her ex-husband too. She had seen the photographs of Tiggy and Charles kissing on the ski slopes, and believed the innuendo she'd read in the newspapers. There was nothing sexual in the relationship. Tiggy is a girl with a big heart who gives everyone great hugs, including the Prince of Wales whom she has known since she was a child.

Tiggy had recently been in hospital for a minor operation, and at the lunch Diana had sidled up to her and said, 'So sorry to hear about the baby.' The clear indication was that Tiggy had been in hospital having an abortion. Tiggy was devastated and rushed out of the room in tears, with Michael Fawcett, the Prince's valet, by her side. Everyone else went on to have a very jolly party with lots of drink, which degenerated into a crazy foam fight, which the Princess enjoyed as enthusiastically as anyone. It was only when they read about it in the press, and libel lawyer Peter Carter-Ruck was instructed by Tiggy four days later, that anyone realised what had happened. She decided to drop the action.

The two boys found life with Tiggy relaxed and uncomplicated and, at times, they found their mother's mood swings very unsettling. They hated the press, hated photographers and disliked being put on show in theme parks. They were also well aware of what the Princess thought about their father. There was nothing she told Andrew Morton that she had not confided in them, particularly William, many times over, and the emotional burden was considerable.

The Prince took the boys on an outing to the Royal Shakespeare Company at Stratford about three years ago, along with Julia Cleverdon and her daughter, Emilie van Cutsem and her youngest son, Bel Mooney and her daughter. Sitting around the table for a pre-performance supper, the Prince started to talk about the Goons and, being of the same generation, Bel Mooney fell into the famous 'Ying tong, ying tong' routine.

'God, aren't parents embarrassing!' said her daughter turning to Prince William by her side.

'Papa doesn't embarrass me,' he replied. 'Mama does.' Gradually he was beginning to see that his father was not as black as he had been painted over the years.

Camilla had become a patron of the National Osteoporosis

Society and her sister Annabel had also become involved. After the success of the soirée at Bowood, Camilla suggested holding another fundraising extravaganza at Talisman Antiques, Annabel's business in Dorset, which was housed in a former brewery. The date was fixed for 13 September 1997, the invitations were specially designed by a leading illustrator, Julia Whatley, and promised 'an evening of enchantment, fascination and the unexpected'. Tickets were £100 each and, although they originally planned to stop when they had sold 500, so many people wanted tickets they eventually stopped at 700. The acts were booked, the ticket money was in, donations had arrived, the cheques had been banked, the catering was organised and, as the excitement of the day grew nearer, there was mounting speculation in the press about whether the Prince of Wales would be there. It was a private event, all the guests were friends, and since the birthday party at Highgrove had been so successful, and the cause of minimal outrage, this could have been another step in the direction of making Camilla a legitimate part of the Prince's life.

Then Dodi and Diana's car ploughed into the tunnel beneath the Seine, and as the fateful news arrived from Paris in the early hours of Sunday 31 August, Charles and Camilla both knew that things would never be the same for them again. Their relationship was forced deeper underground. Dearly though Charles loves Camilla, his sons have always come first, which she understands entirely. She would not have it any other way. Love him as she does, she has always believed that children have to come first.

One of the first repercussions of the accident was the cancellation of the party. Linda Edwards telephoned Camilla the moment she heard and said she felt they ought not to go ahead. Camilla was in a state of shock – desperately sad for Diana, and desperately worried for the Prince, William and Harry. She was concerned that cancelling would mean they wouldn't raise the money they had hoped for, but she agreed there was absolutely no question about it, the event must not merely be postponed, but cancelled, and it would be a long time, she thought, before anyone could think of doing something so light-hearted again.

The staff at the NOS had spent the Saturday getting the tickets and thank-you notes for the donations, each one individually signed by Camilla and Annabel, ready to post first thing on Monday morning. Instead the first thing they did on Monday morning was throw all the tickets in the bin, and start writing to all 700 people to explain why the event had been cancelled and offering to repay ticket money and donations. Very few asked for their money back, and many more donations arrived when people heard the event had been cancelled out of respect for the Princess. It raised £80,000 in all.

The following week was a living hell for everyone. Charles and Camilla spoke at length on the telephone each day – as they do most days, wherever they both might be – and she was a tower of strength. After the funeral he took the boys home to Highgrove, where Tiggy was again on hand to look after them and keep them occupied, but they were both in remarkable control. On the Monday she took them out to follow the hunt by car. On seeing them arrive, Captain Ian Farquhar, Master of the Beaufort, went over to them and, speaking on behalf of the entire meet, said very simply, 'It's good to see you, sirs. I just want you to know that we are all very, very sorry about your mother. You have our deepest sympathy and we were all incredibly proud of you on Saturday. That's all I'm going to say, and now we're going to get on with the day.'

'Thank you,' said William. 'Yes, you're right. We all need to get on with the day.'

The Prince found it harder to continue with normal life. He was very despondent for many weeks and loath to re-engage. When he did finally get back on the road, he was less certain that the crowds he met would be as sympathetic to him as members of the Beaufort had been to his sons. It was a day out in Manchester during the last week of September, and he rang Julia Cleverdon to seek her advice on whether or not he should go. 'Julia, there's the most frightful row going on about Manchester. Half the world says I should do it, the other half says I shouldn't do it. I don't know what to do. If I don't then I'm away, and I've got to face it some time.'

'If you want my advice,' said Julia, 'you should do it, because it's always better to get out there and be seen rather than to stay hidden behind closed doors.'

Julia's advice came from painful experience. By an extraordinary coincidence, her husband had died very suddenly and unexpectedly on a family holiday in Greece, two weeks before the Princess's death. She had made her way back home with the children in a terrible state, and when she arrived her mother said, 'I've had the Prince on the phone four times, he says he must be the first person you speak to as you come in through the door.' At that moment the phone rang again. It was Charles.

'There are not very many people who would care enough to do that,' she says. 'And there was endless support and love and organising life to come to the memorial service to support me.' It touched her deeply.

She had planned to take two months away from the office, but agreed at once to go on the Prince's day out in Manchester, and face the world together.

Julia is also one of the select few to have met Camilla. She had been with the Prince to a Tesco golf tournament to collect a cheque they were giving to the Prince's Trust for a quarter of a million pounds in 1996. He had complained bitterly, which is his standard procedure before going anywhere, almost as if it is his way of combating his natural shyness and getting his adrenalin going. 'Yes, I do agree,' she said. 'Sunningdale is a very way from Highgrove, but you're only going to be there for fourteen minutes. Let's divide fourteen into a quarter of a million. It's probably a rather higher rate than the Spice Girls earn.' And as usual he giggled and his temper was restored.

She was staying at Highgrove overnight, and on the way back the Prince said, 'Julia, I've got a very good friend coming to dinner tonight.'

'Oh, don't worry about that,' said Julia, realising immediately who he was talking about. 'I'll have scrambled egg in the kitchen and go to bed. I'd like an early night.'

'No, I'd very much like you to meet her. It's Mrs Parker Bowles.'

What she found in Mrs Parker Bowles – known by most of the Prince's staff as 'Mrs PB' – was a great giggler, someone who makes life fun, and has a capacity to make Charles talk and laugh about what has happened during the day, while being quite clear that doing what he may not always enjoy is duty. It was clear she was interested in him as a campaigner and that she cared about the causes he cares about. But above all, she was funny and a good raconteur.

The day in Manchester had been very carefully thought through. For six hours, from ten until four, Charles would have to endure the scrutiny of press and public. What mattered most was the backdrop for his first words, which the whole world would be waiting for and judging him by. Julia chose a Salvation Army drop-in centre on one of the most problematic estates in Manchester, which had been built as a result of the Granada community challenge regeneration programme. The estate had been twinned with British Nuclear Fuels, which had built not only the centre, but also an all-weather sports facility with a lot of new equipment.

The Prince was terrified, and so were Julia, Tom Shebbeare, Mark Bolland and Sandy Henney, all of whom had come with him for moral support. None of them had any idea what to expect. They had all had a hand in writing a speech for him, but he had discarded it and scribbled his own notes in the plane on the way up. When they arrived, he straightened his tie in front of the mirror, for perhaps a second or two longer than usual, took a very deep breath, and stepped out to face cameras flashing furiously. At the Salvation Army centre, Julia had deliberately arranged for him to be on his own for a few minutes with ten locals who knew just how much he had done in the area, and what a difference his interest in their problems had made to their lives. It was perfect. They were all loving and anxious about him and he suddenly knew exactly what he had to say when he went into the hall to face the cameras. In the most touching, brave, tear-jerking tribute to the courage of his sons, and to the public who had shown such kindness in what had been an unbelievably difficult time, he won the respect and sympathy of millions.

'I think they are handling a very difficult time with enormous courage and greatest possible dignity,' he said. 'I also want to say how particularly moved and enormously comforted my children and I were, and indeed still are, by the public's response to Diana's death. It has been really quite remarkable and indeed in many ways overwhelming. I think, as many of you will know from experiences of family loss in your own lives, it is inevitably difficult to cope with grief at any time. But you may realise, it is even harder when the whole world is watching at the same time. But obviously the public support, and the warmth of that support, has helped us enormously. I can't tell you how enormously grateful and touched both the boys and myself are.'

Slowly the tide of public opinion began to turn in his favour.

SIXTEEN

Visions of the Monarchy

'It's 1,500 years of breeding. It comes from being
descended from Vlad the Impaler.'
Charles

Every Christmas, the Prince's last engagement before the holiday is
at the two hospices local to Highgrove of which he is patron: the Sue
Ryder Home in Leckhampton and the Cotswold Care Centre in
Minchinhampton. The visit is entirely private and he will not hear
of photographers. 'Absolutely not,' he will say. 'It would be intruding on private grief. These people are terminally ill. I won't have it.'

One year, when his private secretary went to look round one of
the hospices, a fortnight before the visit, so that he could brief the
Prince on the people he would meet, he met a patient who looked as
though he was unlikely to last the night. 'It's a bit unlikely Mr Smith
will still be alive in a couple of weeks' time, isn't it?' he asked the
matron.

'Oh, no,' she replied. 'He's said he's going to meet the Prince of
Wales.'

A fortnight later when the Prince came to visit, Mr Smith was still
alive and did meet the Prince of Wales – and died that night.

For most people it is *what* he is that is so potent. They are excited
by the prospect of meeting the Prince of Wales, the Queen's son, the
heir to the throne of England, Scotland, Wales and Northern
Ireland, a senior member of the Royal Family. But having met him,
what people remember is *who* he is. He may be fundamentally weak
and spoilt, and have a bad temper and be a lousy judge of character;
he may surround himself with people who tell him what he wants to

hear, and cast out those who try and tell him the truth; he may be self-absorbed and self-pitying and have a terrible tendency to whinge. But he has a very big heart, and those that love him do so because, in their view, the goodness of his heart and the integrity of his intentions outweigh any negative aspects of his character.

When Paddy Whiteland – the groom turned odd job man whom Charles had inherited with Highgrove – became ill with cancer, he took care of him. Paddy was in and out of Tetbury hospital, and Charles visited often. The remainder of the time Paddy lived with Joan and Mary Baker, two sisters in the town, who had been his neighbours and once ran the local laundry. When Paddy was home the Prince organised and paid for nurses to look after him, sent Maureen, the housekeeper from Highgrove, to help, and came to see him regularly himself. Paddy died, aged eighty-four, during one night in 1997, and the Prince saw him and paid his last respects the very next morning. He arranged the funeral, a Roman Catholic service in Tetbury Church, swallowing his pride as he did so – the vicar had publicly condemned his adultery, but the local RC church was too small for the sort of numbers expected. Three hundred and sixty people came to the service, including Paddy's eighty-three-year-old sister from Ireland, whom the Prince took under his wing both in the church and at the reception he held for family and friends at Highgrove afterwards.

Paddy had come from very humble origins. 'Fancy me finishing up with the Prince of Wales!' he would say, and adorned his house with signed photographs of the Prince who had done him proud.

On Christmas Eve, 1993, Marjorie Wallace, chief executive of SANE, of which the Prince had been patron since its inception seven years earlier, was told she had cancer. In January, a few weeks into treatment, she wrote to him. Virtually by return post she received a twelve-page, hand-written letter full of love and encouragement, which ended, 'With lots of love, Charles.' In the meantime, he had arranged for Marjorie to be treated, at his expense, by Dr Mohammed Ali, the Indian practitioner of alternative medicine who had treated Dale Tryon some years previously. The Prince had given strict instructions that no bill was to go to Marjorie. Whenever she went through a particularly bad patch of chemotherapy, he would send a huge bouquet of flowers to her home or some other gift like bath oil. When she rang and thanked him, he said, 'Oh, did you like the lilies?' Or the purple and white flox, or whatever it was that he had obviously chosen specially himself.

Then one day he telephoned at nine o'clock in the morning and said, 'I had bad dreams last night and I was really worrying about you so much. How are you?'

She confessed she was not very good at that particular moment. She had huge ulcers all over her mouth, she had no hair and looked dreadful. 'I've been so worried about you,' he said again. 'Would you like to come and have tea? Are you well enough? Don't come if you're not.'

Marjorie said, 'But I look awful,' and he said, 'I don't mind.'

So Marjorie went to Highgrove for tea, where there was just the two of them, and while she sat with her feet curled up on the sofa, with a scarf covering her bald head, they talked of their feelings about death, life and love. Then he said, 'I've got to give you something.' So they wandered through to his office, which was a complete mess, and he started climbing up on a little step ladder to look for things, and he found more bath oil for her and the book on Highgrove – *Portrait of an Estate*, which he had written with Charles Clover – and said, 'I don't suppose you want to read that, do you?' She replied, 'Yes, if you'll sign it.'

Finally he said, 'Who looks after you? Is there anyone to look after you? What do you do when you get home? Would you like some biscuits?' which made her laugh. He then gave her a big cuddle and she set off for home, laden with gifts. But that was not the end to it. Throughout a whole year of treatment, hand-written letters would arrive every few weeks, in which he wrote about philosophy, about life and death, his concerns and sometimes his own frustrations.

In the course of conversation he suggested a visit to see the film *Shadowlands* which he had just seen. It was about the death of C. S.

Lewis's wife Joy from cancer. It was only when Majorie pointed out that she might be a little nervous of the death element that Charles realised what he had been suggesting. Both of them collapsed into giggles.

'Most people,' says Marjorie, 'send a bunch of flowers and a card and then they leave it and hope for the best. The warmth of his friendship and endurance of it really was way beyond the bounds of duty, and he really did help me keep going.' Whether or not it was the ministrations of Dr Ali, or maybe the integrated healthcare she received, Marjorie recovered and is still campaigning as enthusiastically as ever for SANE. In the summer of 1998 she held a big fundraising twelfth anniversary dinner in the new Orchard Rooms at Highgrove, attended by the great, the good and the seriously rich from all over the world. The Prince came and spoke, not only supporting Majorie, but fighting eloquently for the mentally ill and their families.

Such stories are legion, and very little known. As are the scores of lengthy hand-written letters that have gone out to soldiers in his regiments who have had accidents, or the families of people killed in the line of duty. Although he and the Princess went about it in very different ways, and the public perception is therefore quite different, they both expressed great empathy with those who were suffering, and both had an almost magic ability to lift the spirit of those who, for whatever reason, were scraping along the bottom.

The night before a visit to Teeside in March 1994, Charles was persuaded to stop at a school in Middlesbrough on the way, where a child had been brutally murdered the previous day. His private secretary thought it was a good idea; his valet, Michael Fawcett – who very often behaved more like the private secretary than the valet – advised against it. The Prince went to the school, complaining nonetheless that he didn't like intruding on private grief and that was all he was really doing. He was told quite firmly that this was what was expected of monarchy, which of course in his heart of hearts he knew very well. There is nothing the Prince of Wales does not know about the job, but he has always been self-deprecating, and never keen to thrust himself forward on the assumption that people are going to be pleased to see him. Equally, he is genuinely delighted and surprised when they are. The school children in Middlesbrough were no exception. The press was there in force, and he talked to the headmaster and the parents of the murdered girl, as arranged, and then quite unexpectedly, the headmaster asked whether he would go and have a few words with the girl's classmates who had witnessed the attack. Unprepared, but unable to say no, the Prince spoke to the children, privately and most movingly, about what the death of Lord Mountbatten had meant to him and how he had learned to cope, which they clearly appreciated.

He drew on personal experience again when he visited Omagh in Northern Ireland, the scene of the terrible IRA atrocity in August 1998 – the worst outrage in the province since the Troubles began. Twenty-nine people, many of them women and children, were blown apart by a bomb planted by the self-styled 'Real IRA', and over 200 people were injured, many seriously. One of the doctors performing amputations afterwards said he had done so many he had lost count. The Prince spent five and a half hours in the small town, talking to the injured and to the relatives of the dead, meeting doctors, nurses and the people from the emergency services who had had the grim task of collecting the pieces, and visiting the scene where the twenty-nine had died. It was a gruelling day, which he found tremendously emotional and upsetting. Yet he has an ability to soak up the most shocking and appalling grief without cracking up himself. He has his grandmother's strength in these situations. His mother is less good at it. When asked how he does it, he says, 'It's 1,500 years of breeding. It comes from being descended from Vlad the Impaler!' Again, he was doubtful about being there. Wasn't it intruding on people's private grief? he kept asking. But about a thousand people came to see him, and said again and again how grateful they were that he had come. It was clear that there was something healing in his presence.

Monarchy has always had a role to play in national disasters and human tragedy. The Queen Mother, visiting the East End of London during the Second World War, where whole streets had been destroyed during the Blitz, meeting survivors, sent a powerful message that generations of Londoners have never forgotten. The Queen's visit in 1966 to the Welsh mining village of Aberfan, where 144 people, mostly children, were killed when a slag heap collapsed on the primary school, is another picture indelibly etched. Each time the Queen visits a scene of grief, it is an indication that she cares, not just personally, but on behalf of the nation.

The Prince appreciates the value of that role, but he doesn't take the institution of monarchy for granted. He questions its purpose in the modern world. Ten years ago he would never have talked about his thoughts and ideas for the future, believing that it was tantamount to wishing his mother dead; but he has recognised that change can't wait for his succession. It has been becoming increasingly clear to him that modernisation is essential for the monarchy now, if it is to continue to have relevance; and the public reaction to Diana's death made those discussions even more urgent.

Vernon Bogdanor is one of a group which has been advising on these matters for some time. He is worried about making irreversible changes to appease criticism of the monarchy which is based on ignorance about what the Monarch and the Prince of Wales actually do. The real problem with the monarchy, he says, is that it was unable to cope when society began to question the relevance of all its hallowed institutions.

'When the Queen came to the throne in the 1950s, around a third of the population believed she had been chosen by God and there was a tremendous sense of deference. It was a magical institution and you didn't ask questions about it. It was like asking questions about Santa Claus. It was a fairytale, unreal world and when that illusion crashed, as all illusions crash, monarchy wasn't equipped to deal with it. We have moved away from being a society where magic, or even strong religious feelings or deference, play a role, partly as a result of Margaret Thatcher's premiership, although I think it would have happened anyway. We've developed a much more utilitarian attitude to all our institutions. We say, what's the point of it? The fact that something has existed for a long time isn't enough for many people, so the monarchy has to re-establish itself on new foundations. It seems to me that the only way that it can keep going to the twenty-first century is as a practical institution which does a lot of good to the country in a way which politicians can't.'

He is in no doubt at all that monarchy is 'a great benefit which we lose at our peril', pointing out that 'most countries who have become republics have not done so after intellectual argument, but after revolution'.

'The best way of summarising, is that the monarchy represents the nation to itself. There are all sorts of things a sovereign can do which are sullied if done by a politician, because people suspect their motives. The Queen is the only person who has no party history, who has been trained from early times to have no views. The Prince has been trained from birth that if he has views they are not to be publicly expressed. He is not a partisan. Then there are the constitutional functions of the sovereign, in choosing a Prime Minister and deciding whether to dissolve Parliament. Those could be very important if we had proportional representation, because we'd have more coalition governments. It's very important the person who exercises those functions is neutral.

'People talk as if you could have a non-political figure as President. They mention Richard Branson [founder of Virgin records and a host of companies under the same brand] but in practice, the parties would get hold of it, because you couldn't afford to run for election unless you had support of a party, you wouldn't be able to canvas, or get television programmes together. For that you need an organisation and that's best supplied by a party. It is a salutary defence against politicians that the person who is head of state has no political power, has never had it nor is able to seek it or get it, and has no party political motives.'

The Queen is politically very astute and meets her Prime Minister formally for an hour once a week. The Prince of Wales is less so, although he does go to greater lengths than any previous heir to the throne to keep himself informed. He used to see John Major about once every two months, and the two men got on well together. The Prime Minister admired much of what the Prince was trying to do – they were of like mind on many issues – but the Prince did not take account of the intricacies and restraints of government. Over a cup of tea and a plate of Duchy Originals at St James's Palace, he was quite likely to suggest some scheme for dealing with the unemployed, which would involve the government in a fresh commitment of one sort or another, and was frustrated when it could not be done. If there was a famine, a flood, or some sort of disaster around the world, it frustrated him to be told that it would not be possible to send EC surpluses. Lynda Chalker, the former Overseas Minister, was one close contact in the last government whom he would ring, or Douglas Hurd, the former Foreign Secretary, who had delicately to explain why his suggestion about how to stop the shelling in Bosnia, or the despoliation of Romanian monasteries, was not going to work.

The former Tory government did adopt some of the Prince's ideas, but New Labour has gone further, particularly with a scheme for youth unemployment. There has been a lot of contact between the Prince and Tony Blair, and other ministers like Peter Mandelson, since the new government came to power in May 1997. The Prime Minister would like to be thought of as the man who modernised the Royal Family after the death of the Princess, or even as the man who saved it in the week before the funeral. He was certainly the one who created 'the People's Princess'.

Stephen Lamport is well aware of this, and with the diplomacy one would expect from a man of his pedigree, suggests that because the government was so new, it was still learning. 'It may have taken some time for government to understand the rather special and not always self-evident relationship between itself and the sovereign. Government doesn't own the monarchy. They are complementary parts of a system which goes back a very long way and whose history is an important part of why we are what we are. It would be a mistake of any government to think that it could use, own and trade on the monarchy as part of a common enterprise.'

His former boss at the Foreign Office, Lord Hurd, sees no danger in the Prince of Wales getting close to the government; in fact quite the reverse. 'I think one of the weaknesses with the Royal Family is they keep too far away from politicians because they are so worried about being thought to be involved in politics. They should be aware of what's going on. They don't know enough people. They didn't know enough Labour politicians when we [the Tory party] were in power. The whole story of the royal yacht [which was decommissioned, to the family's great sadness, in 1998] would have been different, in my opinion, if people like Robin Cook [Foreign Secretary], Margaret Beckett [Secretary for Trade and Industry] and Tony Blair had been invited on board *Britannia*, because they would have seen how important it was. The Prince ought to be in touch with the younger generation of all the political parties.'

One of the things that rankles most with the Prince, and indeed the rest of the Royal Family, is the notion that they have been pushed into modernising the monarchy by the death of Diana. This is demonstrably untrue, as the politicians, civil servants and expert advisers who have been involved in the process of modernising the monarchy over the years will confirm. Surprisingly, much of the momentum has come from the Duke of Edinburgh. It is true that the process has been given greater urgency by Diana's death, but the Way Ahead group – in which principal members of the family meet to discuss the future – was already in existence, and the Prince had his own groups that were looking at ways of making monarchy more relevant to the current climate. There is, however, an essential conundrum. The monarchy can't react until nearly one hundred per cent of the country wants it to react. Otherwise it will cause controversy and division, which as a symbol of unity it cannot do. Right now, several million people want the Royal Family to behave as Diana did, to wear their hearts on their sleeves, hug Aids patients and stride bravely through fields cleared of land-mines, irrespective of the political sensitivities. Several million want nothing of the sort. They like the dignity and majesty of a traditional monarchy. Several million more want to strip them of their palaces, trains and planes and cut the cost to the nation.

At the moment, the cost of keeping the Royal Family per year is about half the cost of running the vehicle licensing centre in Swansea. The financial benefits alone, in terms of business won abroad, money raised for charity, and tourism in Britain, are incalculable.

John Major's view is that 'We British do not want a bicycling monarchy. It doesn't matter what spin doctors might tell the press. I don't believe that's what they want in Little Rumblington on the Marsh. There was huge emotion at the time of the Princess's death, not surprisingly. This enormously beautiful, attractive young woman who had become an icon, dying in the most tragic and painful of circumstances. So it was an astonishing reaction. But the monarchy's roots are very deep, and to rush to the flip judgement that this has changed the House of Windsor for ever is reckless. The truth is that it is always changing and will continue to do so. But there will be many reasons for these changes, mainly the instincts and judgement of the Queen and Prince Philip.'

'People misunderstand,' says Vernon Bogdanor. 'The style of the Swedish monarchy is much more popular, it's a bicycling monarchy. It is said that the Swedish King was recently asked to provide evidence of his credit card viability in a store. I think people want a bit of glamour and a coach, and so on. What people don't understand is that the continental monarchies interfere much more in government than ours do, partly because of the proportional representation systems. The Belgian King plays a very heavy role in choosing governments. He consults with the equivalent of the Trades Union Congress and the Confederation of British Industry before choosing a Prime Minister.

'Ours is the only international monarchy. It gives a certain colour to Britain that it would otherwise lack. We'd just be a small island off the coast of Europe, but because of our history of Empire and Commonwealth, it gives a certain international flavour which the other monarchies don't have.'

The Prince's greatest fear for the future is the intrusion of the media. He doesn't see how William will ever have a chance of being happy. 'You have absolutely no idea of what it's like,' he will say again and again.

After Diana's death, Earl Spencer said the tabloid press had blood on its hands, and the industry took the message to heart. After some heated debate about whether a privacy law was called for, the outcome was self-regulation, and a strict new code of conduct binding on every editor and publisher in Britain was drawn up by the Press Complaints Commission. Published in November 1997, it was designed to prevent all the excesses of the previous ten years. Every aspect of intrusion that the Prince and Princess had suffered was covered, and the two boys were guaranteed privacy. For example:

Privacy
i) Everyone is entitled to respect for his or her private and family life, home, health and correspondence. A publication will be expected to justify intrusions into any individual's private life without consent.
ii) The use of long lens photography to take pictures of people in private places without their consent is unacceptable. Note – Private places are public or private property where there is a reasonable expectation of privacy.

Children
i)   Young people should be free to complete their time at school without unnecessary intrusion.
ii) Journalists must not interview or photograph children under the age of sixteen on subjects involving the welfare of the child or of any other child, in the absence of or without the consent of a parent or other adult who is responsible for the children.
iii) Pupils must not be approached or photographed while at school without the permission of the school authorities.
v)   Where material about the private life of a child is published, there must be justification for publication other than the fame, notoriety or position of his or her parents or guardian.

Listening devices
Journalists must not obtain or publish material obtained by using clandestine listening devices or by intercepting private telephone conversations.

It was a code, according to the introduction, which 'both protects the rights of the individual and upholds the public's right to know'. The Prince is thoroughly pessimistic, not least because of that very sentence which is supposed to reassure. It won't be long before William finds himself a girlfriend. Girls find him extremely attractive – as the youth of Canada demonstrated when Prince Charles and both boys went skiing in Whistler during the Easter holidays. If he had been any less well protected, the clothes would have been torn from his back by swooning, fainting, sobbing teenagers. At home he is already going to dances and discos in Gloucestershire. And when he finds someone special, the Prince reasons in his gloom, the newspapers could plead it was the public's right to know the identity of the girl who might one day be Queen of England.

William is utterly determined to protect himself. The *Mail on Sunday* published a speculative piece for his sixteenth birthday in July 1998, which was friendly but perhaps presumed too much. William immediately instructed his father's press office to complain to the Press Complaints Commission. He saw what happened to his mother and he is not about to let it happen to him.

William is showing every sign of being a stronger personality than his father. He has very firm ideas about what he wants and a determination to get it – some say there is more than a hint of his mother in him. On the anniversary of Diana's death he refused to go to church on the day, a Monday, unless his father's office issued an announcement calling for an end to the mourning. He agreed a text and Sandy Henney, the Prince's press secretary, read it out on his behalf on the first day of the Eton school term on 2 September 1998. Henney has developed a good rapport with the boys since their mother's death, and William is pleased to be able to use his father's office. It was one of the rare occasions when, under the new privacy rules, the press are allowed to photograph the Princes, and an ideal opportunity.

'They have asked me to say that they believe their mother would want people now to move on – because she would have known that constant reminders of her death can create nothing but pain to those she left behind. They therefore hope very much that their mother and her memory will now finally be allowed to rest in peace.'

Despite his gloom about the future, the Prince has lost none of his fighting spirit. What he took on, with his fiftieth birthday in his sights, was the modification of his style so as to be less confrontational.

The early speeches of the 1980s had been right in establishing the Prince as a man who cared so passionately about issues that he was prepared to take on the giants in society. They had been right for a younger man. With the approach of fifty, it was time for subtler ways. The launch in October 1997 of his initiative for integrated healthcare – taking the best of orthodox and complementary medicine – was clearly different from anything he had done before. The Prince himself explained how he had gone about it in an article in the *Daily Telegraph*.

'Last year I asked a group of leading individuals from different scientific, educational and healthcare backgrounds for their advice on how we could make further progress. We established four working groups and produced a draft report on what seemed to be the main issues, which was circulated for comment to a large number of individuals and organisations with an interest in orthodox and complementary healthcare.

'The results of eighteen months' discussion and consultation are published today in a new report ... The report makes twenty-eight specific proposals for further consideration and development ... But the report is not a definitive blueprint for action. Its purpose is to stimulate a wider public and professional debate about the possible role of complementary medicine within the changing pattern of healthcare in this country.'

The belief that inspired this initiative was that the increased acceptance of complementary medicine 'reflects a growing concern with the use of more and more powerful drugs and a potentially rather impersonal approach to healthcare ... Health should be much more than the mere absence of disease or infirmity; and we should strive to ensure that everybody can fulfil the full potential and expression of their lives.'

The article was published to coincide with a conference at St James's Palace, and was followed in May by a conference at the Queen Elizabeth II Centre in Westminster at which the Prince spoke and quoted Plato:

'The cure of the part should not be attempted without treatment of the whole, and also no attempt should be made to cure the body without the soul, and therefore if the head and body are to be well, you must begin by curing the mind; that is the first thing ... For this is the error of our day in the treatment of the human body, that physicians separate the soul from the body.'

The Prince's views on medicine, 1998 style, took two years of research to prepare, and won admiration from very disparate quarters. It was a far cry from the reaction he had received fourteen years earlier, when he shared much the same thoughts at the BMA's 150th anniversary dinner, and was an indication of a new respect for the Prince of Wales.

SEVENTEEN

Charles and Camilla

'The press has dictated the last fifteen years of my life,
they're bloody well not dictating the next bit.'
Charles

Richard Kay wrote a speculative piece about the Prince and Camilla from New York, at the time Diana's dresses were auctioned, two months before her death. The *Daily Mail* turned it into a lead story, with the headline, 'Charles and Camilla will marry'. When Kay saw what the editor was planning to do with the piece he objected, and the headline was changed to read, 'Charles and Camilla could marry'. Kay was appeased, but when the Prince saw it he was furious. 'The press has dictated the last fifteen years of my life, they're bloody well not dictating the next bit.'

Technically, Charles and Camilla could marry. At one time it would have been impossible for a member of the Royal Family to marry a divorcee, as Edward VIII discovered in 1936. He had to choose between the crown and the American divorcee, Wallace Simpson, and chose marriage. But what made abdication essential then was convention, not law. Times have changed and divorcees are now not only acceptable, they can be remarried in church at the discretion of the bishop. Presbyterian churches are particularly accommodating, as the Princess Royal discovered when she married for the second time, because the Church in Scotland regards marriage as a contract, not a sacrament. Whether it would be acceptable for the man who is to become Supreme Governor of the Church of England to marry a divorcee is open to debate. The only person he would be barred legally from marrying is a Roman

Catholic, and that hasn't changed since the Act of Settlement in 1701. Camilla married a Roman Catholic – and, until he remarried, Andrew Parker Bowles was a member of the Sovereign Military Order of Malta, one of the oldest Catholic lay orders – and their children, Tom and Laura, are Roman Catholic. Camilla did not convert.

There is, therefore, no constitutional obstacle, although while he is still Prince of Wales, under the Royal Marriages Act of 1772, he would need the Queen's permission, which amounts to rather more than a mother telling her son he has her blessing – if ever that were likely to happen. The sovereign acts on the advice of her government of the day, and cannot constitutionally take decisions which might have a bearing on the country without it. The sovereign is the only member of the Royal Family who can marry without consulting or without the need for permission from ministers. If permission were not forthcoming while he was Prince of Wales, Charles could in theory wait until he became King. He could then marry Camilla, and she would automatically become Queen unless an Act of Parliament was passed to prevent this.

In practice, however, as the abdication of Edward VIII demonstrated, the government would still have the upper hand. If the King had decided to go ahead and marry someone he was told the country would find unacceptable, the Cabinet could have simply threatened to resign and refused to carry on as the monarch's constitutional advisers, making the King's position completely untenable. The key to it all is public opinion. Stanley Baldwin, the former Prime Minister, made the point appositely during the debate on the Abdication Bill in December 1936, by quoting from Polonius's speech in *Hamlet*:

> '... his will is not his own.
> For he himself is subject to his birth.
> He may not, as unvalu'd persons do,
> Carve for himself. For on his choice depends
> The safety and health of this whole state.'

If the government felt that public opinion had reached the point where Camilla was acceptable as a wife, but not as a queen, they could theoretically have a morganatic marriage, in which the wife and children, if any, have no claim on the sovereign's rights, status and privileges. Edward VIII had suggested this as a means of keeping the throne and still marrying Mrs Simpson, but his proposal was turned down. Ramsay MacDonald, the former Prime Minister, called it 'degrading to women, offensive to country'. In fact it is unheard of in Britain and in British law, although it happens occasionally on the continent, where sovereigns are required to marry from a narrowly specific range of royal families. If it were going to happen for Camilla, it would require an Act of Parliament, not just in Britain, but in all other monarchies of the Common-wealth. In 1936 they were not keen to support the King, and it is unlikely they would be any more enthusiastic today.

Most senior politicians agree that marriage to Camilla would still be too controversial. It was discussed at great length between the government and the Church, at the highest levels, at the time of the Prince's divorce, and the consensus was that it couldn't happen. As one authority describes it, 'Marrying comes under the heading "too difficult for the stability of the monarchy".'

Edward VIII's solution was abdication, which the Prince of Wales does not consider a possibility. The Princess of Wales hinted at it in her 'Panorama' interview, and as one senior minister at the time said, 'It was one of the most mischievous things that Diana ever did.' The Prince's sense of duty has driven him all his life. He was spoon fed it from birth, and repeatedly reminded of the shame his great uncle had brought upon the family and the misery he had caused. The Duke of Windsor, as he then became, had no more bitter critic than the Queen Mother, whose beloved husband, the then Duke of York, was obliged to step into his shoes to become King George VI. It wrecked his life and his health, and she never forgave Edward for his selfishness in putting a desire for personal happiness above his duty to the country.

Much as the idea of disappearing behind the gates of Highgrove with Mrs Parker Bowles to spend the rest of his life gardening, farming and painting might appeal, Prince Charles has never even allowed himself to dream. Camilla has, and sometimes the tug has been tough for him, but the reality is unthinkable. He is worried enough about William's future happiness as it is. If Charles were to abdicate, he would be exposing William, as next in line to the throne. If for no other reason, he will stay and carry out his duty to the bitter end, to protect his son for as long as he is able.

But there are other reasons. Like George V, George VI and Elizabeth II, he has studied *The English Constitution*, the great and oft-quoted work by Walter Bagehot, the Victorian economist, political analyst and man of letters, whose description of constitutional monarchy and its value to society has been the fundamental model for monarchy and its relationship with government and the people ever since. It was Bagehot who warned that if you let daylight in on the monarchy you ruin its magic.

The Prince of Wales understands the importance of the monarchy being hereditary. Succession is not a matter of choice, it is a duty. 'What suicide is to a man, abdication is to a king,' wrote the novelist Bulwer-Lytton in *The Last of the Barons* in 1843, and Prince Charles recognises that. If the sovereign treats the job as voluntary, then the idea of succession becomes nonsense, and the whole institution would very quickly disintegrate.

Marriage to Camilla, therefore, is not an option, until or unless public opinion changes even more radically than it already has. It is not even something they discuss. What they would dearly like, instead, is public acceptance of her as his companion. He is now fifty, she is fifty-one; they have been in love with one another for many years, their relationship is well known to everyone, and yet they have still not felt able to take a walk in the country together for fear of being photographed; they have not been able to eat in a restaurant, watch a play or an opera, or sit openly side by side in the Tuscan hills and paint together, which they long to do.

Camilla has to behave like an illicit lover, sliding surreptitiously in and out of houses, unable to go shopping or be seen in public places without the protection of friends, and elaborate plans being made in advance. Her life has improved in recent months, and she and the Prince of Wales will soon start spending time together at Birkhall when the Queen Mother is away, but their relationship is still by no means normal. She has all of the disadvantages of fame with none of the perks and pleasures.

Most weeks Camilla spends a couple of nights at Highgrove, and occasional nights at St James's Palace, but London is still a more difficult venue because of constantly being recognised. The Prince now lives in York House, which is attached to his offices, and was once the servants' quarters. The offices are where Edward VIII lived with Mrs Simpson when he was Prince of Wales, and what is now Stephen Lamport's office on the first floor, was once their bedroom. York House was done up by Robert Kime, the interior designer who did Highgrove after the separation. Highgrove is rather bohemian, and homely. York House feels more like a London base than home, although it is comfortable and there are plenty of photographs about to make it personal – snapshots as well as formal pictures of family and friends – and the odd painting of friends.

A surprising number of the photographs in the house are of Diana, including a beautiful black and white one in her wedding dress in the carriage that took her to St Paul's Cathedral, and many more of her with the children taken over the years. On the desk in the Prince's study, tucked into the corner of a photo frame, sits a little snap of Diana with William as a baby. He and the boys talk about Diana a lot; there is nothing forced about it, but if they see something she would have liked, or something that would have made her laugh, they say so. Her memory is being kept very much alive in a healthy and positive way – and it is the good times they remember, not the bad.

William has a self-contained flat at the top of the house, which he keeps locked – and he is the only one with a key – with a bedroom, bathroom, dressing room, sitting room, and his own kitchen, so that he can invite friends back for coffee. He has plenty of friends, in Gloucestershire and London, loves parties, goes to the cinema a lot, and leads a very active social life. Both boys have posters of pretty women and pop groups on their walls – which at one time included the Spice Girls, and All Saints – but, like all children's, their enthusiasms change from one day to the next.

When Harry met the Spice Girls in South Africa with his father early in 1998 he was thrilled. When his father then saw the band back in London at a film premier, he invited them to tea, thinking he had earned himself several brownie points with his children. The girls couldn't come immediately because they were off to Hong Kong but another date was fixed, and the five of them duly turned up in a helicopter at Highgrove, dressed in high platform heels which immediately sank into the sodden ground. They had tea with Harry, William and a couple of friends from Eton who had been given special permission to be out for the day. But by then …'After all the trouble I go to, to arrange the Spice Girls to come round to tea,' said the Prince in complete exasperation, 'they change their minds, fickle little devils. They've now gone on to the All Saints!'

Highgrove is their real home, and it too is filled with photographs of Diana. The Prince spends a lot of money on it, and he is a stickler for detail inside the house, just as much as in the garden. He bought new carpet recently, which was a major expense, and every bill he sees he questions. 'Who authorised that?' he will say accusingly, only to discover that *he* did. He knows precisely how much money he has and how much he spends on the different components of his life, and will always say, 'Good God, everything is so expensive', but it doesn't stop him spending. He is not unlike his grandmother in that respect. But, unlike some members of the family, he is punctilious about paying his bills.

It is an extravagant lifestyle by any standards. He has four valets, two of whom are on duty at any one time, three butlers, four chefs, two drivers, two large houses, and when he goes to Sandringham for ten days a huge container lorry arrives to take his luggage. He also has a Bentley, two Aston Martins, a fleet of Range Rovers and Vauxhall Omegas. He has a few horses too. The polo ponies are now kept at Fort Belvedere, courtesy of his polo playing friend, Galen

Weston, his host when he and the boys were skiing in Canada at the beginning of the year, who is as rich as he is generous. And he keeps three hunters at Highgrove: his, Camilla's and a spare. He also has the two dogs, Tigger and Wigeon.

Life at Highgrove is as relaxed as that kind of lifestyle, with its considerable support system, can be. If any of his friends or staff are staying overnight, the Prince will take them to their room himself, and will say, 'Is that all right? Sorry, but you'll have to use the children's bathroom.' The top floor of the house, the nursery floor, is very simple. It has a big landing and a table in the middle with fresh flowers on it, but the rooms are not huge. 'Oh, I'm so glad they put the lime bath oil in your bathroom,' he will say. 'I do think it's particularly good, but perhaps you'd like to try the rosemary. I'll go and get you some rosemary.'

After the death of the conductor Sir Georg Solti, the Prince wrote at once to his widow, Valerie, inviting her to stay. She readily accepted and enjoyed, she said, her first night's sleep and real relaxation since her husband's death. The Prince was genuinely delighted to have been able to provide some comfort. It is his home, and it's his children's home, and he wants other people to enjoy it and relax in it as much as he does.

Whenever Camilla comes to stay, she brings one of her dogs. She has two Jack Russells, Freddie and Tosca. Freddie is Tigger's son, and Tosca is Freddie's daughter, and sadly relationships between relatives are not all they might be. Tigger and Tosca fight so badly that Camilla usually has to leave Tosca behind. They make a comical sight when they leave: her car is brought to the front of the house, her kit is loaded into it for her and, as she gets into the driving seat, Freddie hops on to the seat beside her, and sits up, facing forward, waiting to be chauffeured home. Not long ago there was great drama in the household. Tosca was expecting puppies, so when Camilla and the Prince went to stay at Chatsworth with the Devonshires for a few days in the spring of 1998, the Prince took Tigger, she took Freddie and left the expectant mother at Highgrove with Kevin, the house manager, who by the end of the weekend had become midwife too. To everyone's huge excitement, the puppies were born in his airing cupboard.

After her divorce from Andrew, Camilla bought a new house in Wiltshire near the picturesque village of Lacock, south of the M4 motorway, which her father, Bruce Shand, moved into for a while, intending to convert the barn. Planning permission was refused, however, and he now lives in Dorset, next door to his other daughter, Annabel, and her husband, Simon Elliot. The Prince helped Camilla financially, paying for some of the alterations, including the installation of a security system, but he seldom visits Camilla at home because the security is still so much better in his own houses. For a while security for Camilla was a major concern. After the Princess died, emotions were running so high amongst the population at large that she was given some protection at her home in the country, and it was impossible for her to go anywhere alone. The Prince put a car and a driver at her disposal, and also sent one of his valets to shop for her and generally help around the house.

He was particularly worried after Camilla collided with an oncoming car while driving to dinner at Highgrove one night in June 1997. The roads between their two houses are very narrow and winding in places, and Mrs Parker Bowles is not known locally as the most cautious of drivers, much like the Prince of Wales, who pushes his Aston Martins almost as hard as he drives his horses.

The accident made the front page of every newspaper, but the details changed from day to day. The two cars hit with such force that Camilla's lost a wheel, and the other one ended up in the ditch. Although unhurt, the woman driving the other car was trapped inside and in need of help. According to one report, Camilla couldn't see the other car and assumed that it had hit her and kept on going. She tried to phone for help, but couldn't get a signal on her mobile phone, so ran up to the top of the hill where she could, and was able to telephone Highgrove. Two royal protection officers immediately set off to rescue her, while someone at Highgrove alerted the local Chippenham police. All arrived on the scene at much the same time. The Prince's protection officers took Camilla back to Highgrove, and the local police were left to find the second car and release the driver. For some time there was a possibility that Mrs Parker Bowles might be charged with dangerous driving or leaving the scene of an accident, but in the end no charges were brought.

At first the headlines read 'Camilla the heroine', who after the crash had helped the other woman out of her car. The next day, having realised for the first time who the driver of the other car had been, the woman corrected a few facts. Camilla had not been a heroine, she said. She had come at her like a torpedo, run her car into the ditch, left her trapped inside, failed to help, and run off never to be seen again. By day three the newspapers had it that Camilla had left the scene because she was responding to special anti-terrorist training, which was just as wide of the mark as the previous stories.

The true facts of the accident were never reported. The reason Camilla hit the other car was because she was momentarily distracted while travelling at speed. The cars struck with a tremendous banging and crashing of glass and metal. Camilla's first reaction was to speak to the Prince on her mobile phone and he immediately sent a car to the rescue. In a state of shock, Camilla then got out of her car and went over to the car she had collided with. She looked in through the window at the woman driver, screamed loudly, panicked and ran off. The Prince's policemen found her sitting by the side of her car in the road, crying. She was bruised and very severely shaken.

The Prince was also shaken, and the accident made him realise how vulnerable Camilla was. Although she has always been very resistant to the idea of protection, she was prevailed upon to agree to it, and to a little help from his office. From that day onward she was taken under the protective umbrella of St James's Palace and became a more acknowledged part of his life. She still values her independence and doesn't want to be wrapped up in cotton wool, but to have her life arranged for her, and to be protected from the media, is very seductive.

As well as giving financial help with the house, Charles also provided a personal assistant, Amanda McManus. The wife of a

Times newspaper executive, she worked part time, helping, amongst other things, with Camilla's correspondence. Amanda fell on her sword, however, in July 1998, when it emerged that she was responsible for a story which first appeared in the *Sun*, reporting that the long awaited meeting between Camilla and Prince William had finally taken place. Amanda made the fatal mistake of telling her husband, who had mentioned it inadvertently to a journalist.

The meeting had taken place at St James's Palace, when William, according to the original story, had arrived unexpectedly to change before going out with friends, and had found Camilla there with his father. The Prince of Wales was absolutely furious that the story should have appeared in the press. The details were such that it had to have come from someone inside St James's, and he wanted to know which member of his staff was the leak. His edict that no one should talk about his sons except to discuss travel and school arrangements had been breached and he was extremely angry.

There was another issue. The tabloid press had been particularly restrained in the year since Diana's death. They had each been fed stories, which were beneficial all round – good for the papers, good for the Prince of Wales – and, while they felt they were being treated fairly and honestly by the Palace, there was no need to play dirty. This was a big story. It looked as though a source was favouring the *Sun*, which enraged the other papers. Suspicion immediately fell on Mark Bolland, as the man with the best contacts in the media, and unless he was to lose the goodwill that had been built up in the previous year, it was essential his innocence be demonstrated.

In fact, it had been no accidental encounter. Prince William had said he would like to meet Camilla, and happened to telephone and say he was coming to London one day at a time when Camilla was staying for a couple of nights. The Prince told Camilla of William's imminent arrival and she immediately said she would leave. 'No, stay,' said the Prince. 'This is ridiculous.'

He then rang William and said Mrs Parker Bowles would be in the house, would that be a problem? To which William replied, 'No.'

By this time William had met Camilla's children, and reckoned that Camilla couldn't be as bad as she had been made out to be if she had produced such nice offspring. They had met during the Easter holidays. The Prince had decided William and Harry should meet Tom and Laura to see if they got on with each other, so while the three of them were staying at Birkhall, he invited the Parker Bowles children to join them for the weekend. Ted Hughes, the Poet Laureate, was also a guest that weekend. The meeting could not have been more successful. William clearly thought Tom at twenty-three was pretty cool, and both Princes, but especially Harry, thought Laura at nineteen was very beautiful. William had seen Laura fleetingly at parties before, but this was the first time they had really spoken and, despite the differences in age, the four of them got on famously. After that meeting they continued to see each other every few weeks or so, either in London or at home in the country.

At about the same time, William and Harry began plotting a surprise party for their father's fiftieth birthday. It started out as a party for the Prince's godchildren and their parents. Tom was his godson, and William therefore wanted to invite Camilla, but he first wanted to meet her in more private circumstances. The Prince had only once spoken to his sons about Camilla. It was in June 1997, when he sat them both down together and tried to explain a bit about the situation, but the boys were very quiet and William was not receptive. He told Tiggy afterwards that William didn't want to know about it.

The Prince had always deliberately kept them away from Camilla – the more so after that experience – hoping that one day they might feel differently and it might be possible to introduce them, but knowing that the initiative would have to come from the boys. He was not sure how much anti-Camilla conditioning William had had from his mother, so he didn't want to force anything, not knowing what he was pushing against. Camilla understood entirely. She had had all of this to go through with her own children, and knew that you had to be patient and wait until the time was right, and then when it was, to just get on and deal with it.

William had heard a lot of terrible things about Camilla from his mother, as he had about his father too – she had spared him little – but he had been beginning to realise that not everything he had heard was true, and his holiday with Diana on board al Fayed's yacht in the South of France in July had been an eye-opener.

Everyone was extremely nervous about the proposed meeting on the afternoon of Friday 12 June. Prince William had said he would arrive at 7 p.m., but typically turned up at York House at about 3.30 p.m. and went straight up to his flat at the top of the house. The Prince went to find Camilla, who was with Amanda McManus, and said, 'He's here. Let's just get on with it. I'm going to take you to meet him now.' So he took her up to William's flat, introduced them to each other and left them alone to talk for about half an hour. At the end of the encounter Camilla came out saying 'I need a drink', but it had been remarkably easy. William was friendly, and Camilla was sympathetic and sensitive and understood the need to let things go at his pace. They met again for lunch a few days later, and since then William has stayed at York House several times when Camilla has been there for the night and they have all had breakfast together the following morning.

The snub to Camilla that afternoon came not from Prince William, who might have been excused, but from Sir Robin Janvrin, the Queen's private secretary designate. Earlier in the afternoon the Prince had interviewed Simon Lewis, the new communications supremo at Buckingham Palace, who took up his post in September 1998. Stephen Lamport and Mark Bolland had been with him, and at the end of the interview, Robin Janvrin came in to chat about how it had gone. When they were done, Stephen and Mark stayed on with the Prince to talk about another matter, and Robin went and sat in the waiting room. When they had finished talking, the Prince said, 'Stephen, before you go, why don't you get Robin back in and I'll introduce him to Camilla because I'm tired of all this nonsense.'

The meeting between William and Camilla had already happened, William had left, and the Prince was feeling rather euphoric. They had talked before about Robin Janvrin meeting Camilla, and he decided to seize the opportunity while they were both in the same building. Stephen went downstairs to the waiting room and said, 'Robin, the Prince of Wales would like you to come back up because he'd like to introduce you to Mrs Parker Bowles.'

Janvrin said, 'I can't possibly do that. I couldn't do it without asking the Queen's permission and making sure it was the right thing to do.' He was not to be budged, and Stephen had no alternative but to go back to the Prince, in a state of some shock, and tell him that the Queen's deputy private secretary was refusing to meet Mrs Parker Bowles.

The language that came from the Prince when he heard this is unrepeatable – he was completely and utterly furious, outraged and affronted – and the hope that the relationship between St James's Palace and the Queen's household would become easier when Robin Janvrin took over from Robert Fellowes became highly questionable. 'In my house ...' he said. 'How dare he be so rude in my house?' However, when the Prince knew that the news of the meeting between William and Camilla was about to appear in print, he telephoned Robin personally and told him to speak to his mother and tell her that it was not a problem, not an issue. Robin complied and there was no fuss from Buckingham Palace when the story appeared.

The Prince is fed up with the hostility from the Queen and her advisers towards Camilla. He is fifty, he has been through a lot, he works extremely hard, and feels it is time his mother showed him a little understanding. His fiftieth birthday party was to be something of a watershed in the relationship. The Queen planned to give an official party for Charles at Buckingham Palace on the night of 13 November for a thousand people to celebrate his public work, at which she would speak. It was for all the people who have been involved in his charities and organisations, and Camilla, quite rightly, was not included. What people wondered all summer, however, was whether the Queen would accept Camilla's invitation to the private family birthday party, which she and a group of the Prince's friends had organised for him at Highgrove on the night of 14 November, his actual birthday. It really mattered to Charles that the Queen should be there.

What is not known is that Harry also met Camilla before the boys' surprise party. Harry is a much less complicated child than William. As someone who knows him well says, 'Harry is just Harry.' He just gets on with life. Being younger, he also appears to have taken in much less of what Diana told him than his brother. He had no qualms about meeting Camilla. About two weeks before the party, after consulting with both boys, the Prince invited Camilla to bring Tom and Laura over to Highgrove for tea one Sunday afternoon. Once again, it was very easy and they liked one another.

The surprise party for their father, held on the night of 31 July, was brought about entirely by William and Harry. It was their own idea, and the Prince was immeasurably touched that they should have gone to such trouble. Sadly the surprise was spoilt by the *Sunday Mirror*, which got wind of what was happening, inadvertently, from one of the guests, and published details the Sunday before. It was an incident which didn't improve the Prince's feelings about the media, but the party was a huge success nonetheless. The boys had wanted to do something special for their father and, since his birthday fell during the school term, fixed a date during the holidays before the family went up to Balmoral. They enlisted the help of Tiggy and Michael Fawcett, the Prince's former valet, in planning the party, but they knew exactly what and who they wanted. They recruited the actors Stephen Fry, Emma Thompson and Rowan Atkinson – all the Prince's friends because, like many entertainers, they have done work for the Prince's Trust over the years – to help them write and put together a revue, along the lines of Atkinson's television comedy series 'Blackadder', in which they appeared themselves, in front of a hundred of the Prince's family and friends. What touched the Prince most of all was that the boys arranged the seating plan themselves, and placed Camilla in the front row of the audience between their father and William's godfather, King Constantine, former King of the Hellenes.

The Queen and the Duke of Edinburgh, though invited, were not able to attend. It was the Queen Mother's ninety-eighth birthday the following day and they were all at Sandringham, but this was no great disappointment because the boys had intended it to be a younger party. Prince Andrew and Prince Edward both came, and also Princess Anne, none of whom had met Camilla for many years. The meeting with Anne was the trickiest. Camilla finds her terrifying, and was very nervous at the prospect, but Anne was quite friendly.

The Prince was incredibly moved – moved to tears – that his children should have gone to so much trouble for him, and Camilla was thrilled to have been invited and touched that William and Harry should both have wanted her to be there. They could not have given their father a more welcome or perfect birthday present, and he stood up at the end of the evening and thanked them both profusely. According to those who were there, he thanked every-one who had had a hand in the evening, with one notable omission – Tiggy.

Tiggy has been posing an increasing problem to the Prince. He recognises the huge debt he owes her for all she has done over the years, and the abuse and vilification from the press she has had to put up with. She was completely invaluable at the time of Diana's death and helped William and Harry in a way that left everyone marvelling and overcome with gratitude. Like the rest of his family, he adores Tiggy, but she does drive him mad at times. She has been hopelessly irresponsible at times and repeatedly found her way into the newspapers, both in her private life and in the course of looking after William and Harry. Whenever they have been in any sort of trouble, Tiggy has not been far away. There were photographs in the press, for example, of Tiggy driving along in a car with a cigarette hanging out of her mouth, while Harry shot at rabbits out of the open window. She had accepted William's invitation to take a picnic to Eton's fourth of June parents' event in 1997, without consulting either the Prince or Princess, who had both been asked by William to stay away because he didn't want the day turned into a media circus. More recently, under Tiggy's supervision, Harry abseiled face outwards down a 150-foot dam wall in Wales, without either a hard hat or a safety line, which the experts immediately condemned as extremely dangerous. The Prince only discovered what had been going on when he saw the photographs published in the press, and he hit the roof. His dilemma is that the boys are very fond of Tiggy, and the last thing he wants to do is take away the emotional support she provides, but she is not the most steadying influence, and she encourages their already rather wild and hedonistic instincts. As the daughter of one of the Prince's friends says of her, corrupting a famous pre-war instruction for country cooks, 'Tiggy shoots a rabbit, stuffs it, skins it, and eats it.'

Diana thought Tiggy was a bad influence on her sons, and there are many people around the Prince who share that view. Whenever he confronts her about some idiocy she bursts into tears and he gets no further. So instead of doing something decisive, he keeps her on and, according to those around him, treats her badly. She wanted to give him a spaniel puppy as an early fiftieth birthday present in July. He told her quite bluntly that he didn't want one.

The Prince is a much easier man when he is at Highgrove. In London he feels hemmed in. There's nowhere for him to walk that's not overlooked by offices. In the country he goes out first thing in the morning with the dogs and it sets him up for the day. For preference, he works from Highgrove, which makes life difficult for all the people who have to drive back and forth from London along the M4 on a regular basis, and tricky for his private secretaries. As one senior politician, who knows the family well, says, 'The difficulty is access. The difficulty for all royal servants is access. They lead these extraordinary lives. They don't operate like a minister where the private secretary sits outside and is the filter, the person who sifts what you see and who you see, which can be maddening. But provided you've got the right people in your team outside in the anti-chamber, it is fine. But the Royal Family doesn't operate like that. The Prince of Wales goes to Highgrove and there's no control, nobody quite knows what or whom he's seeing. None of them is easy to work for because the machine is not smooth running and the co-ordination is not adequate. He's not easy to work for, but none of the important ones are.'

'He's a man of great integrity and great loyalty,' says someone who worked with the Prince of Wales for several years, 'but someone described him to me before I knew him at all as intellectually lazy, and there is a bit of that to him. He sails along, motoring on two or three cylinders instead of everything going properly, he won't always stop and think through all the angles, won't always stop and really get it right. He'll follow his instincts, which he trusts, and bugger the critics. He's a creature of his upbringing, a bit self-centred and a bit inconsiderate, he doesn't really stop and put himself in someone else's shoes. Hugely courteous and well mannered and apparently considerate, but deep down, actually, he knows what he wants out of life, and that is what makes him comfortable.'

Another adviser, who has been working for the Prince in an unpaid capacity, as many do, for well over ten years, finds the inefficiency of his office a serious frustration. 'There was a time when you were trying to do something you just put up with it because they're different from other organisations. They're not a business, not a non-governmental organisation, and not a conventional charity in any sense. It was just one of those endearing hangovers of royalty that they ran an office in this way. Richard [Aylard] improved things and brought it half way into the twentieth century, but I think it's got worse since he left. They are so unprofessional and so unhelpful in terms of managing relationships with the outside world, you wonder what they think the rest of the world expects of them.

'And for people trying to organise activities which involve the Prince, whether it is for a meeting or getting him to write something or just say "yes" or "no", and you go into this absolutely insane system, where you don't get an answer for months and then you're told you'll have to wait, then it's the diary meeting, and we don't do the diary meeting until June, even when you're waiting for a "yes" or a "no" for something in September. It's archaic, and it doesn't seem to make any difference who you are. I, and others, have been battering away at them for years to try and sort it out and they just won't. It's gross exploitation. And there's a slight sense of who

284

needs whom around the place from time to time. Talk to any organisation that has to run itself professionally and use basic standards of administration and good partnership and they just say, forget it, his office is hopeless.'

Julia Cleverdon has a monthly meeting with the Prince of Wales. Looking at her diary on one occasion when Channel 4 was filming about Business in the Community in her office, she said to Bernie, her secretary, 'You're not telling me all these meetings are at Highgrove? It's absolutely impossible. Four hours down there, four hours back. The entire bloody day gone.' The crew had been around the office long enough for Julia to have grown used to the cameras.

The Prince, hearing that she had been on television, asked to see the tape. Julia complied, but knowing that it wasn't so much what she had said as the body language that went with it, she awaited his response with a certain apprehension. He rang her up immediately and said he had never laughed so much in his life. He'd had no idea it was so awful getting to Highgrove.

Although his staff complain about having to go to Gloucestershire all the time, most people relish an invitation to the Prince's home and will drop every other commitment at a moment's notice if an invitation should be extended. An invitation to Highgrove has proved invaluable over the years as a means of thanking people for some task they have undertaken on his behalf, a performance they have given for the Prince's Trust, perhaps, or for people he hopes will do something for him in the future. He holds discussion groups there, and working lunches. During the summer he opens the garden up to special interest groups, or charities, and has a pool of locals who come in to conduct the tours.

Functions at Highgrove were costing the Duchy tens of thousands of pounds per annum in marquee hire, so in 1997 the Prince built a magnificent function room in the park, called the Orchard Room. The Orchard Room was designed not by an architect but by a chartered surveyor called Charles Morris. The Prince was closely involved in the design and although some critics have unkindly likened it to a supermarket, most people think that in time it will blend in well. The Prince is very pleased with the result. It opened in May 1998 with a party the Prince gave for the builders, and he was astonished by the amount of beer they drank.

It was in the Orchard Room that William and Harry staged their father's surprise party but, in the main, it is used by his charities to hold fundraising dinners and receptions. He also has a shop, originally housed in a stable outside the back door, but which moved into the Orchard Room in 1998. Any guests who come to Highgrove find themselves escorted purposefully by their host to buy a few souvenirs before they leave. Since the shop is not open to the public, anyone who fails to buy their Highgrove jigsaw puzzle or place mats may not get a second chance; and not many have the temerity to leave empty-handed.

The shop was set up and run initially by Michael Fawcett, who was at that time the Prince's valet. It was intended as yet another way to raise money for charity – in this case, the Prince of Wales Charitable Foundation, which owns two companies: AJ Carrick, which deals with income from the Prince's children's books, lithographs and paintings, and Duchy Originals, which deals with all the produce. Asking people for money is not something Charles enjoys, but the need to raise money is never-ending and he knows that because of who he is, he has the power to do it.

Michael Fawcett is a man with influence beyond his intellect and extraordinary sticking power. He has been a valet to the Prince since the time of the engagement in 1981; before that he was a member of the Queen's household, which he joined when he was very young. In his spare time he has worked on the selling floor of a department store, but he dresses and behaves as though he were one of its better-bred customers. He is flamboyant, has great style and can be utterly charming and persuasive; he knows what the Prince likes, and is very good at making things happen. He can also be arrogant and domineering and is able to throw his weight about with anyone and everyone, because he knows he has the Prince's backing. He has the Prince's ear, and uses it to damn those people foolish enough to cross him. He is disliked and mistrusted by most people in the office, and over the years there have been suggestions that he was exploiting his friendship with the Prince, who always chose to turn a blind eye.

Early in 1998, it looked as though he had finally come unstuck, but the rejoicing throughout the office was short-lived. Although the Prince's lawyer, Fiona Shackleton, was one of a group who persuaded the Prince that Fawcett must be removed – and the story that he was leaving appeared in the press – he never went. The Prince changed his mind, and Fawcett was kept within the fold, no longer as a valet, but as a consultant organising functions.

'It is an area of weakness in the Prince,' says one of his staff, 'that he does put his trust and faith in people who can deliver what he wants delivered, and is prepared to ignore suggestions that they have cut corners to do it. There is an unspoken, "He's doing what I want. Don't let's make too much fuss about it."'

EIGHTEEN

Victim or Villain?

'How much worse if you happen to be
born into a public position.'
Charles

'The most peculiar thing is that here is this poor wronged creature, of whom I was very fond and a great fan, with a string of boyfriends. He was a man who, at worst, after his marriage was unfaithful with one woman. Yet he is the one who has been cast as the villain of the piece, and she as the poor wronged creature, who, poor little thing, had to go and find succour somewhere, didn't she?

'I've always felt it was rather an unfair perception that the wrong was all on one side.'

These are the words of someone who knew both the Prince and Princess well, who worked with them closely for several years, admired them both in different ways and, most unusually, never fell out seriously with either of them. Most people who knew them both did, and very quickly lost their objectivity. Yet even those people, for the most part, don't apportion blame. There were no villains in this tragedy, only victims, as anyone who saw and understood the reality will recognise. There is no blame or bitterness, despite the damage; simply terrible sadness.

The system played a big part in this whole sad story. The system required the Prince to find a wife and produce an heir, but not just any wife – a wife who was a member of the Church of England, who was pure, with no past experience of men, who was well-bred and who understood the protocol and would be able to share the duties of monarchy. The criteria were unrealistic for the 1980s, and had

Diana not set her sights on the Prince when she was still a schoolgirl, and pursued him with such determination, he might never have found a suitable bride over the age of consent.

Having found a bride, the system then dictated how they would spend their life together, as Charles knew it would, but having been brought up to it from birth, he had no real understanding of how difficult it might be for an ordinary person to handle. Diana should have known the system better than anybody, because she had been around it all her life, but she was little more than a child, in love with a dream. She didn't know the Prince any better than he knew her, but she didn't care. She wanted to marry him, and if anyone had sat her down and told her that she would have to share him with his staff, his family, the United Kingdom and half of the world, plus a diary of immovable dates that could be written in for the rest of their lives, she could not have begun to understand what that might mean. Any more than she could have realised what the loss of her freedom and privacy would mean.

If the system orchestrated an inevitably disastrous marriage, the perception that the Prince was responsible for it came from the media, which the Princess used unscrupulously in the war against her husband. The media took sides, which, in times of falling circulation and cut-throat competition, is not based on fairness and truth, but driven by sales. The public fell in love with a Princess of Wales that the newspapers created. She dressed for them, she performed for them. She was young and glamorous and the public appetite was insatiable. The Prince was balding and boring and predictable, and he'd been around for a very long time.

When Diana went to visit a hospice, she allowed the cameras to follow and the next day's newspapers were filled with photos of her holding a dying child's hand. Cynics would say it was self-promotion; alternatively, one could legitimately argue that it made people think about the dying and the less fortunate. The Prince also visited many a hospice, but out of the respect for the suffering only those who were there knew about it. Instead, he made speeches about the needs of the dying, which went unnoticed as the media focused its attention on his wife; and behind the scenes he worked to find ways of improving their care by bringing all the various professional bodies together who could have an influence on it, and making them find solutions.

These days, when so much of life is visual, most of Charles's words have gone unheard. Diana understood that the medium was the message. She was a child of the tabloid and television era and, although she found photographers too much at times, she knew that her ability to make the media follow her, listen to her and watch her, gave her immense power. She knew that one look could speak volumes. He was still caught in the traces of the past and, emotionally repressed, couldn't begin to engage in the contest. She enjoyed and needed the adulation, and as their relationship began to fall apart, she used the media to arouse sympathy for herself and to punish her husband and his family, whom she blamed for all her unhappiness. The marriage never worked, but in the end, it was Diana's manipulation of the media that killed it.

The irony is that it was a marriage brought about by the media in the first place. Had James Whitaker not been spying on the Prince with binoculars and long lenses in the summer of 1980, and spotted Diana on the riverbank beside him, there might have been no wedding. Once she had been seen, the media tracked her down, followed her, photographed her, telephoned her and built her up into a likely bride, and nothing she said led them to believe they were on the wrong track. She was no fool and quickly learnt that she could use the media to get what she wanted. The hype and the fever of speculation and the intrusion were so fierce that it seemed unimaginable it could continue.

But, of course, it did. An entire industry grew up around Diana. Still painfully young and impressionable, she became everybody's pin-up. Men of all ages fancied her, children thought she was the Princess from a fairytale, young women wanted to look like her, mothers thought she was everything they could have wished for in a daughter, and the media recognised that it could feed all of those interests if it got the photographs and the stories. Designers saw her as a swift passage to fame, as did hairdressers, make-up artists, photographers – their ambitions all achieved through the media. Even psychologists, astrologers and hand-writing experts found themselves caught up in the industry, as the media called on their services to explain what a particular gesture or a snatched remark to someone in the crowd had meant, whether she was healthy or happy or pregnant or what the future might hold.

To blame the media for destroying the marriage is clearly nonsense. The media did not make life easy or pleasant, and it has a great deal to answer for; but the fundamental problem was not the media. It was the fact that these were two people who should never have married. They were both tragic figures in the literal Greek definition of the word – each one brought down by flaws within their personalities, manipulated by forces beyond their control. Each was inadequate, and each needed something that the other was quite incapable of giving. If there had ever been a bond between them, it could have been strengthened by facing a common enemy, in the shape of the media, together. If there had been a bond, they would have given one another confidence, so that invidious comparisons about who did what better would never have wounded with the severity they did. If there had been a bond, they could have had the security to present a united front and use the media to convey whatever message they chose to the world.

But there was no bond. There was nothing more than brief patches of happiness in a morass of misery, and so, given the intrusion, given the comparisons, given the hero-building of Diana and the character-assassination of Charles, the relationship didn't stand a chance.

But what finally fixed the perception of Diana as the poor wronged creature who had to seek succour was the Andrew Morton book. Angry that the Prince had not been able to make her happy, she used a journalist to punish him, and didn't appear to mind that in punishing him she hurt her children too. Of all Diana's actions over the years, this is the most inexplicable – to have deliberately put the sons she adored through the pain of seeing their father attacked publicly, not once but twice, by following up the book with the 'Panorama' interview. Yet no one seemed to see the paradox. She accused the Prince of being a bad father in those attacks, and although she had some increasingly fierce critics in the media towards the end of her life, her adoring public believed everything she said. They didn't seem to question what vilifying Charles in public, and in front of their children, made her.

The Prince remained silent and let the public perception of him, unkind and unfair as it was, persist. He made no attempt to stand up for himself in any way. His staff and friends, who all knew the reality, knew Diana and had watched what went on, were desperate to speak up in his defence, but the Prince forbade it, and was very angry with anyone who attempted to. He was adamant that there should be no criticism of the Princess and no defence of himself or his reputation. And in the absence of a second side to the story, the public had no alternative but to believe that what the Princess of Wales told them about her husband and her marriage was true.

Right to the end, the Prince believed that any attempt to justify or explain could have made matters worse, harmed the boys, and done even greater damage to the monarchy. The 'Panorama' interview was generally thought to be a tit for tat response to Dimbleby. Yet Charles had said nothing in his defence and had in no way spoken disparagingly about Diana during that interview. In admitting his infidelity, without attempting to address any of the other accusations Diana had made via Morton, he merely compounded the problem. The whole undignified business could have gone on indefinitely, and the only winners would have been the media, feasting gluttonously on the seamier intricacies of their lives.

After Diana's death, the opportunity, had he ever wanted to take it, was lost for ever. To tell his side of the story when she was no longer there to answer back, however truthful, however well corroborated by other witnesses, would have been unthinkable. He would rather look forward than dwell on the past, get on with his life and let his children get on with theirs. If he must go to his grave with some people believing that he was to blame for the failure of his marriage and Diana's sadness, that is the way it must be. He knows in his heart that he was no villain. He didn't intend to hurt Diana, any more than she ever intended, at the outset, to hurt him.

The tragedy is that in their own way they did love each other, and in an inexplicable way he still does love her. He still wears her wedding ring, he still kneels down at night and prays for her. She hurt him very deeply and she almost destroyed him, but he knows she was no villain either. She was a victim of the system, as he was. She married him because she craved security, because she didn't want her children to experience what she had as a child. The Prince of Wales, she thought, was the one man for whom divorce would be impossible. He believed the same. He had wanted a companion who would share his life for the next fifty years, and his disappointment that they failed was no less acute than hers.

His attitude is almost impossible for an outsider to understand. If people think him a villain, that's something he will have to live with. His concern is how he will be judged in the next world, and his conscience is clear. He believes that one day history will vindicate him. He knows that the facts – the documentation – papers, diaries, letters, medical reports and tapes are safely stored for the future. When he is dead, and possibly when his children are dead too, historians will discover the truth about his marriage.

But sadly, the documentation will be incomplete. The Prince has discovered that all Diana's papers, which she meticulously kept in a number of safes inside Kensington Palace, have been destroyed since her death.

The Prince was utterly incredulous when he heard that Diana's mother and sister, Lady Sarah McCorquodale, as executors, had instructed Paul Burrell – who was the only person alive who knew the combinations to the safes – to open them and hand over the contents. He did so, and the two women destroyed the lot – letters, medical records, everything.

The Prince's lawyer, Fiona Shackleton, who is acting on the boys' behalf over their mother's will, advised him to have a full inventory of Diana's possessions at Kensington Palace drawn up the day after her death. A number of items had been loaned to Diana following the divorce settlement and it was important to get those back – also to ensure that none of her possessions went missing, as some have. He thought going in so soon was unnecessarily brutal and delayed the process, with the result that these papers, which could have been so illuminating, have been lost for ever.

Much as one can sympathise with the Spencer family for wanting to protect Diana's memory, and for trying to reclaim a little of her for their own, she was a public figure, she belonged to the people, she walked on the world stage, and will go down in history as one of the greatest phenomena of the twentieth century. To have destroyed material that could give future generations an insight into that phenomenon is both misguided and irresponsible.

Diana's will was drawn up in 1993, shortly after the separation but before the £17 million divorce settlement, and the executors were Diana's mother and sister Sarah. She left over £21 million gross, from which inheritance tax of over £8.5 million was deducted. The original will named Patrick Jephson, her private secretary, as an executor with Mrs Shand Kydd. But Diana had amended the will after she fell out with Jephson in 1995, and replaced him with Sarah. She had left no bequests to her mother, brother and sisters, or any of her nephews and nieces, although she left instructions that if she and Prince Charles were both to die before the boys reached the age of eighteen, her mother and brother should be their guardians.

On Fiona Shackleton's advice, and with the agreement of the Queen and the Prime Minister, the Prince of Wales invited John Major, the former Prime Minister, to be guardian to William and Harry, which, on the face of it, seemed a sensible idea. In December 1997, he was involved in a complicated but successful application to Sir Richard Scott, the Vice-Chancellor and Head of the Chancery Division, to vary the will. Not least of their reasons was to protect the unique Intellectual Property aspects of Diana's image; also to give a larger proportion of Diana's inheritance to Harry, who unlike William, will not inherit an income from the Duchy of Cornwall when his father becomes monarch. A third executor was added at the same time, the Bishop of London, the Rt. Revd Richard Chartres, an old college friend of the Prince of Wales, who conducted William's confirmation service. Although Major's role has been to act as honest broker, given the friction between the Spencers and the Royal Family, and with tabloid criticism of the legal costs involved, there must have been times when it made his nightmare years in government feel like a holiday.

Other amendments secured in the High Court, which her mother and sister thought the Princess would have wanted, provided a bequest of £50,000 for Paul Burrell, whom she had described as her rock, 'the only man I can trust', and who was the only outsider present at Diana's burial. He had not been mentioned in the will. Her seventeen godchildren had been mentioned: she had left them one fifth of the value of her chattels shared between them, but the executors decided Diana would have preferred them instead to have something to remember her by, and allocated each one a trinket of sentimental rather than monetary value. Since her chattels today are worth many millions of pounds more than they were in 1993, it was a sensible decision, which none of the godchildren's parents would argue with, but the trinkets that have been chosen are a poor substitute – they include pieces of crockery, and porcelain, a decanter, a carriage clock, hunting figures and a couple of watercolours. The whole business has caused a great deal of bitterness. The chattels belong to William and Harry, who inherited the bulk of their mother's estate, but many of them, including the famous David and Elizabeth Emanuel wedding dress, are currently on display in Earl Spencer's memorial museum at Althorp.

Looking ahead to the future, having watched helplessly as all this happened to Charles and Diana, one member of the Royal family has serious concerns.

'It is probably impossible, I now realise, for a Prince of Wales to have a happy marriage. Charles was handicapped from day one. It is as much to do with the position and the pressures put upon the Prince of Wales and Princess in the modern world, mostly the media, enquiring about every tiny thing in their life. The media will destroy the children too, I have no doubt about that. William can never be a really happy man.'

William seems to have remarkable resilience. Both he and Harry have so far coped with their mother's death very well indeed, and are flourishing. No one can begin to comprehend the pain and confusion they have been through in their short lives, but they do have an elaborate support group of friends and family, and, free from the strain of having constantly to divide their loyalty between warring parents, they have both started to come out of their shells and develop into much more confident, carefree boys. They have grown very close to their father since Diana died, and have made it clear that he is the only blood relative they need.

What is particularly heart-warming for the Prince is that his sons have accepted his love for Camilla Parker Bowles, and are pleased to see him happy at last. The day after William and Harry went back to school in September 1998, Charles and Camilla flew to Greece on their first ever holiday together. There was a great deal of subterfuge involved. The Prince flew back to Balmoral on the Wednesday to lay a false trail, then flew down to RAF Lyneham the following day to collect Camilla. They flew on to Greece in a friend's private plane. The week before, the Prince had almost called it off because he was unnerved by the paparazzi who had followed Camilla to Corfu, where she had been with Candida Lycett-Green as a guest of Jacob Rothschild. Charles and Camilla had been planning a similar holiday in 1997, when Diana, William and Harry were on board the al Fayed yacht in the South of France. But when he saw what was going on there, he called it all off. He feared it would come out in the press, and provide an alternative seemy, seedy spectacle to what was happening in the South of France.

They had planned to go with Candida and her husband, Rupert, also the artist Derek Hill, who helps the Prince with his painting, and was going to give Camilla some tips too. This year Charles was persuaded to stick to his guns and for five days they cruised around the Greek islands, dodging the bad weather, on a small but powerful boat that belonged to another friend. It was a closely guarded secret and the best birthday present the Prince could have asked for. Even better than the sheer joy of being able to spend time with Camilla away from the cameras and prying eyes, was the fact that they went with William and Harry's blessing.

How long the Princes remain carefree remains to be seen. The older they grow, the more interesting their lives will become, and the more legitimate the public interest will be. The Prince once said that Tony Blair, when he was Leader of the Opposition, had told him that the House of Commons had become a bear pit, and that if he was thinking of going into politics today he would probably decide against it.

'How much worse, therefore,' said the Prince, 'if you happen to be *born* into a public position in these intolerable circumstances. My guess is, before long – especially when William leaves school – the press will call for him to become king rather than me. And they will go on doing so until *he* puts a foot wrong – poor chap! And then they'll start on another tack.'

Perhaps the Royal Family are all destined to be victims, and maybe it is we, who demand too much from them, who are the villains.

Index